DIETRICH'S WARRIORS

DIETRICH'S WARRIORS

The History of the 3. Kompanie/1st Panzergrenadier Regiment

1st SS PANZER DIVISION LEIBSTANDARTE ADOLF HITLER in World War II

PETER MOONEY

Schiffer Military History
Atglen, PA

Book design by Robert Biondi.

Library of Congress Catalog Number: 2003114071.

Printed in China.
ISBN: 0-7643-1984-1

Published by Schiffer Publishing Ltd.
4880 Lower Valley Road
Atglen, PA 19310
Phone: (610) 593-1777
FAX: (610) 593-2002
E-mail: Info@schifferbooks.com.
Visit our web site at: www.schifferbooks.com
Please write for a free catalog.
This book may be purchased from the publisher.
Please include $3.95 postage.
Try your bookstore first.

In Europe, Schiffer books are distributed by:
Bushwood Books
6 Marksbury Ave.
Kew Gardens
Surrey TW9 4JF
England
Phone: 44 (0)20 8392-8585
FAX: 44 (0)20 8392-9876
E-mail: info@bushwoodbooks.co.uk.
Free postage in the UK. Europe: air mail at cost.
Try your bookstore first.

CONTENTS

Appendices

Map List

INTRODUCTION

In the early 1930s Adolf Hitler ordered the formation of a squad whose sole purpose would be to protect him. In recognition of their sole link to the Führer, this squad was named the *Leibstandarte* Adolf Hitler. This political squad grew in twelve years from 117 men to a full military armoured Division of 20,000 men. As the growth of the *LAH* began, various components were formed. This included artillery, panzer, reconnaissance and many support *Kompanies*. The backbone of any military formation however, is the infantry. This work will concentrate on one such *Kompanie*, namely the 3. *Kompanie*, 1st Panzergrenadier Regiment *LSSAH*.

This *Kompanie* was formed in the early stages of the Third Reich and remained in existence until the end of the war. In peacetime they were witnesses to the rebirth of Germany as a major European power. When war broke out, they participated in all of the campaigns fought by the *LAH*. This war would take them from their homeland and onto places as far flung as Rostov in Russia, Greece and the shores of the French coast with England.

The 3. *Kompanie* were also witness to immense political changes, but where possible, this work will avoid references to these political changes and the questions that arise from them. The focus of this book is the history of the 3. *Kompanie*, first as members of a protection squad and then as members of an elite fighting formation. This *Kompanie* played their part in forging the reputation of the *LAH* as one of Germany's, and history's, finest fighting units.

Among the ranks that served with the 3. *Kompanie* at one time or another would be, One Divisional Commander (Wilhelm Mohnke), One Brigade Commander (Hinrich Schult), Two Regimental Commanders (Martin Gross and Emil Sator), Three Battalion Commanders (Harry Polewacz, Hans-Joachim Schiller and Albert Stenwedel) and one *Kompanie* commander, other than the 3. *Kompanie*, (Fritz Streipart). Their bravery was without doubt, also. No less than one award of the Swords to the Oakleaves and Knight's Cross (Hinrich Schuldt), six Knight's Cross's, two of these whilst serving with the 3. *Kompanie*, (Hermann Dahlke, Martin Gross, Wilhelm Mohnke, Harry Polewacz, Heinrich Springer and Albert Stenwedel). There was also six German Crosses in Gold awarded, none whilst with the 3. *Kompanie*, (Martin Gross, Wilhelm Mohnke, Harry Polewacz, Hans-Joachim Schiller, Hinrich Schuldt and Günther Zaag). The rank achieved by some of the former 3. *Kompanie* members would include the following, two *Brigadeführer*s, one *Standartenführer*, four *Obersturmbannführer*s, four *Sturmbannführers*, one *Hauptsturmführer*, two *Obersturmführer*s and four *Untersturmführer*s. Every one of these men help to forge the *LAH*'s and the Waffen-SS's excellent fighting reputation. They would also have left their mark upon the 3. *Kompanie*.

Detailed information on this *Kompanie* is not readily available. Therefore, I have had to trawl through various other works and extract what information is on hand. This has been backed up with first hand accounts from surviving members of the 3. *Kompanie*. Surviving maps from this period have also been invaluable in determining the course that this unit took on its' varied journey through the Second World War. Where necessary, I have had to detail the actions of the I Battalion, 1st Panzergrenadier Regiment of the *LAH*. This is the Battalion that the 3. *Kompanie* were part of.

I would like to thank those surviving members of the 3. *Kompanie* who have helped me with my research and in some cases provided excellent photographs. They were Heinrich Springer, Gerhard Dilling, Günther Junker, Max Schmidt, Heinz Kirsch, Hans Komischke and Gerhard Franz. Ralf Tiemann, the former Ordnance Officer of the *LAH*, has also been a constant source of help, information, provided photographs and he also gave permission for his work on the *LAH* to be used.

Other people have helped in various ways, people such as former *Obersturmbannführer* Hubert Meyer for the photograph of Harry Polewacz. Erwin Bartmann, the former member of the *LAH*'s 4. *Kompanie* for his recollections of the battle for Rostov and also for providing photographs from his collection. *Kameraden* Hans

Vogel for various photos from the first Russian campaign. Patrick Agte for permission to use various photos as listed. Nick Adams who provided the 1938 photograph of Albert Stenwedel. Gabriel Gorman who provided the photographs of Hans Komischke. The U.S. Army Military History Institute for the photograph of the Jadgpanzer IV in the Ambleve River. Bob Carruthers and the crew at Cromwell Productions Ltd for transforming my sketches into proper maps. Tim Hagger and the people of Holiday Extras for finishing the maps. Karen Ovenden for translation work. Mark Yerger for permission to use the photograph of Hans-Joachim Schiller. Lou Malcolm of the Geography and Map Library, Indiana University for the map of Rostov from 1941. James Mcleod for the recollections and photographs of former 3. *Kompanie* Commander Gunther Zaag. And of course, John Fedorowicz of J.J. Fedorowicz for his permission to use the five volume history of the *LSSAH* as a basis for this work. Every effort has been made to obtain original photographic sources.

Two people deserve special mention for their enthusiasm and help in various ways. Firstly, Peter Witt, the son of Fritz Witt and the nephew of Franz Witt, who provided excellent photographs and also provided invaluable information on aspects of the 3. *Kompanie*'s history. He also very kindly took the time to proof read the manuscript and gave valuable feedback on this. Secondly, Justin Horgan, who has been a close friend for a number of years and has provided photographs, help with research and help with locating former 3. *Kompanie Kameraden*. This included the former 3. *Kompanie* Commander Gerhard Dilling, which was not an easy task. He also was responsible for introducing me to people such as former 3. *Kompanie* Commander, Heinrich Springer and former *Oberscharführer* Max Schmidt. Without these people, this project would not have been completed and I am indebted to all of them.

Last, but not least, are my wife Sandra and my two children Alanna and Karl. This project has taken a number of years and my family has been a constant source of support and understanding. If there was a award for patience, then my Wife deserves it!

Abbreviations List

AuE	Ausbildungs und Ersatz
Bat.	Battalion
B.E.F.	British Expeditionary Force
Hiwis	Hilfs Willige: volunteer helpers

LAH/LSSAH	*Leibstandarte* Adolf Hitler
OKW	Oberkommando der Wehrmacht
Pz.Div.	Panzer Division
Reg.	Regiment
SS	Schutzstaffel
SS VT	SS Verfügungstruppe
StuGs	Sturmgeschütz assault guns
R.A.D.	Reichsarbeitdienst: Labour Service

Rank Structure Changes

SA and SS Ranks before 17/07/33	***SA and SS Ranks after 18/07/33***	***SS Ranks after 15/10/34***
SS (SA) Mann	*SS (SA) Mann*	*Schütze*
		Obershütze
	Sturmmann	*Sturmmann*
	Rottenführer	*Rottenführer*
SS Scharführer	*SS Scharführer*	*Unterscharführer*
	SS Oberscharführer	*Scharführer*
SS Truppführer	*SS Truppführer*	*Oberscharführer*
	SS Obertruppführer	*Hauptscharführer*
	SS Haupttruppführer	*Sturmscharführer*
	SS Sturmführer	*Untersturmführer*
	Obersturmführer	*Obersturmführer*
Sturmführer	*Sturmhauptführer*	*Hauptsturmführer*

In the early days of the SS, a *Kompanie* was known as a *Sturm*. A *Zug* (Platoon) was known as a *Trupp*. From the above list you can discern that a *Truppführer* would have commanded a *Zug* (Platoon) and a *Sturmführer* would have commanded the *Sturm* (*Kompanie*). As the SS expanded, it was necessary to insert further ranks between these main ranks. The control would have stayed the same. Therefore, the *Haupt* (main) *trupp* (*Zug*) *führer* (leader) or *Sturmscharführer* would been the senior NCO. The *Haupt* (main) *sturm* (*Kompanie*) *führer* (leader) would have commanded the overall *Sturm* or *Kompanie*. As the war progressed, it was not uncommon to see lower officer ranks in command of a *Kompanie*, and there are also plenty of examples of NCO's in charge of *Kompanie*s in the field during periods of high casualties.

Gratitude

Any person who wishes to research the history of the 1st SS Panzer Division *Leibstandarte Adolf Hitler*, cannot do so properly without consulting the six-volume (five written and one photographic) history of the Division that was compiled over a period of more than a decade. There were two main people responsible for this compilation; they were former *Standartenführer* Rudolf Lehmann and former *Sturmbannführer* Ralf Tiemann. Together they managed to construct a very thorough record of one of Germany's and one of history's finest fighting units. Without this compilation, a huge gap would exist in the history of the Second World War. This gap would have no-doubt been filled with inaccuracies and misrepresentations. I think for that reason alone, anyone wishing to research the Second World War owes these men a great deal of gratitude. I have listed a short summary of each of these individuals service in the Waffen-SS.

Rudolf Lehmann

Date of birth: 30.01.14 *SS number: 111 883*

Born in Heidelberg, Lehmann joined the *Leibstandarte* in 1933. He stayed with the *LAH* until October 1934 when he then left to attend an SS Officer candidacy program at the Jüterbog training grounds. This lasted until the end of March 1935 and was quickly followed by a year-long course at the Bad Tölz *Junkerschule*. In 1936 he obtained the rank of *Untersturmführer* and was assigned to the *SS-Standarte Germania*, first as a *Zug* leader and then as the *Kompanie* Commander. It was whilst with the *Germania Standarte* that he was awarded the Second Class Iron Cross (Poland) and the First Class Iron Cross (Western Campaign 1940). He returned to the *LAH* during October 1940 as part of the main staff. He spent a spell in hospital that began in August 1941 and lasted until the early part of 1942. He then attended a General Staff Officer course held at the *Reichsakademie* in Berlin. He returned to the *LAH* as the First General Staff Officer. He was awarded the German Cross in Gold during November 1943 in recognition of his bravery. This was followed in February 1944 by the award of the Knight's Cross to the Iron Cross, at the time he was holding the rank of *Obersturmbannführer*. He stayed as the main staff officer of the *LAH* until March 1945 when he took command of the 2nd SS Panzer Division Das Reich, during the battles in Hungary. His bravery was further recognised in May 1945 by the award of the Oakleaves to the Knight's Cross. Rudolf Lehmann died on the 17th of September 1983. Ralf Tiemann continued the work that Lehmann began on tracing the complete story of the LAH after his death.

Left: Rudolf Lehmann seen here with the rank of *Obersturmbannführer*. He was the person responsible for tracing the complete history of the LAH. He died in September 1983 before the work was complete. (Ralf Tiemann) Right: Ralf Tiemann photographed in 1941 with the rank of *Obersturmführer* just before he moved to the LAH's Panzer Regiment. He completed the five-volume history of the LAH alongside Rudolf Lehmann and has been a great help in this project. (Ralf Tiemann)

Ralf Tiemann

Date of Birth: 06.08.18 SS number: 353 109

Born in Bad Salzelmen, Magdeburg, Tiemann served with the R.A.D. during early 1937. He then joined the SS in November 1937 as a member of the *Germania Standarte*. In April 1939 he attended the *SS-Junkerschule* at Braunschweig and left with the rank of *Standartenoberjunker*. By November of the same year he was a *Zug* Leader in the 5. *Kompanie* of the II Battalion within the *LAH*. During the campaign in the west in 1940 he obtained the rank of *Untersturmführer*. In March of 1941 during the campaign in Greece, he became the II Battalion Adjutant. With the invasion of Russia in June, Tiemann was serving with the 7. *Kompanie*. During these early battles in Russia he received two wounds. The first was in July at Uman when he received a head wound. The second was in September at Cherson when he was wounded in the lung. By November 1941 he had reached the rank of *Obersturmführer*. By this stage he had been awarded the Bulgarian Cross 1st Class

(April 1941), Iron Cross Second Class and the Infantry Assault Badge (June 1941) and the First Class Iron Cross (October 1941).

At the start of 1942 Tiemann moved to the *LAH*'s Panzer unit as the Adjutant. By March he was holding the post of *Kompanie* Commander of the 3. Panzer *Kompanie*. In October of the same year he had reached the post of Regimental Adjutant within the *LAH*'s Panzer Regiment. In 1943 he took part in the battle for Kharkov in March and then in April he became the commander of the 7. Panzer *Kompanie*. During the mighty tank battles near Kursk in July 1943, he received his third wound. This time it was shrapnel wound to the left shoulder. He also gained promotion to *Hauptsturmführer*. In August of the same year he became the 1st Ordnance Officer for the *LAH*. In August he also was awarded the Silver Wound Badge and the Panzer Assault Badge. This was followed in October by the award of the German Cross in Gold.

In the early part of 1944 he attended various General Staff courses. By November 1944 he was holding the rank of *Sturmbannführer* and the 4th General Staff Officer of the 6. Panzer Army. This was followed a month later by the move to the 1st General Staff Officer of the *LAH*. He spent the first month of 1945 in Zossen and then moved to the post of 1st General Staff Officer within the 2nd SS Panzer Division *Das Reich*. This was during the final battles in Hungary and Austria. His final post was that of 1st General Staff Officer within the I SS *Panzerkorps*. He past into American captivity during May 1945. He received a fourth wound whilst in captivity, this was a bullet wound to the heart during July 1945!

I think it is fair to say that both Rudolf Lehmann and Ralf Tiemann are more than qualified to record the history of the 1st SS Panzer Division *LSSAH*.

CHAPTER ONE

BIRTH OF A LEGEND

The framework of this work is centered round the 1st SS Panzer Division *Leibstandarte* Adolf Hitler. The birth of this legendary Division can be traced to the 17th of March 1933. On this day 117 people assembled in Berlin-Kreuzberg at the Friesenkaserne. They were sent by the SS leadership who had hand picked volunteers from various SS units. They were first called the *SS Stabswache* Berlin. During April they were transferred to the Lichterfelde barracks and were titled *SS-Sonderkommando* Berlin, this unit contained 1 *Sturm* (*Kompanie*). On the 10th of May 1933 the *Sonderkommando* Zossen was formed, this was a training unit. This was followed on the 8th of July 1933 by the forming of the *Sonderkommando* Juterbog; this was another training unit. On the 2nd of August 1933 the *Sonderkommando* Zossen was amalgamated into the *Sonderkommando* Berlin. The *Sonderkommando* Berlin now had 2 *Stürme*. Within two weeks of this date, mid-August 1933, a third *Sturm* (*Kompanie*) was added. This is the birth of the 3. *Kompanie*. This *Sturm* was commanded by *Sturmführer* Emil Sator.

Emil Sator: The First Commander of the 3. *Sturm/Kompanie*

Date of Birth: 26.07.05 SS number: 11 736

Emil Sator started 1933 with the rank of *Sturmführer* (equivalent to *Hauptsturmführer*). He held this rank when he took command of the newly created 3. *Sturm* in mid-August 1933. He moved to the 4. *Sturm/Kompanie* on the 7th of October

1933 and stayed there until the 9th of December 1933. It is known that on the 1st of November 1934 he took part in the *LAH*'s officer training program held at Jüterbog, he was holding the rank of *Hauptsturmführer* at this stage. It is not known what this officer done between 1934 and 1944, but by that stage he was holding the rank of *Obersturmbannführer* and was in command of the Panzergrenadier AuE. (training) Battalion 18. As far as can be determined, he survived the war.

The Honour of Carrying the Führer's Name

During September 1933 this unit took part in the party rally at Nüremberg. They wore the Adolf Hitler cufftitle for the first time and were renamed *Adolf Hitler Standarte* on this day. The first banner to bear the Führer's name was also presented on this day. On the 8th of September the 3. *Sturm* listed 167 men in its ranks, 139 of these had joined the SS before the 1st of January 1933. A full list of these 167 men is not available. On the 7th of October 1933 the *Sonderkommando* Jüterbog was absorbed into the *Adolf Hitler Standarte*. The unit now had one full Battalion containing four *Kompanies*. The 3. *Kompanie* was now commanded by *Sturmführer* Wilhelm Mohnke, with Albert Stenwedel, Heinrich Lindner, Rudolf Scheide and Harry Polewacz as his *Zug* commanders.

Wilhelm Mohnke: Second Commander of the 3. *Kompanie*

Date of birth: 15.03.11 SS number: 15 541

Wilhelm Mohnke was one of the first 117 men to join what became the *LAH*. At the time he held the rank of *Truppführer* (*Oberscharführer*). He took command of the 3. *Sturm/Kompanie* on the 7th of October 1933, with the rank of *Sturmführer*. Just prior to this, in June 1933, he had attended a Platoon Leaders course at the Infantry Firing School at Döberitz. He stayed with the 3. *Kompanie* until 1934 when he moved to command of the 5. *Kompanie*. For details of the rest of Wilhelm Mohnke's career, see later in this book. He did however finish the war with the rank of *Brigadeführer* and was the third commander of the *LAH* Division.

Albert Stenwedel: Platoon Leader in the 3. *Kompanie*

Date of birth: 10.09.08 SS number: 28 762

Born in Hamburg he became one of Mohnke's *Zug* Führers in the 3. *Sturm/Kompanie*. He was holding the rank of *Scharführer* (*Unterscharführer*) at the time.

On the 22nd of July 1934 there was a dozen Ausbildungs (training) *Kompanie*s formed. Albert Stenwedel was in the 11. A. *Kompanie*, holding the rank of *Obertruppführer* (*Hauptscharführer*). He followed this in 1935 by obtaining the rank of *Untersturmführer*. In April 1937 he attended an MG-*Zugführer*'s course at the Heer's school in Döberitz. On the 15th of May 1938, Stenwedel left the *LAH* to become part of the cadre that formed the *Der Führer Regiment*. By September 1939 he was in the 6. *Kompanie* of the 4th *SS Regiment Der Führer*. By May 1944 he was the commander of the 11. *Kompanie*/27th SS Mountain Regiment within the 13th SS Division *Handschar*. It was with the *Handschar* Division that Albert Stenwedel was awarded the Knight's Cross to the Iron Cross on the 3rd of May 1945. He was commanding the II Battalion at that stage with the rank of *Sturmbannführer*; he survived the war.

Rudolf Scheide: Platoon Leader in the 3. *Kompanie*

Date of birth: 24.12.08 SS number: 2 351

Rudolf Scheide was one of the original 117 men who formed the *LAH*. He was serving with the *Sonderkommando* Zossen in May 1933. He was also holding the rank of *Scharführer* (*Unterscharführer*) when he was with the 3. *Kompanie*. By the 7th of April 1934 he was holding the rank of *Sturmführer* (*Untersturmführer*) and he took over the command of the Motor Vehicle *Kompanie*. By October 1934 he held the rank of *Hauptsturmführer*. By August 1936 he was the *LAH*'s Regimental Engineer. On the 15th of September 1938 he formed the Light Infantry Column. He was back in the post of Regimental Engineer by 1940. He was on the staff of the *LAH* in 1941 with the rank of *Sturmbannführer*. He ended the war holding the rank of *Standartenführer* within the SS-WVHA (SS main administrative office) as part of the *Verkehrswesen* (transportation) section.

Heinrich Lindner: Platoon Leader in the 3. *Kompanie*

Date of birth: 14.06.09 SS number: 18 241

Very little is known about this officer. He held the rank of *Scharführer* (*Unterscharführer*) in 1933 whilst with the 3. *Kompanie*. After the 3. *Kompanie* he became an *Untersturmführer* in 1935, *Obersturmführer* in 1936 and *Hauptsturmführer* in 1937. He was also one of the men who left the *LAH* in May 1938 to form the *Der Führer Regiment*. Towards the end of June 1944 he was serving in the

Right: Wilhelm Mohnke photographed in 1933 not long after the forming of the LAH. At that stage he was holding the rank of *Truppführer*, equivalent to *Oberscharführer*. (Patrick Agte)

Below: Rudolf Scheide photographed with a group of other LAH officers on December 17, 1935. He is in the first row and numbered 13 (third from the left). At that time he was holding the rank of *Hauptsturmführer*. Other officers associated with the 3. Kompanie are also in this photograph. They are *Hauptsturmführer* Hinrich Schuldt (No.19), *Untersturmführer* Albert Stenwedel (No.21) and *Hauptsturmführer* Wilhelm Mohnke (No. 23). (Patrick Agte)

Left: Albert Stenwedel pictured in 1933 holding the rank of *Scharführer*, equivalent to *Unterscharführer*. (Justin Horgan) Right: Albert Stenwedel photographed in 1938 just after he left the LAH to help form the cadre of the newly created 4th SS Regiment "Der Fuhrer" in Austria. (Nick Adams)

Allgemeine-SS with the rank of *Obersturmbannführer*. He survived the war and died in 1973.

Harry Polewacz: Platoon Leader in the 3. *Kompanie*

Date of birth: 31.03.09 SS number: 35 952

Polewacz was also one of the original 117 men who formed the *LAH*. In June 1933 *Truppführer* (*Oberscharführer*) Polewacz attended a Platoon Leaders course at Döberitz. He joined Mohnke's 3. *Kompanie* in October 1933. On the 7th of April 1934 Sturmführer (*Untersturmführer*) Polewacz was with the newly formed Recruit

Kompanie. When the Training *Kompanie*s were formed three months later, he was commanding the 8. A. *Kompanie* and holding the rank of *Obersturmführer*. By August 1939 Polewacz was commanding the 10. *Kompanie* and holding the rank of *Hauptsturmführer*. He was awarded the Second Class Iron Cross on the 8th of September 1939 and the First Class Iron Cross on the 5th of June 1940. He followed this by the award of the German Cross in Gold on the 19th of December 1941. He then received the Knight's Cross to the Iron Cross on the 23rd of December 1942 as commander of the II Battalion of the SS-Regiment *Nordland* within the 5th SS Panzer Division *Wiking*. He was the commander of the *Nordland Regiment* by January 1943 and it was with this unit that he was killed on the 12th of January 1943.

Another Name Change for the *LAH*

The title *Leibstandarte Adolf Hitler* stayed until the 13th of April 1934 when the name changed to *Leibstandarte SS Adolf Hitler*. In June of 1934 the *LAH* were involved in "The Night of the Long Knives". A six-man firing squad was hand picked by Dietrich to carry out the executions of the SA high command in Munich. The orders for the executions came direct from Hitler. Many books have been written about the *LAH* death squads shooting people in Berlin. The *LAH* official history gives a detailed account of this period and states that the *LAH* were confined to barracks during this period.

The *LAH* expanded further on the 17th of October 1934. The training *Kompanie*s at Juterbog were dissolved and used to form a third Battalion within the *LAH*. The 3. *Kompanie* remained within the I Battalion. The *LAH* had a total of 13 *Kompanie*s at this stage. The commander of the 3. *Kompanie* at this stage was *Hauptsturmführer* Hinrich Schuldt; his junior officers were *Untersturmführer* Martin Gross and Fritz Streipart.

Hinrich Schuldt: The Third Commander of the 3. *Kompanie*

Date of birth: 14.06.01 *SS number: 242 677*

Hinrich Schuldt was born in Blankenese, near Hamburg. His military experiences began during the 1920s when he was a member of the *Reichsmarine*, where he obtained the rank of *Leutnant*. He joined the SS in 1933 and the following year he was given command of the 3. *Kompanie*. Schuldt's military career would see him

Right: Harry Polewacz seen in July 1934 holding the rank of *Obersturmführer*, almost a year after his service with the 3. Kompanie. (Patrick Agte)

Below: Harry Polewacz, on the right, pictured in July 1941 in the Ukraine alongside Hubert Meyer. By this stage Polewacz was serving with the 5th SS Division "Wiking". (Hubert Meyer)

reach the rank of SS-*Brigadeführer* und *Generalmajor der Waffen-SS* and Commander of the 2nd Latvian Brigade and later the 19th Latvian *SS-Freiwillige* Division. It was with this Division that he was killed on the 25th of March 1944. His death was as a result of wounds he received whilst with his men at the front line. He was a popular and respected officer and during his time with the Waffen-SS he was awarded the Swords and Oakleaves to the Knight's Cross, the German Cross in Gold and the 1st and 2nd Class Iron Crosses. Besides commanding the 3. *Kompanie*, he also saw action with *Germania*, *Totenkopf*, his own *Kampfgruppe* Schuldt and the 2nd Latvian *Freiwillige* Brigade. Hinrich Schuldt is an excellent example of the type of soldier that fought in the ranks of the Waffen-SS. He displayed courage on numerous occasions and was an example to his men. The 3. *Kompanie* no doubt benefited from his leadership qualities in the early stages of their existence.

Martin Gross: Platoon Leader in the 3. *Kompanie*

Date of birth: 15.04.11 SS number: 6 684

Martin Gross was born in Frankfurt and he joined the SS in May 1933. He served with the 3. *Kompanie* as a Platoon Leader at the end of 1934 with the rank of *Untersturmführer*. By 1937 he was holding the rank of *Obersturmführer*. He took part in the *LAH*'s action in Austria and the Sudetenland before the war. He was serving with the 1. *Kompanie* by the 28th of August 1939. He was awarded the Second Class Iron Cross on the 1st of October 1939. By May 1940 he was the *Kompanie* commander of the 1. *Kompanie* with the rank of *Hauptsturmführer*. He won the First Class Iron Cross on the 20th of July 1940. In April 1941 he took command of the 5. *Kompanie* and it was with this *Kompanie* that he was badly wounded in the battle for Rostov. After his convalescence he was posted to a staff job. He then took command of the II Battalion of the *LAH*'s Panzer Regiment. By January 1943 he was a *Sturmbannführer*. He was awarded the German Cross in Gold on the 28th of March 1943 for actions around Kharkov. This was followed on the 12th of July 1943 by the award of the Knight's Cross to the Iron Cross for actions during the Kursk offensive. The men under his command succeeded in destroying no less than ninety enemy tanks in one engagement. When the *LAH* went west, Martin Gross stayed on the eastern front and moved north to the Riga area in Latvia. He commanded his own *Panzerbrigade* and by November 1944 he was holding the rank of *Obersturmbannführer*. By the end of the war he was commanding the 12th SS Panzer Regiment within the *Hitlerjugend* Division, with the rank of *Obersturmbannführer*. He survived the war.

The only known photograph showing the entire 3. Kompanie. This photo dates from 1934 when Hinrich Schuldt was in command; he can be seen in the front row (ninth from the left). Martin Gross can be seen three places to the right of Schuldt. (Patrick Agte)

Fritz Streipart: Platoon Leader in the 3. *Kompanie*

Date of birth: 08.07.07   SS number: 43 880

Fritz Streipart was one of the first 117 men to join the *LAH* in March 1933. There is little information on this officer in the years between his service with the 3. *Kompanie* and the start of the Second World War. By November 1944 he had reached the rank of *Hauptsturmführer* and was the commander of the 5. *Kompanie* within the *LAH*'s Panzer Regiment. He ended the war with the rank of *Sturmbannführer*. He survived the war and died in 1989.

The *Leibstandarte*'s Pre War Military Actions

On the 1st of March 1935 elements of the *LAH* marched into the Saarland at Bruchmühlbach. The *LAH* continued to grow with the additions of heavy machine gun and *Panzerspähwagen Kompanie*s. In 1935 the *LAH* listed 2551 members. In August of 1936 the *LAH* performed various official duties during the Berlin Olympic Games. Three members of the 3. *Kompanie* served as orderlies at official functions between 1935 and 1938. They were Ernst Kraumendahl, Franz Heurich and Schwerdfeger. These early years of the *LAH*'s existence consisted for the most part of drill, weapons training and vehicle driving skills. As the unit was conceived to guard the Führer, they performed various guard duties and were present at many high profile events. Sports were greatly encouraged within the *LAH* and they had many award-winning sports teams. Of note were the rowing team and the boxing team. Rudi Maule, of the 3. *Kompanie*, was a member of the *LAH*'s rowing team in 1937.

On the 12th of March 1938 the *LAH* took part in the march into Austria. They moved through Linz and by the following day they were in Vienna. At the start of April 1938 the 3. *Kompanie* were in Innsbruck. On the 15th of May 1938 some members of the *LAH* left to form the 4th SS *Regiment Der Führer*. In October of the same year the *LAH* also took part in the march into the Sudetenland. This was after the political settlement at Munich regarding this matter. In March 1939 the *LAH*, who were now designated an Infantry Regiment (mot.), were part of the forces that moved into the area of Bohemia and Moravia. The *LAH* occupied the Ostrau and Witkowitz areas. The *LAH* spent the rest of their time up to the end of August 1939 performing honour guards and continuing with training. The Training *Kompanie* was commanded by *Hauptsturmführer* Hans-Joachim Schiller during late 1939, he would soon take over the command of the 3. *Kompanie*. Also in this training *Kompanie* at that time was Günther Zaag, he would also command the 3. *Kompanie* later in the war, and Hans Komischke who would move to the 3. *Kompanie* during July 1940.

Left: Hinrich Schuldt pictured in 1942 as an *Obersturmbannführer*. At that stage he was commanding the 4th SS Infantry Regiment "Totenkopf" and had been recently awarded the Knight's Cross. (Author's collection) Right: Martin Gross photographed in 1943 holding the rank of *Sturmbannführer* and after his award of the Knight's Cross. (Justin Horgan)

Above: Fritz Streipart photographed in early 1934 while serving with the 1. Kompanie, and just prior to his move to the 3. Kompanie. At that time he held the rank of *Rottenführer*. He is seen in the back row, second from the left. (Justin Horgan)

Right: Fritz Streipart photographed in mid-1944. At this time he was holding the rank of *Obersturmführer* and was commanding the LAH's 5. Panzer Kompanie. (Patrick Agte)

On the 24th of August 1939 the *LAH* was put on alert due to the increasingly deteriorating political climate and the expectation of forthcoming hostilities. Over the next four days the *LAH* moved to their designated area of Namslau, close to the German/Polish border. The 3. *Kompanie* were commanded by *Hauptsturmführer* Wichmann at this stage.

The Polish question had been brewing since March 1939. In April a plan had been drawn up by the OKW, under the code name 'Case White', that detailed the army missions for the attack on Poland. The twenty-one year peace that had stood since the end of the First World War was about to come to an end.

Hauptsturmführer* Jochen Wichmann: Fourth Commander of the 3. *Kompanie

Date of birth: 09.12.09 SS number: 61 569

He is first listed as an *Untersturmführer* in March 1935. By November of the following year he had achieved the rank of *Obersturmführer*. On the 20th of April 1939 he had reached the rank of *Hauptsturmführer*. After leaving the *LAH* he moved on to service with the *Totenkopf Standarte* in early 1940, the Replacement Battalion East in late 1940, the Training and Replacement Battalion 31 in 1943 and finally the 16th SS Division *Reichsführer-SS* in 1944. He ended the war with the rank of *Sturmbannführer*.

CHAPTER TWO

THE START OF THE SECOND WORLD WAR: POLAND

The attack on Poland was to be one of almost complete encirclement. Army Group South, under von Rundstedt, contained three Armies and was responsible for the main attacks. The 8th Army would advance east towards Lodz. The 10th Army would move towards Warsaw, while the 14th Army would advance southeast towards the Galician region. Army Group North, under von Bock, contained the 3rd and 4th Armies. They would push through the Polish corridor and down from East Prussia. The *LAH* were part of the 8th Army under Blaskowitz and they had the 10th Army close by. Within the 8th Army the *LAH* were subordinated to the 17th Infantry Division, who was part of the XIII *Armeekorps*. Mobility was to be the key and emphasis was placed on the need for speedy advances.

The Polish army facing them had realised the vulnerability of their country and had prepared a serious defensive strategy in 1938. The Pomorze Army was in the Polish corridor, the Poznan Army was on the western border with the Lodz Army in front of Lodz. To the south were the Cracow and Carpaty Armies, with the Modlin and Narew Armies in the north. The Polish plan was designed to hold of the Germans until help arrived from the west.

Week One: Engagement and the First Casualties

The *LAH* moved across the border on the 1st of September 1939. Their march route was from Namslau to Gola, via Kronstadt and Pitschen. The main objective was the bridge at Gola. This was taken after brief fighting and the advance continued. By the end of the first week's fighting the *LAH* were at Pabianice. They had moved via Burzenin and had also forced a crossing of the Warthe river. In this first week the 3. *Kompanie* had seen action in the following areas – Nalepa (1st September), where *Oberscharführer* Rudi Schiller, *Rottenführer* Werner Mohr and *Rottenführer* Kurt Schwertfeger were killed. Stolec (3rd September), where *Obersturmführer* Franz Fischer, *Rottenführer* Kurt Michaelis, *SS-Mann* Kurt Berger, *SS-Mann* Willi Lange and *SS-Mann* Bruno Schmidt were killed. Pabianice (7th September), where *SS-Mann* Robert Bruning was killed. These men would be the first of many casualties to be suffered by the 3. *Kompanie* in what became known as the Second World War.

Week Two: Lodz and on Towards Warsaw

There was heavy fighting in the Pabianice area and the *LAH* met their first real stiff resistance, they even had to give ground. There was help from army units and the

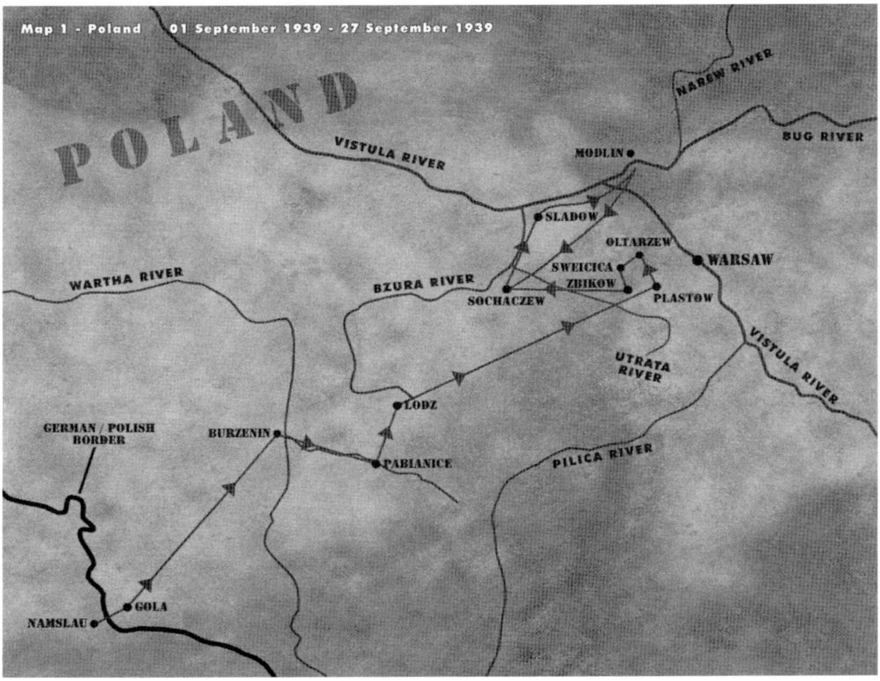

Map of Poland

resistance was finally broken. The 3. *Kompanie* were responsible for capturing a factory in this area. After the fall of Pabianice the way to Lodz was open. In a surprise move the city of Lodz was surrendered to the 17th Infantry Division on the 8th of September. On this day, the 3. *Kompanie* suffered the deaths of *SS-Mann* Adolf Thiede and *SS-Mann* Mathias Frick. The Polish army had moved out of this area and was retreating fast towards Warsaw. Elements of the German army were now on the outskirts of the capital; the final moves were taking shape.

The *LAH* were moved to the west of Warsaw. They were detached from the XIII *Armeekorps* for this move and attached to the XVI *Armeekorps*. Upon arrival at the designated area of Nadarzyn they were subordinated to the 4th Panzer Division. This move was complete by the 9th of September, the day on which *Sturmmann* Hans Ellmerer was fatally wounded. Their orders were to form part of the blocking force that was to be placed to the south and west of Warsaw to prevent any enemy retreats. They were sent to the Domaniew area near the Utrata river. They reached this area in piecemeal fashion and were immediately involved in heavy fighting. The 3. *Kompanie* fought at Oltarzew, as part of the I Battalion, against sizeable enemy forces. The *LAH* eventually gained the initiative and more than 1000 enemy prisoners passed into captivity from this area. On the 10th of September the 3. *Kompanie* lost *Sturmmann* Werner Schönrock and *SS-Mann* Walter Boysnen, both killed at Oltarzew.

A short lull in the fighting was used for rest and repair. Then on the 12th of September the *LAH* were involved in heavy fighting with retreating Polish forces and on this day the 3. *Kompanie* were fighting at Pilaszkow where *Sturmmann* Ernst Augustin, *Sturmmann* Ernst Bantow, *SS-Mann* Siegfried Dreher, *SS-Mann* Erich Pfannkuchen and *SS-Mann* Hans Nitzsche were all killed. Immediately after this the 3. *Kompanie* were placed as Battalion reserve, but elements were used to relink the 1. and 7. *Kompanies*. These 3. *Kompanie* soldiers entered the battle and helped to retake the town of Sweicice. Repeated counterattacks were made by the enemy and due to increasing pressure the *LAH* were ordered back to the Domaniew area to allow a better defence. The 3. *Kompanie* were to secure the town of Zbikow and to link up with the 31st Infantry Division. The following day saw the *LAH* moving slightly north to the Sochaczew and Kutno areas. They would be part of the 8th Army's battle for the area north of Warsaw.

Week Three: Actions Around the Bzura River

These moves were started and by the 14th of September the I Battalion had moved to the left towards the Bzura River. The 3. *Kompanie* were involved in heavy fighting at Sochaczew against enemy forces that were trying to break through to Warsaw. It was here that *Untersturmführer* Karl Wilhelm Janssen was killed along with *Unterscharführer* Erich Jadecke, *Sturmmann* Heinrich Eggers and *SS-Mann* Harry Nehring. On the 16th of September the I Battalion crossed the Bzura river and captured the town of Julianopol, where *Unterscharführer* Otto Felleckner and *Sturmmann* Günther Kube were added to the 3. *Kompanie*'s list of losses. The Battalion was then placed as the reserve unit.

It was on the 16th of September that the commander of the Polish 17th Division was captured; he had the attack plans with him. The German plans were amended to make better use of the available forces. The main objective was to close any escape route to Warsaw. The I Battalion was attached to Attack Group Hartlieb (part of 5th Panzer Brigade). Their orders were to attack towards Sladow; the move to this town was via Trojanow, where on the 17th of September, *SS-Mann* Heinz Pioch was killed. On the 18th, Sladow was reached and the 3. *Kompanie* lost *Rottenführer* Willi Kutz. With this, elements of the *LAH* were at the river Vistula. Due to enemy pressure these elements were surrounded. Supplies were sent to help them hold that area. The following day the II and III Battalions broke through. The defeat of the enemy in this area netted over 2000 enemy prisoners. After this heavy fighting a short rest was allowed. The first reports arrived of *LAH* soldiers being murdered and mutilated after being captured.

The Modlin Forts and the Final Stages

North-east of Warsaw the Bug and Vistula rivers meet, close to where they meet is the Modlin area. The Polish forces had constructed fortifications during the pre-war years to help defend this area. These fortifications became the *LAH*'s next objective. They were moved to the area south of here and placed under the XV *Armeekorps*. This *Korps* was commanded by *General* Hoth and they were preparing to surround the forts from the south. The *LAH* moved to the Kol. Lubiec area on the 21st and they were placed under the 29th Division. They were ordered closer to the forts and by the 24th they were opposite Fort V., they had moved via the Dubrozyn area. Their move to this area gave them the entire defensive responsibility for this area.

Hitler visited the town of Guzow on the following day and Dietrich was among those that met him. On the 26th of September the I Battalion were relieved by elements of the 221st Division. This Battalion was placed as the Regimental reserve in the Brzozowka region. The 27th of September saw the surrender of Warsaw. The *LAH* were relieved the following day and sent to the Sochaczew area. They spent the next few days resting and carrying out repairs. Some Polish forces continued fighting into the first week of October.

The First Victory and Counting the Cost

The end of the Polish campaign provided a welcome rest for Germany's forces. In just over five weeks they had advanced 300 miles into enemy territory. They executed a double pincer move on Poland's forces and completed their destruction on the Bzura river. The *LAH*, who had advanced 170 miles, had taken part in many decisive battles. They could now consider themselves as battle proven. The training had produced the required results, although they had been criticised by some for their methods. They, like their Army *Kameraden*, had paid the price in fallen comrades. Besides this, the German forces had been informed of Britain and France's decision to declare war on them on the 3rd of September 1939. The reason given for the declaration of war was Germany's invasion of Poland. On the 17th of September, Russia invaded Poland from the east. Britain and France failed to declare war on Russia for this action. The prospect of a Second World War was weighing heavily upon the men of the German forces.

The *LAH* had lost over 100 dead and almost 300 wounded during this campaign. The 3. *Kompanie* themselves had suffered at least thirty casualties, the last of which was *SS-Mann* Otto Hohnke on the 23rd of September, at Modlin, and *Rottenführer* Hans-Joachim Opelt on the 24th.

The German victory had been so rapid that the western powers did not have enough time to effectively mobilise their forces. A new method of warfare was born and with the dawn of Blitzkreig, the western powers watched ... and waited.

CHAPTER THREE

PAUSE AND PREPARATION

The first day of October 1939 saw the *LAH* ordered southeast into Prague. The moves began the next day and by the 4th of October they were in Prague's Wenzel square. They took part in a parade and were warmly greeted by the population. At the start of November the *LAH* were moved to the Bad Ems region. They conducted war games and training, particular attention was paid to night fighting. On the 23rd of December 1939 Hitler visited his namesake unit and gave a short speech. Part of the speech read as follows, "As long as I have the honour to stand at the spearhead of this battle, it is for you, the men of my *Leibstandarte*, an honour to be the spearhead of this battle."

The first few months of 1940 were a relatively quite phase for the *LAH*. On the 17th of April 1940 they were renamed Reinforced *Leibstandarte SS Adolf Hitler*. At the end of April the seeds of the *LAH*'s Panzer unit were laid in the form of an integral Sturmgeschütz Unit. The training also shifted emphasis towards river crossings. A motorcycle platoon was also formed prior to the start of the campaign in the west. The purpose of this platoon was to perform fast mobile duties. This included four motorcycles from the 3. *Kompanie*. They would be responsible for capturing some of the vital bridges in the opening stages of the campaign.

Due to the casualties suffered during the Polish Campaign, replacements were sent to the various *Kompanie*s within the *LAH*. Amongst the replacements sent to the 3. *Kompanie* were Max Schmidt (joined 1st September) and Heinz Kirsch (joined 30th of August). Max had been called up initially in April 1938. On the 1st of September 1939 he was posted to the 1. Ersatz (replacement) *Kompanie* and was given the identification mark 1. E.L.A.H. 306. Due to basic training Max and Heinz had missed out on the fighting in Poland. They were sent from the replacement *Kompanie* in Berlin to the 3. *Kompanie* at the start of November 1939, during its' time in Prague. They were then moved to Bad Ems at the end of November. In a conversation with the author, Max and Heinz recalled being present when Adolf Hitler visited the *LAH* and made his famous speech mentioned above. They felt proud to be present during this occasion. The 3. *Kompanie* were commanded by *Hauptsturmführer* Hans Joachim Schiller at this stage.

CHAPTER FOUR

THE FIRST CAMPAIGN IN THE WEST: 1940

France and Britain declared war upon Germany, on the 3rd of September 1939. This left Hitler with the problem of having to eliminate this new threat from the west. At the time, the western powers expected an attack from Germany immediately after the end of the Polish campaign. What did develop was a 'phony war' that had little or no offensive actions by either side. What were taking place behind the scenes during this time were intensive attempts to find a solution to the problem. All of the nations involved had vivid memories of the last conflict and they wanted to avoid a repeat of that conflict. As the winter months of 1939-1940 progressed, the chance of a diplomatic solution passed by. The British sent their B.E.F. to Europe and along with their French Allies they prepared for the expected German attack.

The Allies anticipated a repeat of the German First World War attack plan and they positioned their forces accordingly. The best Allied troops were sent north and positioned opposite the Low Countries. Two further Allied reserve lines were established, one of which was opposite the Ardennes region, further south. In the years of peace since the end of World War I, the French and Belgians had been busy constructing formidable defensive fortifications. The French had their Maginot Line, which was considered by all to be impregnable. The Belgians had built Eben Emael, a fortification situated on high ground that gave it commanding views of the surrounding countryside. The Allied intelligence anticipated a quick and decisive victory over Germany, and they had good reason to believe this. Firstly, they had

Left: Max Schmidt photographed in 1940 just before he left the 3. Kompanie to join the 5. Kompanie. He was holding the rank of *Sturmmann* at this stage and had been awarded the Second Class Iron Cross. He would finish the war with the rank of *Oberscharführer* and holder of the First Class Iron Cross. Max helped immensely in this project and unfortunately died in April 2001, on the same day he was born in 1920! (Justin Horgan) Right: Heinz Kirsch photographed as an *Oberscharführer*. He served in the 3. Kompanie during 1940, and moved to the 5. Kompanie in November 1940 along with Max Schmidt. (Heinz Kirsch)

the luxury of numerical superiority in men and machines, although, at the time, they over-estimated the numerical strength of the German tanks. Secondly, the Allies were equipped with modern tanks and planes that did, at that time, outclass the German machines with regards to armour and weaponry. The task facing the Germans was indeed a formidable one.

On the German side a plan was drawn up, initially based on the Schlieffen Plan, which was of World War I vintage. This would have drawn the Allies into the Low Countries and then a secondary attack would swing behind the bulk of the Allies towards Paris, thus encircling them in a pocket of annihilation. Through an unfortunate accident, a copy of these plans had fallen into the hands of the Allies. Therefore, a quick change was needed. Erich von Manstein, who at that time was Guderian's Chief of Staff, devised a variation of the original plan. He submitted his proposal on a number of occasions throughout the winter months, only to have them rejected. Manstein finally got the opportunity to explain his proposal, which

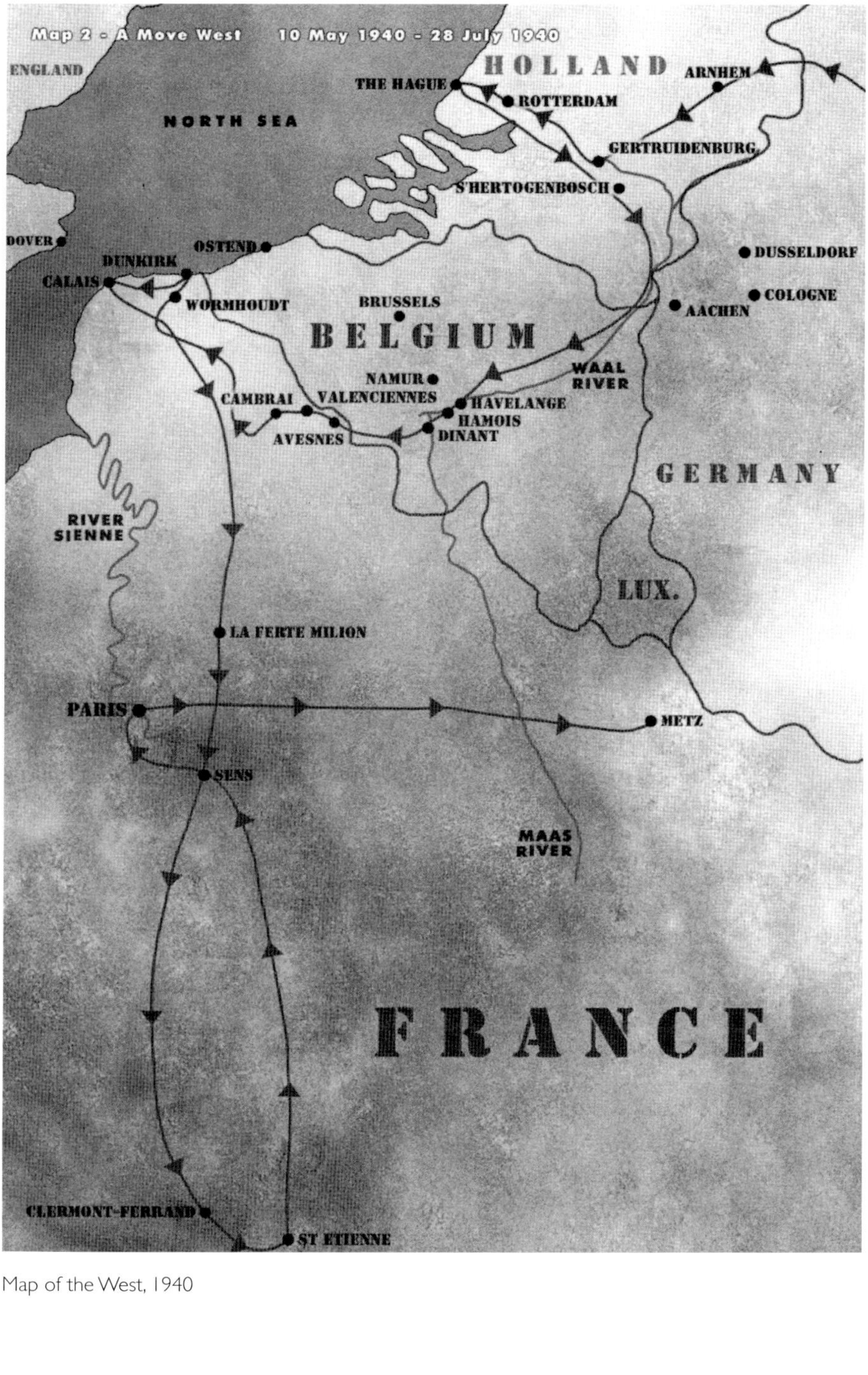

Map of the West, 1940

was different to the ideas of General Staff direct to Hitler during February 1940. Hitler accepted the plan, but took the credit himself!

The basis of the forthcoming campaign was as follows. There would be a diversionary attack in the Low Countries, just as the Allies anticipated. The Allies would then move forwards against this attack. The shift of the main thrust however, would now be in the Ardennes region. An area that was considered to be 'tank-proof' and an area that was not covered by the Maginot Line; the campaign was given the code name 'Operation Yellow'.

The German forces were split into three Army Groups and positioned as follows; Army Group A would move through the Ardennes. They had XXXXI and XIX *Panzerkorps*, together with the XIV *Armeekorps*. Their objective was to cross the Meuse River at Sedan. Army Group B would advance through Belgium and Holland, and they were given three Panzer Divisions to aid their task. Army Group C would be opposite the Maginot Line.

The *Leibstandarte* were part of Army Group B and were attached to the 18th Army. They were subordinated to the 227th Division. The *LAH*'s orders were to break through the Dutch positions on the Issjel and Nieder Rhine rivers, and advance towards Rotterdam. *Fallschirmjäger* troops would be dropped behind the lines to hold key positions until the *LAH* linked up with them. The I Battalion was directly subordinated to the X *Armeekorps*. They were to attack Bocholt moving via Aalten, Lichten, Groenlo and Eibergen. They would then be placed at the *korps* disposal. The lessons learnt by all of the German troops in the Polish Campaign would be put to good use.

The Moves Begin: Holland

The alert went out to all troops on the 9th of May 1940. Then at 05:05 a.m. on the 10th, the code word Danzig was given to signal the start of the offensive. The 3. *Kompanie*, together with the rest of the I Battalion, moved out at 06:00 a.m. The move was mainly on foot. By that evening they had reached Oosterhuizen. The I Battalion went on to occupy Ruurlo; here they were subordinated to the 207th Division and were ordered to the Arnhem area. All their missions had been achieved. They had taken over 1000 prisoners. The following day the I Battalion were attached to the *SS Der Führer Regiment* and billeted in Oosterbeek. Their orders were to attack towards Wageningen, positioned slightly west of Oosterbeek.

For this attack, the I Battalion had the right flank. They were responsible for a patch of woods outside the town. The town was captured by the *Der Führer*

Regiment before noon. In the evening the I Battalion were re-attached to the *LAH*. The 13th of May saw the *LAH* move towards Gertruidenburg whilst subordinated to the XXXIX *Armeekorps*. Gertruidenburg is over fifty miles south west of the Arnhem-Oosterbeek region. The fast pace of the advance was key to the success of the German plans. For one member of the 3. *Kompanie*, this was experienced at first hand. Max Schmidt was seeing his first action of the war and he remembers the orders to move out of the Arnhem area. One of the bridges was damaged and all that was left intact was a water pipe, which ran directly under the bridge. They were ordered to cross the river by any means. Max watched as some of his *Kameraden* crossed this pipe on a motorcycle! The driver and passenger would use their feet to steady themselves. He remembers that a few people ended up in the river, but plenty of people did make it across. Towards Getruidenburg the *LAH* were ordered to capture the vital bridge over the Wilhelmina Canal. This bridge was taken under fire. The next day they moved to Moerdijk where they crossed the bridge over the Maas River. Here they were greeted by elements of the 7th *Flieger* Division who had taken the bridge.

The next objective was Rotterdam. Paratroops had landed near the bridge leading into the city and were holding it against repeated attacks. The Dutch surrendered in the evening after a bomber attack on the city. Following this the *LAH* moved into the city to link with the paratroops; who had been holding out for three days. The *LAH* had difficulty in locating survivors. The Dutch were still fighting. When they reached the Delft area they linked with the main paratroop force. It was around this time that *General* Kurt Student received a wound during an exchange of fire. The capture of this city netted 3500 prisoners. On the 15th of May the push continued into the Hague. The securing of this area added another 7000 prisoners to the total.

Belgium and France

The *LAH* were relieved on 16th by the X *Armeekorps*. They took part in a parade in Amsterdam and then moved back to Arnhem for a short rest and repair period. Between the 18th and 19th of May 1940 the *LAH* moved towards northern France as part of the SS-VT. They reached the Evelette, Hamois, Havelange and Barvaux areas, centered on the N16 Highway and were subordinated to the 20th Infantry Division. They then stopped at Barvaux and awaited orders. This was followed by a quick move towards Avesnes then north east through Le Quesnoy.

This photograph dates from 1940 during the western campaign and was taken whilst the 3 Kompanie were in Holland. The key symbol and 3. Kompanie markings can be clearly seen. The names of these 3. Kompanie men are not known. (Gabriel Gorman)

They were ordered to move to the Valenciennes area and take up defensive positions. The I Battalion where in the centre with the III Battalion on the right and the II Battalion on the left. The enemy had blockades set up over the La Rochelle River. Reconnaissance was sent out, the enemy resistance was growing. On the 23rd of May the *LAH* pushed forward slowly. The 3. *Kompanie* were involved in trying to clear the enemy from positions at Sebourg. They managed to get within fifty metres of the enemy, but could advance no further due to enemy pressure. They eventually disengaged in the evening. The *LAH* were then relieved by the 1st and 8th Infantry Divisions. Their next designated area was at Lumbres where they were attached to XIX *Armeekorps* under Guderian. They were to assist in the 1st Panzer Division's attack on the Dunkirk area, with a specific objective of Watten. The attack began on the 25th of May 1940.

The Push Towards the Coast: Watten and Wormhoudt

At this stage in the campaign the German Armies encirclement of the enemy was almost complete. A few days earlier, the British tank forces had launched an attack into the flank of the main German armoured advance. This caused considerable panic in the German High Command and was an example of what damage could have been done to the German plans, if the Allies had have been more coordinated. Further north, in the *LAH*'s area of responsibility, bridgeheads had been established over the Aa river at St. Omer and also the Canal de l'Aa. This day saw Hitler issue his famous halt order. Max Schmidt recalls everyone's astonishment at this order. The troops on the ground were told that Hitler considered the British to be Germany's 'Blood Brothers'. They were told 'not to kill our blood brothers'. Max has contemplated since, how different things would have been if they had have been allowed to continue with the pursuit of the British at this stage in the campaign. The German forces in the area were ordered onto the defensive. The *LAH* were at St. Momelin. The 3. *Kompanie*, together with the rest of the I Battalion were in reserve at Nordausques. Sepp Dietrich, however, had different ideas.

The Wattenberg heights east of Watten had a commanding view of the area, and therefore were important to both sides. The III Battalion was ordered to gain this area. This was accomplished within forty-five minutes. The result was that the enemy withdrew from southern Watten. Dietrich had to explain his decision to disobey a direct *Führerbefehl*, or Führer Order, to Guderian. His explanation, "from the top of the Wattenberg you can look down on everything. I prefer to look down on the enemy, rather than let them look at me". Due to the success of the action, Guderian backed him. The *LAH* stayed in this area until the 26th of May 1940.

The following day the *LAH* moved over the Canal de l'Aa. They were subordinated to the 20th Division. They were facing the British 48th Division and their advance was towards the Wormhoudt area. Bitter fighting took place throughout the day. The III Battalion was at La Couche with the I Battalion and the 3. *Kompanie* positioned at l'Erkelsbrügge. The Belgian Army surrendered on this day. The pursuit continued on the 28th of May with the 3. *Kompanie* moving along the line north of Esquelbecq-Westcappel-Rexpoede. The 2. *Kompanie* where on their right. The II Battalion was fighting further south. The British 44th and 48th Divisions were giving strong resistance backed up with artillery; the fire was coming from Wormhoudt and Esquelbecq.

The 3. *Kompanie* suffered losses around the Wormhoudt area on this day. They included *Untersturmführer* Werner Linde, *Rottenführer* Herbert Sollman, *Sturmmann* Werner Sprecht, *Sturmmann* Ernst Lindenberg and *SS-Mann* Bernhard Pietsch. Max Schmidt was fighting alongside *Sturmmann* Werner Sprecht on this day. They came under fire from three British soldiers. Max and Werner jumped into a hole for cover. As they were still under fire, they attempted to move to better cover. It was during this move that Werner received his mortal wound. Werner did ask for help, but it was of no use and he died shortly after this. This experience left a deep impression upon Max that remained with him for a long time. Another person who left a deep impression upon Max from this time was the *Kompanie* Chef, *Hauptsturmführer* Schiller. He recalled having good memories of fighting under Schiller in the battles taking place during this period.

Just before noon, Sepp Dietrich and Max Wünsche visited the I Bat.; they also intended to visit the II Battalion. On route they came under attack and became trapped in a ditch close to the enemy positions. Their vehicle caught fire after being hit and both of them had to smear themselves with mud to protect them against the heat. A number of *Kompanie*s tried to rescue them but they came under fire and suffered losses. Eventually, in the afternoon part of the 2. *Kompanie* successfully rescued them.

Wormhoudt, itself, was taken by 19:00 hours that day. The enemy tried many counterattacks, but all were repulsed. An hour later the men of the *LAH* left the town. This day has been remembered by many survivors of the *LAH* as the hardest day yet in the western campaign.

The 29th of May saw the *LAH* occupy Wormhoudt. The 20th Infantry Division ordered the attack to continue towards the Yser River. Their objective was the Winnezeele and Bambecque areas. The 3. *Kompanie* suffered the loss of *SS-Mann* Fritz Frobel and *SS-Mann* Theodor Noll during this day's advances. The II Battalion was on the right flank with the I Battalion on the left. Both Battalions fought against ever increasing resistance. The enemy were fighting for their lives and trying to escape whilst delaying the Germans. The II Battalion captured the ground on both sides of the N16 Highway. The I Battalion captured the railway embankment at Rexpoede. This fighting continued into the following day and many counter-attacks were stopped. Contact between the two Battalions was lost, but the I Battalion pushed forward and also reached the N16 Highway. The two Battalions relinked. The Regiment was subordinated to the 9th Panzer Division and ordered to continue the pursuit of the enemy. This was changed and they stopped for the night.

The Enemy's Retreat to the Coast at Dunkirk

The enemy was routed and was fleeing towards Dunkirk. They left behind vast quantities of equipment. Equipment was not the only thing that they left behind, as

Max Schmidt recalls. The pursuit of the enemy was so fast that Max and some of his 3. *Kompanie Kameraden* came across some chickens that were cooking on a spit. The enemy must have just left the area, as the chickens were still warm. They stopped and quickly consumed the ready prepared meal so thoughtfully cooked by the Allies!

On the 31st of May the Reg. were attached to Group von Kleist and ordered to Calais. This area was reached on the 1st day of June 1940. During these two days, the 3. *Kompanie* suffered more losses. This time, *Sturmmann* Erich Rokitta (31st of May) and *Rottenführer* Günther Kell (1st of June) were added to the casualty list. The second and third days of June were spent on rest and repair.

According to the *LAH*'s official history, the famous key symbol appeared for the first time. The original idea came from the III Battalion who wanted to use the Baltic Cross symbol, their commander was W. Trabandt who was awarded the Baltic Cross in World War I. He refused the idea and quickly drew a key symbol, the *dietrich* (no mention was made of Sepp at this stage). The key symbol was used as the III Battalion opened the Prosna sector in Poland and also the Ijssel positions at Zutphen; This symbol was soon used by the whole Regiment. When Dietrich saw it he liked it. The shield was added later and then when Dietrich was awarded the Oakleaves to the Knight's Cross the oakleaf cluster was added. The use of symbols had appeared in general during the western campaign and although unofficial, it did greatly aid recognition and orientation.

During the 3rd and 4th of June, the last English bridgehead was destroyed. Many questions have been asked as to why the Germans did not immediately continue their pursuit across the English Channel. The facts were that Germany's surface fleet had been effectively crippled in the recent Norwegian campaign. Additionally, there were still sizeable French forces to the south with the remaining Allies having around 2000 tanks left in operation. There had also been an immense strain put on the men and especially the machines of the German armed forces. They had been fighting continuously for weeks and had covered long distances; they simply were not in a position to mount this type of operation. There was the political situation to weigh up also. Any invasion of England would be costly. Hitler had hoped that the defeat of the bulk of the British forces in France would help bring Churchill to the negotiation table. The job was not done yet and the complete defeat of the Allies was needed.

A Move to the South and Defeat of the Enemy

The remaining French Army composed of sixty-six Divisions, were expanding their defensive positions from the mouth of the Somme river to the Maginot Line. The German orders were to attack the enemy before they could prepare extensive defenses. The attacks began on the 5th of June 1940. The *LAH*'s march began the following day. They moved via Moeuvres and Marcoing, stopping just north of Peronne, they were attached to XVI *Armeekorps*. This position was in the World War I Somme battlefields. On the 7th the Reg. split into march groups A to F. The 3. *Kompanie*, together with the rest of the I Battalion were in March Group E.

The orders were to advance after the retreating enemy. The *LAH* moved towards the N38 Highway near the town of Mery, the I Battalion was the reserve unit. The move continued to Combles and Longueval. Here they were attached to Army Group B. The objective was to push across the Oise and Ourcq rivers. By the 9th of June the *LAH* were moving towards Soissons, they were now subordinated to the XXXXIV *Armeekorps*. One French Corps and two English Divisions were being surrounded at Abbeville. Von Kleist had captured the southern area and the 6th Army where moving towards Compiegne. This day and the following day saw the Regiment fighting through enemy positions at St. Quentin and Chezy. They were part of 72nd Infantry Division, and were successful in capturing prisoners from the French 11th Division.

The I Battalion fought up to the Clignon stream. During the 11th of June, in preparation for the attack across the stream, the II and III Battalions were moved to either side. The enemy where positioned on the high ground to the south of the stream. The stream was crossed, but progress was slow. The 72nd Infantry Division were trying to push the enemy over the Marne. An enemy strongpoint had developed around a chateau building on the high ground. The enemy were shelling the *LAH* and inflicting losses. The II Battalion under Mohnke ordered a feint attack to the north with a corresponding one to the east. Support was given by the mortars and artillery. The chateau fell at 17:00 hrs, the *LAH* then moved towards Montreuil via Brumetz and Coloumbs. Coloumbs was taken after a brief fight and reconnaissance was sent out to Montreuil. This route was becoming congested with the 72nd Infantry Division's horse drawn wagons, a halt was ordered. The *LAH* deployed to the Ste. Aulde area and held the *Korps* area to the north west.

The Marne river was reached on the 12th near Ste. Aulde. The enemy had blown the railway bridges. The high ground at Le Mondel and east of Caumont was occupied by the II Battalion They could observe the enemy moving up to the bend in the Marne and inflicted heavy losses on them. The I Battalion moved south from Dhuisy and captured Tanquex on the west bank of the Marne. The II Battalion pushed on and forced a crossing near the railway embankment. The pioneers had erected a foot ridge less than an hour later. Messy was captured the same evening. Also that evening, orders arrived from the XXXXIV *Armeekorps*. The *LAH* were to leave their present formation and join Group von Kleist at Eterpilly. On the 12th of June, *Rottenführer* Henry Peters was added to the list of 3. *Kompanie* casualties.

The *LAH* moved via Ferne and Bouresches and were in place by the 13th. The following day was used for rest. The radio announced that German troops were marching through Paris, it was clear that the enemy were crumbling. The Seine River had been crossed on both sides of Paris. Von Kleist was pursuing the enemy towards Lyon and the Rhone Valley. Some German units were ordered to the Swiss and Italian borders. Guderian was ordered to swing east and attack the Maginot Line in the rear. The German plans were coming to fruition.

The *LAH* stayed in their positions until the 16th of June. They were then ordered to the Provins area. This was completed the same day and they were attached to the 9th Panzer Division. The following day they moved towards Sens via the Seine. On route they were ordered to Touchy via Jaigny and Alliant. The final order was to move to St. Amand via S. Sauveur, here the *LAH* were placed under *Panzergruppe* von Kleist. This was the day that the new French President Marshall Petain announced that France would lay down its' weapons. The Government sent a message via the Spanish Foreign Ministry appealing for an Armistice. While the politics were being decided, the soldiers continued with their job.

On the 18th the *LAH* were ordered to Decize via Brinon and Rouy. The bridge at Decize had been destroyed so they moved west towards Nevers and Moulins. The bridge at Moulins was destroyed as the *LAH* approached it. The Allier River was crossed at Villeneuve and advance elements were sent to Souvigny. After this town was taken the I and II Battalions occupied it. The III Battalion and the Artillery stayed on the east bank of the river. The pursuit of the enemy continued the following day. The *LAH* captured the town of St. Pourcain as the enemy was still erecting defences. As they moved through the town the enemy resistance stiffened. The bridge at the far end of town was blown before they could take it, but a crossing was made further down the river. They held the town under ever increasing enemy fire from the opposite riverbank. They eventually overrun the enemy taking 950 prisoners. The advance continued towards Gannat, by that evening, the *LAH* were holding the line from Begues to Peyrolles.

There was no time for rest and on the 20th of June they were ordered to a new line from Riom to Maringes. The II Battalion had Riom and the I Battalion had Pont-du-Chateau, whilst the III Battalion were in reserve. The I Battalion captured their objective and sent reconnaissance towards Clermont-Ferrand. They reported back that the airstrip was still occupied by the enemy. The 2. *Kompanie* engaged in a long battle for the airstrip. The 3. *Kompanie* were behind the 2. *Kompanie* at the airstrip. When the airstrip was taken it netted hundreds of intact planes along with some tanks and other vehicles; over 250 prisoners were taken also. In front of them lay Clermont-Ferrand. There were thousands of enemy troops still in the town. An *LAH* NCO was responsible for disarming an enemy barracks. Inside there was a Brigadier-General, seventy other officers and 2000 fully armed men. With this the town was occupied, although this proved to be a sizeable task as the town had 130,000 occupants and a large amount of captured material.

The 22nd saw the *LAH* ordered east towards the Feurs-Montrand Meylieu area. There was an estimated nine to eleven enemy Divisions in this region. The men moved towards La Foullouse where they met resistance at an enemy roadblock. This was cleared with some difficulty as the enemy had tanks. These were destroyed by the artillery and a further 400 prisoners passed into captivity. They moved towards St. Etienne on the 24th and took this town with a pincer movement. The 3. *Kompanie* were on the western flank of the pincer and advanced through Villars and St. Geriet and onto the southern part of St. Etienne.

The 24th of June 1940 also saw the signing of the Armistice. This brought the western campaign to an end. In the space of forty-four days Germany's forces defeated the Dutch, Belgian, French and English Armies. Over 1,500,000 prisoners had been captured in addition to vast amounts of material. This had only been possible with the help of the Luftwaffe. The *LAH* themselves had been placed under the control of over two dozen different commands in this time and had seen a total of twenty-two days combat. The fact that they performed their tasks well shows the flexibility that the German forces enjoyed. This was a distinct advantage over their adversaries. The plans that were drawn up months ago had been brought to fruition. The enemy had not been prepared for this type of warfare. The key to this victory was co-operation. Germany had shown what could be achieved when the ground forces and the air force worked closely together.

The German forces had achieved their victory over modern equipped armies who possessed superior weapons. This victory is one of the fastest and most complete victories in the history of warfare. The Germans had advanced from their borders to the coast of France in around six weeks. This is something, which their predecessors had been unable to achieve in over four years of fighting during World War I. The fact that the British had escaped at Dunkirk would present problems later on, but at this stage, celebration was on every German soldier's mind. The *LAH* could take pride in the fact that they had played their part in this stunning victory. The cost to them was 500 dead and wounded with the 3. *Kompanie* suffering at least ten casualties.

CHAPTER FIVE

OCCUPATION AND EXPANSION

The *LAH* spent the days between the 25th of June and the 2nd of July 1940 resting. With the campaign over, the job of occupation and of course celebration was next. They stayed in the Clermont-Ferrand area until the 3rd of July. They then spent five days moving to Paris via Feurs, Pouilly, Luzy and St. Honore.

In between this, on the 5th of July Sepp Dietrich was awarded the Knight's Cross, for the capture of the bridgehead near Watten. When the *LAH* reached Paris they were billeted in the southern suburbs. Max Schmidt remembers being billeted in one of the suburbs of Paris during this period. They were only permitted into the city under supervision.

The rest of July was spent in this area where they prepared for the victory parade. On the 24th of July they were ordered to the Metz region, a move that took four days. They were placed under the XXXXIV *Armeekorps*.

At the start of August the Regiment was reorganised and moved up in status to a Motorised Brigade. These orders were issued in August and the new formation was now to be known as *Verstärkte* (reinforced) *Leibstandarte SS Adolf Hitler*, or verst. *LSSAH*. During this time preparations were made for the planned invasion of England, code named Operation Sealion. Also during August the *LAH* received the new field insignia, this was a copy of Hitler's personal pennant. A ceremony was carried out to receive the pennant. The honour formation was under *Sturmbannführer* Witt. Witt had recently returned to the *LAH*, initially commanding the III

Battalion, and Heinrich Springer recalled that to have Fritz Witt back in the *LAH* was something very special as Witt was regarded as a very competent soldier.

From August to December the *LAH* stayed in Metz. Elements did perform various ceremonial duties in Berlin for state visits, etc. On the 26th of December 1940 Adolf Hitler went to Metz and attended the *LAH*'s Christmas celebrations. He gave a speech and Dietrich presented him with a recording of the *LAH*'s actions. Max Schmidt was present at this celebration and remembers saluting in front of the Führer. He stated that he was always impressed when seeing the Fuhrer in person. It was during the expansion of the *LAH* that Max Schmidt and Heinz Kirsch left the 3. *Kompanie* and joined the 5. *Kompanie*, during November 1940. Max left the 3. *Kompanie* with the rank of *Sturmmann*. Heinz had been unable to gain any rank at this stage due to some minor offenses, which are common to any soldier in any army. Firstly, he had a guard violation. Then he was due on parade and he had been spending time with some female company, which delayed his return. Lastly, he was on leave and when he returned his rifle butt plate was dirty. Heinz finished the war with the rank of *Oberscharführer*. Max finished the war with the rank of *Oberscharführer* and holder of the 1st Class Iron Cross.

During the end of 1940 and the early part of 1941, a lot of political movements had taken place. Future intentions of all nations were being sounded out. One aspect was the Soviet Union, Hitler's main target. Other events however, would force Hitler to change his priorities. During the early part of 1941 the 3. *Kompanie* were commanded by *Hauptsturmführer* Schiller.

CHAPTER SIX

THE BALKANS

The situation further south in the Balkan region had deteriorated towards the end of 1940 when the impatient Mussolini attacked Albania and Greece. The Italian military fortunes were not good and the Greeks quickly gained the advantage and were in the process of routing the Italians. A German plan already existed for a possible campaign in this region. Hitler ordered the attack plans into being in order to remove the threat from the south. The plan was given the name Operation Marita and would involve the Germans moving via Bulgaria and Yugoslavia. The Germans did get as far as the southern Bulgarian border, but then the Yugoslavian Government changed sides and adopted an anti-Axis stance. The forthcoming operation would have to be fought through a hostile Yugoslavia. The plan had the Germans advancing down the eastern side of Yugoslavia with the Italians advancing in the west. The German forces were in place towards the end of March.

The Germans were not alone in their moves during March 1941. The British used the developing situation as an excuse to get involved. They sent a large number of British and Commonwealth troops to the area to aid the Greeks. These forces were under the control of General Sir Henry Maitland-Wilson. The Commonwealth contingent consisted of the 6th Australian Division and the 2nd New Zealand Division. Facing them was the German 12th Army under *Feldmarschall* Siegmund Wilhelm von List. Within the 12th Army were a number of formations including *General* Georg Sturmme's XXXX *Korps*. It was within this latter formation that the *LAH* would fight.

Hans Komischke photographed later in the war when he held the rank of *Unterscharführer*. He joined the 3. Kompanie in July 1940 from the 1. Kompanie. He would later serve in the 26th SS Regiment within the 12th SS Panzer Division "Hitlerjugend". (Gabriel Gorman)

On the 10th of January 1940 the *LAH* were ordered to move to the Balkans. An advance party was sent out a few days later with the bulk of the *LAH* staying in Metz until the start of March. They left Metz in the first week of March and moved to an area north of Bucharest. Here they were attached to the 12th Army. From the 12th to the 17th of March they moved to the southern edge of the Transylvanian Alps, in an area between Campulung and Stelpini. On the following day the *LAH* began their move into Bulgaria. By the 20th they where in their designated area that was northwest of Sofia, they were attached to the XXXX *Armeekorps*. They billeted in various areas, the I Battalion billeted in the Citen-Studena areas. On the 26th of March the I Battalion was given Fritz Witt as their new commander. On the 30th of March, the *LAH* where moved to the Radomir area. The I Battalion was billeted in the towns between Popovo to Bugjevec. On the 5th of April new orders were issued that detailed a simultaneous attack on Greece and Yugoslavia. The attacks were to begin the following day.

The *LAH* did not cross the Yugoslavian border until the 8th. By the 10th, the I Battalion was in positions between the towns of Bitolj and Florina. The 1. *Kompanie* had orders to move to Lazec and Medzidli-Kenali, they would then turn east and link with the 3. *Kompanie*. The 1. *Kompanie* prevented the destruction of a bridge and moved into the town of Niki. This was the first town to be reached on Greek soil. The 3. *Kompanie* were part of *Kampfgruppe* Witt.

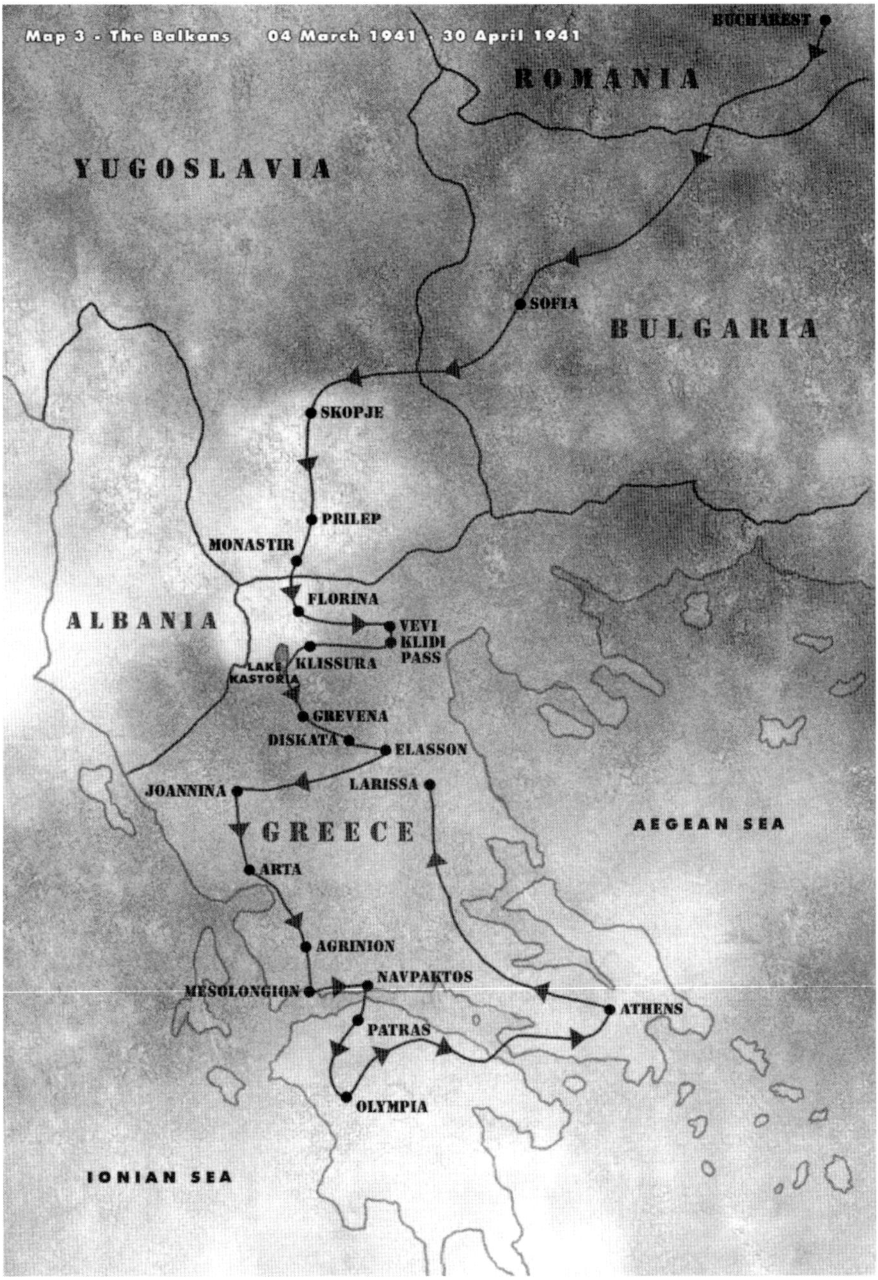

Map of Greece

The following day the 3. *Kompanie* were in Niki with their intended advance route being in a south easterly direction from Niki. Whilst in Niki, the men of the 3. *Kompanie* enjoyed a quick break in the fighting. They camouflaged the vehicles and then proceeded to engage in washing themselves in the stream. Karl Hojas of the 3. *Kompanie* remembers that whilst doing this the men of the 3. *Kompanie* watched a spectacular site. A formation of British bombers was approaching their positions from the south. There were German flak batteries also in the village and they proceeded to engage the enemy bombers. They managed to bring some of the bombers down. Karl Hojas and his 3. *Kompanie Kameraden* were given orders to move at once. They left the stream and mounted the vehicles still dressed in the swimwear. He remembers that they dressed on route to the next objective. It was a chaotic experience for them and on route to their objective they had to deal with aerial attacks from British fighters and road obstacles such as damaged bridges. After a few hectic hours of advance, they halted and assessed their situation. Karl Hojas's report does not mention any casualties, and the casualty list provided to the author by Max Schmidt does not list any losses in this area.

Vevi and the Klidi Pass

The 3. *Kompanie*'s route of advance was along the main road running from Niki through Marina and Itia and on towards Vevi. Just south of Vevi there is a fork in the road. The left side arcs uphill towards Vevi, whilst the right side goes towards the Kliddi pass. The 3. *Kompanie* were given the task of moving through this area and setting up a blocking position at the end. An assault group was sent out from the 3. *Kompanie* under the command of *Untersturmführer* Franz Witt, Fritz Witt's brother. The column of 3. *Kompanie* vehicles were led by a motorcycle and followed by a car with Franz Witt in it. There was also a self-propelled flak vehicle and various other vehicles following. The motorcycle suffered a puncture and moved off the road. This put *Untersturmführer* Franz Witt's car in the lead of the column. It was just after this that his car went over a mine that exploded. The two other occupants of the car, *Oberscharführer* Georg Koch and *Rottenführer* Eugen Brandhoff were killed instantly; Franz Witt was badly wounded. All hell was let loose as a firefight began between the 3. *Kompanie* men and elements of the Australian 6th Division. The 3. *Kompanie* dismounted their vehicles and took up positions in the near-by ditch. Enemy machine gun fire rained down on them. Medics were called and began to attend to Franz Witt. The enemy fire was intense and it forced the men to retreat to better cover. It wasn't until late that night that the 3. *Kompanie* freed themselves. By this stage *Untersturmführer* Franz Witt had died from his wounds. His brother and Battalion Commander, Fritz Witt, was made aware of the day's occurrences. He visited the body of his brother and was left visibly shaken. At the end of this day the 3. *Kompanie* where in position near the Vevi railway station.

The following day saw the capture of Vevi. Extensive reconnaissance was carried out during the previous evening and a good picture had been built up of the enemy positions and strengths. On the 11th of April the 3. *Kompanie* suffered further losses with the following *Kameraden* receiving wounds, *Scharführer* Fritz List, *Sturmmann* Helmut Fiuster and *Sturmmann* Roderich Geserich.

Franz Witt: Platoon Commander of the 3. *Kompanie*

Date of birth: 21.09.13 SS number: 30 300

Franz Witt served with the *Hitlerjugend* from October 1930 until 1932. On the 1st of May 1932 he joined the SS and served with the 1. *Sturm*, II *Sturmbann*, *SS-Standarte* 30. He had also been serving an office apprenticeship from the 1st of April 1930 until the 31st of March 1933. On the 10th of May 1933 he moved to the *LAH* with the rank of *SS-Mann*. On the 17th of October 1934 he had reached the rank of *Oberscharführer*. By April 1935 he was serving with the 1. *Kompanie*. Just after the start of World War II would see Franz Witt participate in the second war time Officer candidate's course at Bad Tölz from October 1939 to March 1940. He then served with the IV Battalion of the *LAH*. In the early autumn of 1940 he was promoted to *Untersturmführer*. He was posted to the 3. *Kompanie* of the *LAH*. It was with this *Kompanie* that Franz Witt was killed in April 1941 in Greece. It is not known what awards he obtained, but it can be determined from photographs that he was wounded at least once as he is seen wearing the Black Wound Badge.

The *LAH* Push Towards the Klidi Pass

The next objective after Vevi was the Klidi Pass. An attack was launched on the morning of the 12th of April towards this pass. Against stiff resistance the 1. *Kompanie* took Hill .997 and the 3. *Kompanie* took Hill .1009 with the help of the 2. *Kompanie* and heavier support from some Sturmgeschütz. The 3. *Kompanie*'s attack route was through an enemy mine field and this was quickly cleared by

Franz Witt photographed in May 1933 just after he joined the LAH. (Peter Witt)

Franz Witt seen in 1935 holding the rank of *Oberscharführer* when he was serving with the LAH's 1. Kompanie. (Peter Witt)

This photo shows a group of Officer candidates at the Second Wartime Course held at Bad Tölz between October 1939 and March 1940. Franz Witt is in the first row on the extreme right under the fire equipment. For a list (incomplete) of the other candidates in this photo, see appendix 8. (Peter Witt)

Franz Witt pictured in late 1940 - early 1941 holding the rank of *Untersturmführer* and now serving as a Platoon Leader in the 3. Kompanie. (Peter Witt)

supporting Pioneer troops. The battle for this high ground was intense and numerous enemy machine gun nests had to be cleared, fixed bayonets was the order of the day for the 3. *Kompanie*. The enemy soldiers were retreating fast over the many surrounding hills. Later that afternoon the 3. *Kompanie* came across a railway tunnel that contained British and New Zealand forces. A Sturmgeschütz was brought up and helped to persuade the enemy to surrender (after firing). There were over 250 prisoners taken.

This intensive battle resulted in further casualties for the 3. *Kompanie*. *SS-Mann* Hans Rambow was killed by enemy shellfire. *Sturmmann* Arthur Lietz, *Sturmmann* Friedrich Schumacher, *SS-Mann* Karl-Heinz Seller and *SS-Mann* Walter Weber were also killed. *Unterscharführer* Siegfried Richter was wounded when he was shot through the shoulder. He went off to the aid station helping to support *Rottenführer* Johann Huntschel who had been seriously wounded in the jaw. Also wounded on this day was *Unterscharführer* Johann Ohlrogge.

The town of Klidi was taken by the 7. and 1. *Kompanies*. *Kampfgruppe* leader Fritz Witt was on hand to enjoy the commanding view that this town had over the Macedonian Plain. He stood there with some of the *Kompanie* Commanders including *Hauptsturmführer* Hans-Joachim Schiller of the 3. *Kompanie*. The retreating enemy could be seen clearly from this high point. Shortly after this the 3. *Kompanie* moved off towards the road junction west of Sotir. The forces dug in

The top photograph shows the German cemetery at the Klidi Pass in Greece. The bottom photo is an enlargement of the bottom left-hand corner of the cemetery. Franz Witt's grave can be seen clearly, the inscription reads: 'SS Ustuf. Witt. 3.LSSAH'. His grave, along with others was moved in 1959 to a cemetery near Athens. (Peter Witt)

This photograph dates from autumn 1940 and shows the newly promoted *Untersturmführer* Franz Witt together with his brother Fritz Witt, then serving with the "Deutschland" Regiment, not long after he was awarded the Knight's Cross. Also in the photo is Albert Schuch who at that time held the rank of *Obersturmbannführer* within the Allgemeine-SS. He would later serve in the Waffen-SS and by June 1944 was holding the rank of *Sturmbannführer*. (Peter Witt)

for the night with the 3. *Kompanie* providing defense at a fork in the road near Xinon-Neron.

On the 13th of April enemy tanks were sent up against the *LAH* positions. 88mm Flak guns engaged and destroyed a number of them within the space of a few minutes and at ranges in excess of 2000 metres. Soon after the *LAH* were relieved by the 73rd Infantry Division. This ended the battle for the Klidi Pass. The capture of this Pass opened up the gateway to Greece. Over 500 prisoners were taken as well as tanks, trucks and guns. This action is widely accepted as the *LAH*'s finest battle. The enemy had been able to observe the *LAH*' every move. This proved to be the decisive battle of the Balkan campaign. *Obersturmführer* Pleiss, *Chef* of the 1. *Kompanie*, was awarded the Knight's Cross for his part in the battle. Max Schmidt, who was now with the 5. *Kompanie*, was awarded the 2nd Class Iron Cross during this fighting for taking thirty English soldiers prisoner. The 3. *Kompanie* added the name of *Sturmmann* Werner Gotz to its' list of dead on the 13th of April.

The Klisura Pass and Victory in the Balkans

By this stage the battle was by no means over, but the men of the 3. *Kompanie* and the rest of *KG* Witt got a well-earned short rest. The next objective was the Klisura Pass. The *LAH* moved to Lake Kastoria over the Klisura Pass. It was here that Kurt Meyer's men came up against a demolished bridge. They came under concentrated attack from enemy positions above this area. They were not able to press the attack forwards until the following day, when small groups fought their way up the slopes. The objective was captured that evening. As the *LAH* got closer to Lake Kastoria they came under attack from Hill 800, positioned west of Zubjakos. The III Battalion was moved up to Korisos and on the 15th of April a two-pronged attack was launched on Hill 800 from the west and east. The objective was taken that afternoon with the help of dive-bombers. Kurt Meyer was awarded the Knight's Cross for his actions at the Klisura Pass.

On the 16th the *LAH* continued their advance towards the south. They moved through Argos-Orestiakon, here the enemy had blown the bridge and the *LAH* had to construct a bridge to continue the advance. The march continued through Kivotos and other towns until they reached Grevena. Here they stopped for the day. On the following day they were ordered to move to Joanina. Heavy rains had begun to fall and reduced the roads to thick mud. Due to this, the move took three days.

On the 20th of April they reached the summit of the Katara Pass. They were surprised to be offered the surrender of the Greek and Macedonian Army. A hasty radio message was sent to locate Dietrich. He reached the area and was taken to Votanasi to meet General Tzolakoglou and negotiate peace terms. Due to the difficulty in translation, the final declaration was signed back at the Katara summit under torchlight. The following day Dietrich and the authorised Greek Commander went to Larissa where final negotiations were held with *General* Jodl. Orders arrived for the *LAH* to close the Albanian border. Whilst this situation was developing, Kurt Meyer executed a crossing of the Gulf of Patras on the 25th of April. Orders had arrived for the securing of this area as British forces were escaping into Corinth and onto freedom. He used two fishing boats to cross the Gulf and capture some of the enemy, including three officers. The pursuit continued into Corinth and Olympia and finally into Tripolis. On the 30th the II Battalion reached Pyrgos and with this the actions in Greece came to an end.

The Greek surrender to the Germans had not pleased Mussolini and he demanded a change to the surrender terms. He even went as far as to refuse to stop his troops fighting with the Greeks further west. The Greek's were not happy at these developments as they felt that they had already defeated the Italians. Hitler became involved, and much to the annoyance of the German Army's High Command, he arranged for a victory parade to be held in Athens in which the Italians could take part. Some reports state that as the Italians passed, the Greeks turned their backs on them. Mussolini ordered that the Greeks had to surrender to the Generals at the front. The Greeks finally agreed to avoid further losses. Over the next few days the *LAH* politely held the Italians back from pursuing the Greeks. The *LAH* were holding border crossings at Perat. They were also ordered to assist in the Greek surrender ceremony. An Italian motorcade would be passing through the *LAH*'s positions, and orders were received that allowed for the passage of the motorcade only, protection was provided for the Greeks. This motorcade passed through on the 28th of April 1941.

Between the 29th of April and the 3rd of May, part of the *LAH* was given a rest. Preparations were made for a parade through Athens on the 3rd. From there the *LAH* moved to Larissa. The move was completed by the 6th. The rest of May was used for extensive repairs on the vehicles and rest for the men. On the 9th of May 1941 *Reichsführer-SS* Heinrich Himmler made a brief visit to the *LAH*. Among the *Kompanie*s that he visited were *Hauptsturmführer* Schiller's 3. *Kompanie*. Present at this visit was Himmler, Karl Wolff, Fritz Witt and Jochen Peiper, among others. It was around this time that the *LAH* first started to use the title 'Division'. Evidence exists that show it appearing from the 15th of April 1941. At the start of June the *LAH* moved to the Wischau area, near Brno, within the Bohemia and Moravian Protectorate. On the 7th of June 1941 the restructure of the *LAH* into a Division began.

The Greek campaign had been completed within the space of a month. As before the *LAH* had fought with determination and skill. The areas that they were fighting in consisted of many steep hills and mountains. They had found themselves fighting in a role more suited to specialised mountain troops. This did not prevent them from executing some outstanding victories. Two men in particular will always be associated with the Greek campaign. Gerd Pleiss for his actions at the Klidi Pass, and Kurt Meyer for his actions at the Klisura Pass and the Gulf of Patras. These actions were a portent of things to come for the men of the *LAH*. This determination to succeed in the face of apparently unobtainable objectives was becoming typical of the Waffen-SS. They had fought against worthy adversaries including British and Commonwealth troops. Again, close co-operation with the forces of the Army and Luftwaffe had made this possible. The rest period for the forces of Germany would be a short one. The next task was already decided.

For the *LAH*, they had to start their reorganisation into a full Division before the next campaign, a process that lasted until the summer of 1942. Until that point, they remained a strong Brigade. As this was taking place the men of the 3. *Kompanie* not only considered what was coming next but they also had to deal with their losses from the Greek campaign. This amounted to at least one officer and eight other men killed, together with seven wounded. The 3. *Kompanie* had been in the thick of the fighting and could be proud of the part that they played in this victory.

CHAPTER SEVEN

OPERATION BARBAROSSA: THE INVASION OF THE SOVIET UNION

The German High Command had been working on a plan to attack Russia since August 1940. Hitler saw America's entry into the war as inevitable. He estimated that they would have entered by 1942 at the latest. He wanted to remove the Russian threat before this happened and therefore hopefully persuade England to agree on peace terms. He was also riding on the success wave in the wake of the victories that his armies had enjoyed over their adversaries to date. He did not rate the Russians very highly and this, together with the victories, left Hitler with an air of arrogance towards his next opponent. Due to the climate and road conditions, an attack on Russia would have to be made within a restricted time-window. Hitler's venture in the Balkans had delayed the planned attack date and therefore, reduced the available time-window. The Blitzkrieg tactics would be tested once again. This time however, they would be fighting over a huge and mostly inhospitable area. The expectations were high, as was the tension for the German troops.

Stalin had virtually ignored all of the warnings that he was given regarding the German attack. He did not expect an attack as he did not think that Hitler would be in a position to attack so soon after the Greek campaign. There were around two million men positioned on the border, with a further one million being positioned further back from the border. The Soviet forces were grouped as follows. In the north was the North West Front with the Kalinin Front just behind this. In the middle was the West Front with the Reserve Front further back. In the south

This photograph was taken on the 9th of May 1941 and shows *Reichsführer-SS* Heinrich Himmler visiting the 3. Kompanie. The 3. Kompanie commander *Hauptsturmführer* Schiller is on the extreme right, Sepp Dietrich is next to Schiller and the I Battalion commander Fritz Witt is third from the right with Himmler next to him. (Patrick Agte)

was the South West Front, with the South Front being placed further back and to the south. The emphasis of the Russian strength was in the south. The Russian troops were at this stage in the war poorly led as they had lost most of their experienced Commanders in Stalin's purges of 1937-1938.

Hitler's forces were divided into three Army Groups; North, Centre and South. Army Group North would attack towards Leningrad, Army Group Centre would attack towards Smolensk and then Moscow and Army Group South would attack towards the Black Sea and the cities of Kiev and Rostov. Army Group South had the strongest forces. Germany's forces had almost two years fighting experience that would serve them well in the opening phases. They had tested and proved the new method of warfare. They had every reason to believe that Blitzkrieg would serve them well in Russia also. They pitched over three million men, just under 3500 tanks and around 3000 planes against Stalin's forces who numbered around three million men in the opening phases, 20,000 tanks (this figure was not known at the time), and around 10,000 planes. The forthcoming battle would indeed be a monumental one.

The *LAH* themselves, were attached to *Panzergruppe* 1 which was part of Army Group South. This Army Group would be attacking between the Carpathian Mountains and the Pripet marshes. Their first objectives were the city of Kiev and the Dneiper river. Between the 9th of June and the 26th the *LAH* made preparations for the offensive. The 3. *Kompanie* were part of a march group that moved to the Ostrowiec-Konskie area towards the end of the month, just ahead of the bulk of the *LAH*. Around this period, *Hauptsturmführer* Schiller had *Untersturmführer*

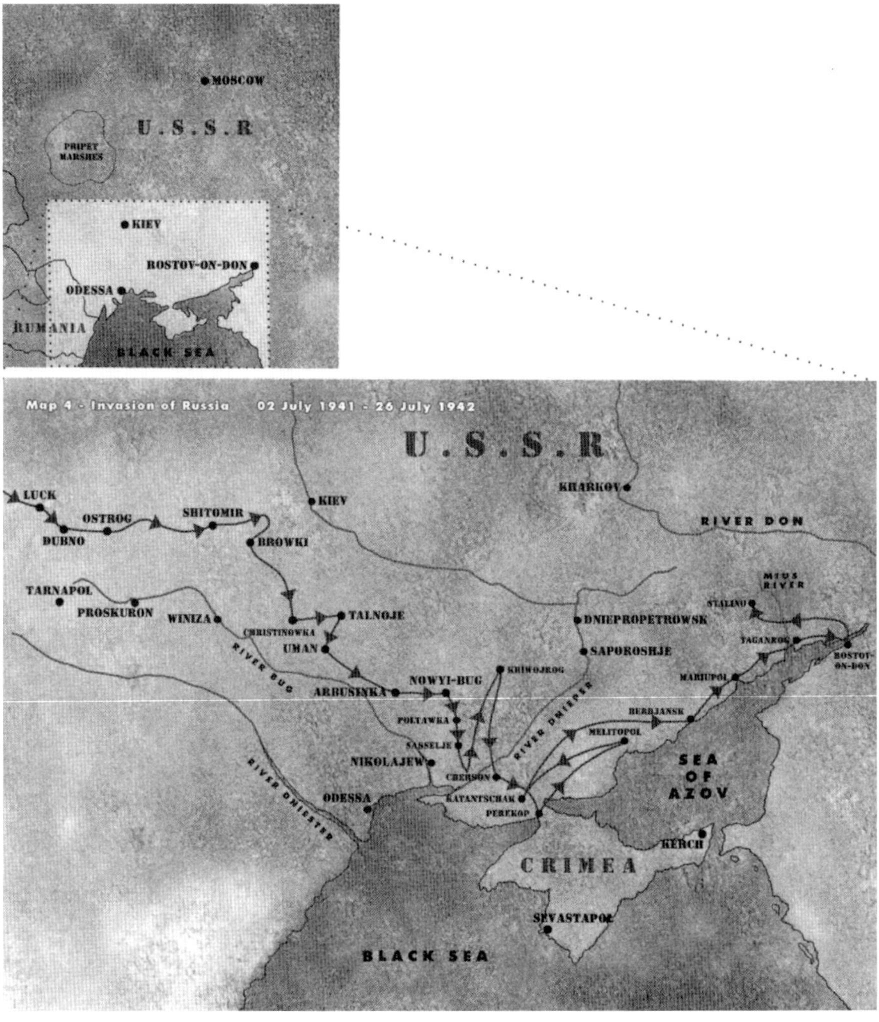

Invasion of Russia map

Franz and *Untersturmführer* von Wallfeldt as his junior officers. There is no information on either of these officers.

The First Battles Against the Soviets: Portents for the Future

The main offensive started on the 22nd of June 1941, but the *LAH* did not take part until the 30th, when they moved 150 kilometers to Samosz. They received their first march orders on this day. The III *Panzerkorps* had come up against stiff resistance in the Rowno area and their supply route was severed. The *LAH* were to break through to them and re-open their supply line. These moves were begun over the next two days. They moved up to the Luck area and began to attack the enemy's flank near Dubno. The fighting was difficult. On the 2nd of July Heinrich Springer took some men from the I Battalion and linked up with the III *Panzerkorps*, who had been cut-off. They returned the following day. *General* von Mackensen was very surprised to see them. They then made a return trip two days later and gave the III *Panzerkorps* the new attack plans. This was an excellent accomplishment.

On the 3rd of July the I Battalion moved to the Zastowie area. Kurt Meyer came across the gruesome scene of murdered German soldiers for the first time. Their hands had been tied and they were all naked. The officers who were nearby had also been trampled on and dismembered. The *LAH*'s official history states that Dietrich strictly forbade any reprisals.

On the 4th of July the *LAH* were subordinated to the III *Panzerkorps* and advanced towards Horyn via Horbakow. The roads were reduced to thick mud due to heavy rains. Horbakow was reached on the 5th. On the following day the XXXXVIII *Panzerkorps* succeeded in breaking through to Miropol. On the 7th the *LAH* were ordered to protect their northern flank as far as Korzec. This order was quickly changed and the II Battalion had to clear a forest near Ostrog of enemy forces that were disrupting supplies. No enemy troops were found and the *LAH* were ready to go towards Miropol again by the 8th. Enemy positions were encountered on the way and dealt with.

On the 9th of July they were ordered to attack Shitomir via Romanow and Buki. The I Battalion moved south of the Romanow-Wysoki-Piec road and were to proceed towards Shitomir, they moved on to Teterew. Due to bad road conditions the bulk of the *LAH* requested a move north towards the Rollbahn Nord so that they could continue the advance. This move started on the 10th and when they reached the Rollbahn, they were ordered to attack towards Sokolow. This attack was launched at midday on the 11th. The Russians cut the Rollbahn between Sokolow and Shitomir and they were also mounting heavy attacks towards Sokolow. The German forces shifted emphasis to meet the threat. The fighting was confused and the need to be alert was essential. The 12th of July saw the IV Battalion engage in an intensive battle for the forest near Sokolow. The following day they pushed into Henrykowka.

The 3. *Kompanie* where in the Adamowka area, south east of Sokolow around this time. On the 13th of July they began their attack across the Rollbahn towards Dolzyk. Due to mounting enemy pressure coming in from their left, they were forced to dig in during the night. The 4. *Kompanie* were able to reach the men of the 3. *Kompanie* that same night. Then on the following day an officer from the 4. *Kompanie* took some men from the 3. *Kompanie* and under *Hauptsturmführer* Schiller's orders, they went towards the town to determine the enemy positions and strength. It was during this mission that the officer of the 4. *Kompanie*, *Untersturmführer* Quassoswki, had his foot blown off by enemy shellfire. It was on this same day, the 14th of July, that the Russians abandoned the town of Dolzyk.

The rest of the 14th and 15th of July were spent repulsing enemy attacks. The *LAH* were then ordered to move further east towards Kiev. The I Battalion had the area from Shernowka to Goremitschi. The bulk of the *LAH* positions were along the Irpen River. As the enemy withdrew, the plan was changed to exploit this advantage. The emphasis was switched from east to southeast. The pursuit and destruction of the enemy was the priority. These positions were maintained against enemy pressure until the 22nd. The *LAH* were then ordered to move south towards Uman. The march began over the next two days. In front of the *LAH* the XXXXVIII *Armeekorps*, which included the 11th and 16th Panzer Divisions, had moved towards Uman. There were large enemy forces trying to break through to the east from the west. They forced a gap between the 11th and 16th Panzer Divisions from Sokolowka to Cybulow. The *LAH* were ordered to close the gap. This was achieved on the 25th of July.

The next objective was the encirclement of Uman. The *LAH* were to move to the east with the 11th Panzer Division. The 16th Pz. and 16th Infantry Divisions were to move to the west. The moves began on the 27th and continued against heavy enemy attacks up to the 1st of August.

Hans-Joachim Schiller: The Fifth Commander of the 3. *Kompanie*

Date of birth: 24.03.07 SS Number: 23 814

The 3. *Kompanie* were undergoing a change of *Kompanie* Commander on the 1st of August 1941. *Hauptsturmführer* Schiller was badly wounded and these wounds prevented him from staying in the field. Schiller had commanded the 3. *Kompanie* for almost two years. Max Schmidt recalled that Joachim Schiller was a popular commander and much liked by the men of the 3. *Kompanie*. It can be determined that Schiller served with the 5. *Kompanie* during October 1934 and then the 6. *Kompanie*. By April 1939 he held the rank of *Obersturmführer* and was in command of the 2. A. *Kompanie*. After his service with the 3. *Kompanie*, he went on to serve as the Adjutant to the *LSSAH* in early 1943. He followed this by commanding the I Battalion with the rank of *Sturmbannführer* in late 1943 and 1944. During Normandy, he commanded his own *Kampfgruppe*. It is known that he ended the war with the rank of *Obersturmbannführer* and holder of the German Cross in Gold. In addition to the above listed awards, he also held the Second Class Iron Cross, the First Class Iron Cross, General Assault Badge, Infantry Assault Badge and the Black Wound Badge. Max Schmidt recalled that he was wounded in the final fighting in Berlin. It is known that he survived the war and was responsible for building up the East German Army, with a final rank of *Oberst*, or Colonel. He lived until the early 1990s.

Another Change of Command for the 3. *Kompanie*

Hauptsturmführer Schiller's replacement was the I Battalion Adjutant, *Obersturmführer* Heinrich Springer. Springer had already amassed an impressive military record before joining the 3. *Kompanie*. He had joined the Allgemeine-SS on the 1st of June 1936; he was placed with the 9./50 *Sturm*. On the 1st of November 1937 he joined the 3. *Kompanie* of the *Germania Standarte*. He took part in the annexation of Austria before the war started. On the 15th of November 1938 he began his officer training at the Bad Tölz *SS-Junkerschule*, which lasted until mid-August 1939, leaving with the rank of *Standartenoberjunker*. He was assigned to the *LAH* at the start of November and then on the 9th of November 1939 he was promoted to *Untersturmführer*. Up until joining the 3. *Kompanie* his war-time exploits included action in France, where he received the 2nd Class Iron Cross whilst fighting near Dunkirk on the 8th of June 1940. He was wounded for the first time on the 10th of June (thigh injury) and again on the 21st of June (hand injury).

He did not receive the Black Wound Badge until the 3rd of October 1940, when he also received the Infantry Assault Badge in Bronze. Just prior to joining the 3. *Kompanie*, he received the 1st Class Iron Cross for his exploits in linking up with the III *Panzerkorps*.

Obersturmführer Springer felt that it was an honour to be asked to replace *Hauptsturmführer* Schiller. When he took over the 3. *Kompanie*, Springer found them to be in a good state of combat readiness and training. He remembered that the NCOs had led the men well and their skills had been passed on to the men of the 3. *Kompanie*. Around this time they had worked closely with the reconnaissance unit and they were therefore used to advancing at a very fast rate. They were usually to be found at the spearhead of many of the attacks. Springer considered the 3. *Kompanie* to be very good.

The Fighting Around Uman

By the 3rd of August 1941, the I Battalion was around Nowo Archangelsk, with the rest of the *LAH* spread out down to Marianowka. There was intensive fighting, which continued until the 7th. All the enemy attacks were defeated and huge amounts of men and material were captured. Over 3200 prisoners were taken along with tanks, artillery and planes. There were still four Russian Armies to defeat around the south of Uman. After this battle, *General* Kempf paid tribute to the men of the *LAH* for their successes in this area.

The 9th of August saw the *LAH* move further south towards Wossnesensk and Nikolajew, in the general direction of the coast with the Black Sea. The I Battalion reached Jelanez that night. The advance reached as far as Bobry before orders were received to change direction. The 16th Pz. Div. were to advance on Nikolajew, the *LAH* were to move further east and south towards Cherson. The *LAH* were currently in a favourable position and the opinion was that this was a mistake. After a days rest the march resumed. The enemy were still trying to make their way east. The march was conducted under artillery fire.

Sasselje and the Link-up with 'Panzer' Meyer

By the 14th the situation had become very confused. Kurt Meyer's *Aufklärungs-abteilung* had reached as far as Sasselje, but they had then become surrounded by the strong enemy forces in this area. *Obersturmführer* Springer was ordered to link

Above: *Hauptsturmführer* Hans-Joachim Schiller (to the right of Dietrich) photographed in 1940 after being awarded the Infantry Assault Badge. Also in this photograph is the officer who would replace Schiller as the commander of the 3. Kompanie, the then *Untersturmführer* Heinrich Springer (to the left of Dietrich). Clear photographs of Schiller are very hard to find. (Erwin Bartmann)

Right: This photograph was taken on the 12th of April 1941 and shows the Battalion commander, Fritz Witt explaining one of the attacks to Himmler and Dietrich. Also in the photograph is Heinrich Springer (on the extreme left); then holding the rank of *Obersturmführer,* the rank he held when he took over command of the 3. Kompanie. (Peter Witt)

up with Kurt Meyer. This task was not an easy one; they also had the problem of having to use old maps that dated from the First World War. These maps did not show many of the villages with the result that the 3. *Kompanie* did not know where they were. As they advanced they noticed some electricity pylons on the horizon. They moved towards these and determined that they were running in a southerly direction. They moved alongside these pylons and after fifteen kilometres they reached Sasselje. Kurt Meyer was glad to see them and said to Springer, 'Hein, you are here with your 3. *Kompanie*. Have you enough ammunition'. Heinrich Springer confirmed that they did have enough.

They knew that the Soviets were already in the south and east of the village. They held a briefing to determine what they could do. Springer came up with the suggestion that they would wait until dusk, at around 6:00 p.m. They would then fire a signal flare. At this point they would fire in the direction of the enemy for three minutes using all of the available weapons. This was agreed and then subsequently carried out. Springer recalls that these, 'shock tactics' must have caused great alarm for the Russians as there was a deathly silence once the firing finished. The next morning, all that was left behind by the Russians was some camouflaged netting.

Over the next two days, Meyer and Springer's men successfully held the town against repeated enemy attacks. The enemy was trying to make it to the relative safety of the east and they did not expect this German strongpoint, which they were determined to smash. The Russians attacked from all sides during their countless attempts, but due to the relentless efforts of the German soldiers in Sasselje, every enemy effort was defeated. The men of the *LAH* were also assisted by men from the Infantry Reg. 60. The II Battalion of the *LAH* eventually linked with the men at Sasselje on the 16th of August, but by then the situation was under control. It was on this day that Nikolajew was taken by the 16th Panzer Division with a further 4000 prisoners and enemy materials being taken.

The Thrust Towards the Black Sea

Between the 17th and 18th, the 3. *Kompanie,* together with the rest of the I Bat., were ordered to move east as far as the Ingulez River, the other Battalions were ordered south towards Cherson. This town was taken the following day by the III and IV Bats'. The I Battalion had reached and taken their objective of Ssnigerjowka on the Ingulez river. By the 20th the Black Sea had been reached by the men of the

LAH. It had been an eventful first three weeks for *Obersturmführer* Springer and his newly acquired 3. *Kompanie*, they had fought well but the task was not complete yet. The *LAH* were ordered to move north-east to the Kirowograd area for a short rest period. The actual move was delayed until the 24th. The I Battalion were stationed in Perepelizyno, the rest of the *LAH* were stretched down as far as Ssedrewka.

At the start of September the *LAH* were removed from the XXXXVIII *Armeekorps* and placed under the 11th Army. *General* Kempf paid a visit to the *LAH* and gave them a good farewell. They were to move southeast on the 8th of September towards Orlowa. Some elements crossed the Dneiper River and due to delays, two *LAH* groups were inadvertently formed. The first group contained the I, III and Reconnaissance Battalions under Dietrich and were known as Group East. The second group contained the II and IV Battalions under Keilhaus and were known as Group West. As the 3. *Kompanie* were part of the I Battalion, we will follow the movements of Group East.

The *LAH*'s 'Group East' in Action in the Crimea

Group East moved south towards the Crimea. They were ordered towards Preobrashenka to deal with the strong enemy positions in this area, they reached it by the 12th. A day of rest followed and then on the 14th the attack began. With the help of the 73rd and 46th Infantry Divisions they began to move towards the hills. Due to enemy pressure a frontal assault was ruled out. The plan was changed to cut the enemy off on the hills. By the 16th the I Battalion were holding defensive positions around Ssaljkoff, the III Battalion were in Nowo Dimitrjewka. An attempt by Panzer Meyer to storm over a footbridge near the isthmus was successful, but they pulled back under heavy attack. In the evening Group East were ordered north-east to Melitopol. The Group von Boddien were under heavy enemy attack and needed assistance. Due to fuel shortages and present engagements, the order could not be carried out. Dietrich asked for the Group West to be returned. On the following day attempted enemy landings by sea were repulsed. On the 18th the I Battalion moved to Melitopol and took up position to the left of Group von Boddien. This area was heavily defended by the enemy so little progress was made, the present positions were held. They stayed in these positions until the 21st of September when they were relieved and ordered to Kalantschak. The two elements of the *LAH* were reunited on the 23rd of September.

Between the 23rd and the 29th of September, the *LAH* took part in the attacks of the isthmus at Proebreshenka and Perekop. This attack was difficult due to the presence of strong enemy forces and strong fortifications in the area. The enemy was attacking with tanks and aircraft. Perekop was taken by the 73rd Infantry Division on the 26th, with the 46th Infantry Division fighting around Armiansk. A breakthrough in this area was proving difficult, as the use of motorised units was not possible. On the 27th the *LAH* were ordered to move northeast.

The Re-united *LAH* Move Further Eastwards

Dietrich was summoned to von Mansteins HQ on the 28th. The situation was that the resources at the disposal of LIV *Armeekorps* were too small to occupy the Crimea; a moving of forces was necessary. In the north the Russians had opened a 15 kilometers gap in the lines held by the Rumanians. The *LAH* were to help the 11th Army, to the north of Melitopol, in plugging the gap. The *LAH* moved up on the 29th and by the evening the I Battalion had taken Hill .78, north-west of Nowopetrowka. On this day the situation worsened in the Wessjoloje sector and elements of the *LAH* were sent to assist. The bulk of the *LAH* were fighting around Dnjeprowka. The I, II and III Battalions were moving east towards Nowo Dnjeprowka. Orders came through for them to move to Mentschekur, the IV Battalion were already in Wessjoloje. The attack proceeded east and by the 2nd of October a line from Hf. Adamowitsch to Mentschekur was reached. The I Battalion were in the area of the middle of the Fullhorn-See. On this day the 11th Army and Panzer Group 1 were able to break through the Dneiper bridgeheads. The enemy was too involved in trying to stop the counter-thrust going on with the help of the *LAH*. On the 3rd of October von Manstein sent a congratulatory note to the 11th Army in which the successes of the *LAH* were mentioned.

From the 4th the pursuit of the enemy continued to the southeast towards Berdjansk. The first objective of Terpenje was reached; here the Reconnaissance Battalion under Kurt Meyer raced the retreating Russians for the bridge in the town. The bridge was blown just before they reached it, at the time it was full of Russian soldiers. The I Battalion reached the west of the town in the early afternoon. They assisted in increasing a bridgehead over the river made by Kurt Meyer's men. The next town reached was Kolonie Romanowka. Here the Reconnaissance Battalion captured the staff of the Russian 9th Army. By the end of the 6th the I Battalion was in this area.

Mariupol and the Sea of Azov

The following day the *LAH* were ordered to move to Mariupol and attach themselves to the XIV *Panzerkorps*. They succeeded in capturing Berdjansk, which had been abandoned. Two enemy columns were sighted moving close to the town. The Reconnaissance Battalion attacked one of the columns and caught them by surprise. They did not expect an attack from this direction. By the 8th they had reached Mariupol. On the way, they had passed numerous columns of retreating enemy. The advance into the city stopped at the Kalmiuss River where a bridgehead was set-up. This city is situated on the Sea of Azov and is an important seaport. At the time of its capture, there were 250,000 inhabitants. The securing and administration necessary for the city was a sizeable one. Relief was sent in the form of the 13th Panzer Division. The Russians attacked the city with planes. 4500 prisoners were taken but many others had escaped to the east. *Obersturmführer* Springer recalled that the brave men of the 3. *Kompanie* took part in the attacks towards Berdjansk and Mariupol and onto the Sea of Azov.

The Thrust Towards Taganrog

The next target was Taganrog. The march began on the 10th of October after the 13th Panzer Division took over Mariupol. On the march route, the *LAH* captured the towns of Kotlomin and Jefremowka. Strong enemy forces were observed moving along the same route. The I Battalion received orders to attack the enemy's flank. The III Battalion continued the advance whilst the II and IV Bat's backed up the I Battalion The advance continued to the Mius River which was reached on the 12th. The river was flooded at this stage so the bridges over this river were essential for the continuation of the advance. The enemy was moving across the river in strength, retreating east. The I Battalion was ordered west and the *Aufklärungs* Battalion moved south. The enemy on the east bank was putting up stiff resistance. Springer remembers that the east bank was higher than the west bank and therefore the Russians could observe all of the *LAH*'s movements. Fritz Witt stated to Springer, 'Hein, if you take this, you will be a *Hauptsturmführer*'.

By nightfall the 3. *Kompanie* were at the river north of Nikolajewka. Springer ordered a squad to cross by raft and during the night, the entire 3. *Kompanie* managed to cross the river. They then pushed forward in intensive fighting that included hand-to-hand combat. They secured an important area of high ground to the north of the town, which the enemy decided not to attack. The rest of the I Battalion was pushed across the river at this point. The 3. *Kompanie* also managed to get as far as the northeast part of the town. The capture of this town was essential as the next objective of Taganrog was already being called for. The following day the emphasis was placed on the 3. *Kompanie*'s crossing. The II Battalion were moved over this bridge whilst a second bridge was put up to ease the traffic flow. The 3. *Kompanie* had by now reached the centre of Nikolajewka and had orders to clear the town of enemy to allow the speedy advance towards Taganrog. It was considered a life or death matter. Enemy air attacks were put in over the next two days. By the 15th the town had been taken and secured. Defensive positions were set up on the southern edge of the town. It was during this battle that the 3. *Kompanie* listed six men as missing. It was on the 15th of October 1941 that *Obersturmführer* Springer received his third wound in action, this time it was a wound to the shoulder.

The attack on Taganrog was suspended until the 17th due to enemy pressure on the Korps northern flank. On this day the I Battalion moved west of the main Taganrog road with the intention of taking the south of the city. The rapid capture of Taganrog was achieved by the 19th of October. The I Battalion 's final positions were the harbour area.

On the 20th of October the *LAH* began their move north-east of Taganrog, with the 3. *Kompanie* and the rest of the I Battalion on the extreme left of the line of advance. They battled through strong enemy forces for the next six days. By this stage the line from Alexandrowka, held by the I Bat., to Mogila Chotschkaja had been reached. These positions were held until the 16th of November. The cold was having its' effects on the men and machines. At night the ground froze and the vehicles got stuck. During the day heavy rains also jammed the vehicles with thick mud. Morale was very low at this stage. The fighting had temporarily ceased due to the weather. The Russians were aware of the importance of the nearby city of Rostov and their preparations for its' defence were more important than trying to engage the advancing Germans. There were some harassing attacks put in against the *LAH*, but nothing too serious. In this period the *LAH* moved to the Tusloff River area in preparation for the attack on Rostov.

Pause Before Rostov and the First Russian Snows

During this period, Heinrich Springer recalled that the men of the 3. *Kompanie* built small bunkers in the ground with wood and straw, to protect themselves from the cold and snow, which had begun to make an appearance. The temperature was well below zero. They kept guard during the long nights and kept communicating between each bunker. These dark days, both in the physical sense and the mental sense, were days when the *kameraderie* of the men was strengthened. The continuous fighting, which had been raging for four months, was taking its' toll on the men. The sort of kameraderie mentioned above is forged in times of trouble and lasts a lifetime. Sixty years after the event, former members of the 3. *Kompanie* are still close friends. This sentiment can be appreciated by any soldier in any army. *Obersturmführer* Springer recalled that to the men, it seemed that the Russians had endless supplies of ammunition. In these dark days the men of the 3. *Kompanie* turned their thoughts to their fallen *Kameraden*. This did not help their morale, but the orders for the capture of Rostov were issued, which helped turn the men's thoughts to other things. On the 28th of October 1941, *Sturmmann* Erich Wildenstein of the 3. *Kompanie* was killed. On the 31st of October 1941, the 3. *Kompanie* had a strength of one officer, ten NCOs and fifty men.

The Move Towards Rostov Begins

The city of Rostov is situated on the Don River and it is a vital communications and traffic centre for the Caucasus. It had immense value to the Russians and the capture of the city was vital to the German plans. The attack began on the 17th of November with the *LAH* positioned on the northern wing moving east. Heinrich Springer painted a graphic description of the situation on this day. He stated that it was cold and foggy on the morning of the 17th of November. The tanks could not attack in this weather and therefore the start time of the attack was delayed. As they waited for the fog to clear, Heinrich Springer, Gerd Pleiss (Commander of the 1. *Kompanie*) and Heinrich Heimann (Commander of the 2. *Kompanie*); shared a bottle of rum that warmed them inside; their thoughts were of the battles of yesterday, today and tomorrow. The fog lifted at around 10 a.m. With this the artillery opened fire and the attack of the III *Panzerkorps* began. The first hour of the advance was very good. Suddenly the Russians began a heavy artillery attack of their own. During this attack, Gerd Pleiss was heavily wounded by a piece of shrapnel. He died the same day. Springer recalled that once the *Kompanie* Commander dies, the soul of the *Kompanie* is dead. Everybody was aware of this.

On the first day of the attack the battle was very hard and they quickly realised that the Russians were determined to hold Rostov at all costs. The 13th and 14th Panzer Divisions were adjacent to them, along with the 60th Motorised Infantry

Division. Springer recalled that this line-up looked very imposing on the grassland. It reminded him of the pre war exercises held on Lüneburg Heath. The difference this time was that they were not using blank ammunition.

The 3. *Kompanie* pushed ahead towards Rostov itself. They came across Russian trenches on this first day and they overran these enemy positions with ease. They then occupied the trenches and used them against the enemy. Springer remembered that the trenches offered very good protection. On the following day a large group of enemy T-34 tanks came against their positions. The men of the 3. *Kompanie* watched from the trenches as the German tanks engaged the Russians and destroyed tank after tank. In these first two days of the attack towards Rostov, the 3. *Kompanie* suffered no losses.

Heinrich Springer's Promotion to *Hauptstürmfuhrer* and the Next Task

The *LAH* captured Ssultan Ssaly on the 19th and pushed on towards Rostov. On this, the third day of the attack, the enemy was mounting stiff resistance. Dietrich arrived during the attack and Heinrich Springer reported to him that the 3. *Kompanie* were in the process of attacking Rostov. Dietrich got out of his command car and gave Springer new epaulettes and informed him that, 'as of today my boy, your are a *Hauptsturmführer*. Carry on and you will lead'. This was for his actions in establishing a bridgehead over the Mius River during October. Springer recalled that it was a very dangerous place for Divisional Commander to be. Later the same day the I Battalion Commander, Fritz Witt, told Springer that a bridgehead was to be captured over the Don River. The Bridge that spanned the river was to be captured intact. The honour of taking the bridge was to fall to the men of the 3. *Kompanie*. For this attack they would be assisted by a group of Pioneers from the 2. *Kompanie*/ Pioneer Battalion and a signals communication group. They all decided to wear captured Russian clothes and use captured Russian weapons.

The Capture of Rostov and the Don Bridge

During the morning of the 20th of November the attack on Rostov began and the nearby airstrip was quickly taken. The men of the Pioneer *Kompanie,* travelling with the 3. *Kompanie*, overpowered an attempted Russian attack and the rapid advance into the city continued. Newly promoted *Hauptsturmführer* Springer recalled that at this stage the city was in mayhem with large amounts of Russian soldiers and civilians making their way towards the bridge. The German advance had been fast and there were guards standing at some of the official buildings in a relaxed stance. Once the 3. *Kompanie* got into the confines of the city; intensive house to house fighting ensued. It was during the advance further into the town that *Hauptsturmführer* Springer had a very close shave. A Russian officer appeared ten feet in front of him and drew his pistol. He proceeded to point the pistol at Springer and pull the trigger! The gun did not fire and very quickly, another 3. *Kompanie Kameraden*, Franz Frohlich, shot the Russian officer. There was no time to stop and think about what had just happened and the rapid advance continued. They got to a position where they could look down on the large bridge below. They could see the large groups of civilians and supply trains moving over the bridge.

The 3. *Kompanie* and the Pioneers made it to the railway station where a train was destroyed. The accompanying Pioneers also managed to stop a convoy of Russian trucks, which blocked the bridge; the fighting continued into the evening. It was during the evening that the 3. *Kompanie* moved onto the bridge from the direction of the city. What lay in front of them was a daunting task. The bridge itself was around 1650 feet wide and was prepared for demolition by the Russians. All around them were enemy soldiers and the bulk of the rest of the *LAH* were still fighting outside the city. A Russian train full of soldiers came out of the city and attempted to make it across. *Hauptsturmführer* Springer saw an opportunity to turn this to their advantage. He gave the order for all of his men to open fire on the train. The hail of fire punctured the engine and the steam gushed out of the multitude of holes. The loss of pressure brought the train to a halt. Wasting no time, The 3. *Kompanie* and the 2. *Kompanie* Pioneers quickly advanced across the bridge using the ensuing confusion as their cover. The Pioneers concentrated on removing the wires to the demolition charges. The Russians were not expecting any Germans to be this far forward and the 3. *Kompanie* managed to get to the opposite end of the bridge and overpower the bridge guard unit positioned there. The 3. *Kompanie* had got to the southern end of the bridge with no losses.

At the southern end of the bridge the Pioneers pushed on further in order to destroy the railway lines leading into Rostov. Springer and his 3. *Kompanie* searched for the bridge guards. There was a large red house on the south bank. They went into the house and began to search the ground floor. There was no one to be seen so they went up to the first floor. It was here that the 3. *Kompanie* discovered thirty Russian soldiers eating a meal. Springer shouted out to them 'Stoi, hands up'. The Russians were very surprised and the food they were eating fell from their mouths.

The 3. *Kompanie* removed the Russian weapons and sent the enemy soldiers over to the north end of the bridge. The 3. *Kompanie* had done their job and captured the gate to the Caucasus.

With the bridge captured, they quickly set up a small bridgehead, but they were coming under increasing pressure from the enemy; the losses to the 3. *Kompanie* were starting and worse was to come. They became temporarily cut-off, but a re-link was made later that night. At this stage the 3. *Kompanie* were engaged in hand to hand fighting. Reinforcements were urgently needed to exploit the success; there was however, simply not enough men available to carry out this task. In the early hours of the 21st of November, orders were given from Korps level detailing that the bridgehead was to be abandoned. This was a painful order for the men of the 3. *Kompanie* and the 2. *Kompanie* Pioneers to adhere to as they had suffered a lot of losses. The withdrawal was carried out during the relative safety of darkness with the wounded and then the dead men being removed from the bridge. The Russians wasted no time in re-linking the demolition charges and destroying the bridge. The hard won objective paid for in 3. *Kompanie* blood was lying at the bottom of the Don River. The rest of the *LAH* were moving closer to the city with the I and III Battalions in the centre. The *LAH* eventually took the rest of the city during the course of the day. Part of the war booty included over ten thousand enemy troops and over fifty enemy tanks.

Recollections of another *LAH* member

Erwin Bartmann was at this time serving with the 4. *Kompanie* of the *LAH*. He recalled that the 1. and 3. *Kompanie*s tended to be the *Schützen-Kompanie*s, or attack *Kompanies*. The 2. and 4. *Kompanie*s were in support. Bartmann's *Kompanie* were ordered to advance on Rostov to help the attack. They were advancing alongside Wehrmacht tanks in the early stages. The tanks came to a stop at an enemy tank ditch, but the *LAH* were ordered to move ahead. The Wehrmacht tank commander was astounded that the *LAH* would proceed in an attack without tank support. The answer he received was that the *LAH* needed to get into the city and they could not waste vital time, tanks or no tanks!

Bartmann recalled that they advanced into the city past the railway station and witnessed the debris of the earlier 3. *Kompanie* fighting. This included one of the Russian trains. Erwin Bartmann was ordered to go across the bridge by the Battalion commander, Fritz Witt, and lay telephone lines so that communications could be established with the 3. *Kompanie* on the other end. When he got half way across, he was ordered back by Fritz Witt as by that stage the bridge had been captured. He returned to the building being used as the headquarters. There he reported to Fritz Witt who was with three other officers. Witt told one of the officers to go and get some of the champagne that had been captured in the Crimea, so that they could have a celebratory drink. The officer returned with four bottles of champagne. Fritz Witt then pointed to Erwin Bartmann and asked the officer why there was no bottle of champagne for Bartmann. Fritz Witt stated that he wanted everyone in the room to celebrate the capture of the bridge and that included Bartmann, so the officer had to go and fetch another bottle so that they could all join in. Even after the capture of the city, Erwin Bartmann recalls that it was still a dangerous place. The *LAH* had almost exhausted their ammunition supplies and he remembers that there was a wooden bridge situated about 100 yards away from the main bridge. They could see Russian soldiers crossing this wooden bridge with their horses, but all they could do was to fire intermittent bursts of fire at the enemy. He also recalled a near fatal situation for himself. He was with three other *Kameraden* and they approached a high wooden fence with a door in it. They tried to open the door, but were unsuccessful. They were standing opposite the door talking when the door was opened and a Russian soldier fired some shots from his pistol. The man standing beside Bartmann was hit four times and died on the spot. The door was closed again and all attempts to open it failed!

Consolidation on the Northern River Bank

On the morning of the 21st of November, *Hauptsturmführer* Springer went to see Fritz Witt at the Battalion Headquarters. Fritz Witt asked how he was doing and then enquired about a wound on Springer's head. During the course of the fighting, an enemy bullet had pierced his helmet and shot off his left eyebrow! Fritz Witt remarked on how lucky he had been and he then got Springer to sit down and give him an assessment of the fighting strength of the 3. *Kompanie*. At this stage they had thirty men left. Witt remarked that, 'hopefully we will come here again, but at the moment the III *Panzerkorps* situation is critical'. Heinrich Springer and Fritz Witt had known each other for a long time. Springer had fought under Witt as Battalion Adjutant and then *Kompanie* Commander. He could see the worry in Witt's eyes at this moment.

Rostov street plan map 4a

The Battalion Headquarters was situated in a multi-story building on the north bank of the Don River, which was frozen at this time. The Russian soldiers were firing on the building from the south bank with snipers. Springer was moving from floor to floor in an effort to determine the location of the snipers. It was during these endeavours that he was hit in the shoulder with an enemy bullet. He felt hot under his Russian jacket in the area of his left shoulder. The bullet had passed right through him and Springer found the bullet; it was a .50 calibre shell! This was Springer's fifth wound. He went back down the stairs to Fritz Witt, where a medic was called for. The wound was serious enough for Springer to be sent back home. As they waited on the ambulance arriving, Fritz Witt and Heinrich Springer shared a drink from a bottle of Crimean champagne, which had been captured from the harbour at Taganrog.

Evacuation for Heinrich Springer, and the 3. *Kompanie* Casualties

Hauptsturmführer Springer was placed in one of three ambulances, along with some of his wounded *Kameraden* from the 3. *Kompanie*. They were moved towards the main medical station in Taganrog. They proceeded through Rostov and their previous battle sites. Outside of Rostov the ambulances stopped and Springer became worried. He got the medics to help him out of the ambulance. It was foggy again and Springer discovered that they were moving north towards the enemy positions instead of west towards their own lines at Taganrog. Springer took command of the ambulance section and ordered them to move west. They had to reach the airport at Taganrog as some of the 3. *Kompanie* men were heavily wounded. Once they reached Taganrog airfield they were flown to Dnjepropetrowsk in a Ju 52 and then by train to a hospital in Jauer by Liegnitz in Schlesien. He was awarded the Gold Wound Badge on the 26th of November 1941.

Heinrich Springer: Sixth Commander of the 3. *Kompanie*

Date of birth: 03.11.14 SS Number: 291 700

On the 12th of January 1942 Heinrich Springer was awarded the Knight's Cross to the Iron Cross for the capture of the bridge over the Don River at Rostov. He also received the Russian Front Medal in May 1942, along with other soldiers of the German Armed Forces. It was on the 1st of June 1942 that *Hauptsturmführer* Springer was given command of the 1. *Kompanie*, 1st Regiment *LSSAH*. He was promoted to *Sturmbannführer* in June 1943 and he would also see service with the 12th SS Panzer Division *Hitlerjugend* as the Divisional Adjutant. Later he would serve as the First Ordnance Officer of *Feldmarschall* Model's Army Group B, where he would be closely linked to another famous bridge during the Allied Market Garden Operation; that being the one that spanned the Nieder Rhine at Arnhem. He also took part in the fighting in the Ardennes at the end of 1944. This talented and highly respected SS officer survived the war and has helped immensely in the tracing of the 3. *Kompanie*'s history.

Defensive Fighting on the Ssambek River: Winter 1941-1942

Back in Rostov towards the end of November 1941, the massive operation of clearing and securing the area began. Von Mackensen, who was commanding the III *Armeekorps*, sent a congratulatory note to the men on their successes in taking Rostov. Although Rostov had been reached, the battle for the city was not finished.

Hauptsturmführer Heinrich Springer pictured after he received the award of the Knight's Cross to the Iron Cross for his successful leadership and actions in capturing the bridge at Rostov. (Heinrich Springer)

This photograph shows the bridge that spanned the Don River at Rostov. This formidable objective was successfully captured by Heinrich Springer and the men from the 3. Kompanie, with help from the LAH's pioneer troops. (Patrick Agte)

This second photograph from Rostov shows one of the LAH's assault guns fighting its way through the city. This was an intensive battle that was still raging after the bridge had been captured. (Patrick Agte)

Right: Erwin Bartmann photographed with the rank of *Sturmmann*. He would end the war with the rank of *Unterscharführer*. He was responsible for trying to link with Springer and the 3. Kompanie during their battle for the bridge at Rostov. (Erwin Bartmann)

Below: An Opel Blitz of the LAH negotiates the Russian 'roads' in early autumn 1941. These road conditions would worsen significantly as winter progressed and cause the German Army many problems. (Hans Vogel)

Along with the above note, von Mackensen sent another one to the Divisional Commander. It stated that there were strong enemy forces still present in the area. This presented a strong threat to the Mariupol area. This situation was considered more dangerous than the loss of Rostov. If the enemy did break through at Mariupol, then the III *Armeekorps* would be cut-off. Some units were pulled out of the Rostov sector and sent north to the I Pz. Army. A new line behind the Mius River was ordered. Although the men of the *LAH* and indeed the other elements of the III Pz. Army had suffered much up to now, von Kleist considered the next few days to be a testing time for the men. These new defensive positions were taken up on the 22nd of November. Although they did not know it, they would be in this Donez region for the next seven months.

The fighting in the Rostov area had been a hard battle. The German forces had captured over 135,000 prisoners, 1500 tanks, 2000 artillery pieces, nine armoured trains and 111 planes. When the attack had begun, the Korps were fighting against odds of 2:1. When they went over to the defensive, this rose to 4:1. The *Korps* suffered over 1000 casualties. The fighting qualities of the German soldier, at this stage in the war, needs no further explanation.

On the 25th of November the *LAH* repulsed a strong enemy attack in the southwest of Rostov. Some enemy forces made it across the river, but they were

This photograph shows a group of LAH vehicles starting to move out during their advances deeper into Russia during the autumn of 1941. (Hans Vogel)

pushed back. The enemy numbers were far superior to the defenders of the *LAH*. At this stage the average *Kompanie* was down to thirty-five men. Within the next few days all of the Battalions of the *LAH* were subjected to attacks, fortunately these were all repulsed. The planned withdrawal did not happen, as there were no reserves left. The only sensible, albeit bitter, decision was to abandon Rostov and take up new positions west of the Ssambek River.

The moves began at the start of December but were quickly halted as Hitler prevented any further backward moves. Von Runstedt was relieved of command after asking for a change in the orders. A great deal of argument followed regarding the situation for the troops and the logic in keeping them where they were. The order to allow moves to a better position was finally given the following day. The delay had cost valuable lives and the loss of a capable commander. A report on the strength of the *LAH* at this stage shows them as having approximately 10,000 men and 15% of their vehicles combat ready.

The new defensive positions were as follows. The I and IV Battalions were on the right from the railway line on the Ssambek to Balka Popowa. The II Battalion were in the middle and the III Battalion were on the right, south of Ssambek. Hitler visited this area on the 2nd of December and met with Dietrich to assess the situation. Over the next week the Russians tried to break through these positions. They were under the impression that the Germans were on the retreat. They threw twelve divisions and six brigades against the four weak divisions of the III *Panzerkorps*. The *LAH*, 13th and 14th Panzer Divisions and the 60th Division stood side by side and repulsed these attacks. The fighting then died off as winter set in.

Up to this point the *Korps* had advanced 1200 kilometers into enemy territory. They had fought over eighty enemy units, seventy of which were Divisions. They had taken almost 140,000 prisoners, 1500 tanks, over 2000 artillery pieces and large quantities of smaller weapons. The losses for the *LAH* up to this point stood at 1700. The *LAH* had been fighting for three months non-stop. Due to the *LAH* losses, the IV Battalion was merged with the I Battalion in the last week of December and renamed Group Witt.

At the start of 1942 Dietrich was awarded the Oakleaves to the Knight's Cross. The *LAH*'s official history mentions the use of two British prisoners of war as Hiwis. An order for these men to be returned to Berlin followed. They were accompanied to Berlin by two officers from the *LAH*. Here the officers were astonished to discover a room full of other British, American, Canadian and New Zealand troops who had agreed to fight for the forces of Germany!

Above: Congestion on the Russian roads, LAH style! This photograph also dates from the same period and shows a column of mainly heavy vehicles from the LAH; one of the motorcyclists from the previous photo can be seen in the bottom left corner. (Hans Vogel)

Right: This photograph shows the church that was situated in the Ssambek area. This church was a familiar sight to many of the LAH veterans during the winter of late 1941, early 1942. (Hans Vogel)

Right: This second photograph also shows the same church, only from the opposite side. It was heavily damaged by the Russians as they shelled the LAH's positions. The damage can be clearly seen. Erwin Bartmann recalls that the church was very beautiful and it was a great shame to see the results of the Russian shelling. (Erwin Bartmann)

This photograph shows the command car of Sepp Dietrich temporarily stopped during the advances into Russia. Dietrich is sitting down in the front of the car beside the open door. (Hans Vogel)

The LAH's Fiesler Storch pictured around the same time. It was another familiar sight to the men of the LAH, and was used for reconnaissance and other tasks. (Hans Vogel)

The Murder of Six 3. *Kompanie Kameraden*: Taganrog, October 1941

On the 28th of March 1942, a disturbing discovery was made in the former G.P.U. building in Taganrog. The bodies of six men from the *LAH* were found down a well in the grounds of the building. Initially there was little to identify the bodies, except for a mug that had one person's name on it. The name belonged to that of *Sturmmann* Steiner of the 3. *Kompanie*. The former 3. *Kompanie* Spiess, *Hauptscharführer* Ferdi Husser, and the existing 3. *Kompanie* Spiess, *Sturmscharführer* Bruhn, were called to identify the bodies. They were identified as *Sturmmann* Gehrken, *Sturmmann* Lippke, *Sturmmann* Schwillinsky, *Sturmmann* Steiner, *SS-Mann* Mehnke and *SS-Mann* Plotz. These were the six men listed as missing from the 3. *Kompanie* on the 15th of October 1941.

An autopsy was performed on each man to determine the cause of death; the following findings were made.

Sturmmann Gehrken had four fingers of his right hand missing. His skull was shattered, but there were no gun shot wounds on the body.

Sturmmann Lippke had been shot in the right temple.

Sturmmann Schwillinsky had a shattered skull and no gun shot wounds were found.

Sturmmann Steiner had a shattered skull and broken spine, no gun shot wounds. *SS-Mann* Mehnke had been shot in the rear right hand side of the head. He also had a shattered rib cage and his right hand was missing.

SS-Mann Plotz had a broken spine and a shattered left rib cage. No gun shot wounds.

The bodies were placed in coffins and buried in the church cemetery near the lighthouse in Taganrog.

Preparations for the Move to France: Mid-1942

The *LAH* stayed in these positions until May. There was a major Russian offensive launched in January 1942, but it only briefly threatened the left flank. On the 15th of May 1942 the orders were received that detailed the increase of the *LAH* numbers. A further Infantry Battalion was added together with Panzer, Flak and Pioneer units. The *LAH* were to move to Mariupol for a period of rest, this began on the 23rd of May. Three days later the Russian Front Medal was awarded for the winter campaign of 1941-1942. At the start of July there was a move to the new area between Stalino and Mariupol. From the 15th of July 1942 they were retitled 1st

SS Division (motorised) *Leibstandarte Adolf Hitler*. This was prior to the birth of the Waffen-SS, official from 21st of October 1942. In a letter to the author from Ralf Tiemann, it was confirmed that Joachim Schiller assumed temporary command of the 3. *Kompanie* during early 1942. Listed as serving with the 3. *Kompanie* at this stage was *Untersturmführer* Eberhard Stehr. It can assumed that he was serving as Schiller's Platoon Leader at this stage. The period of 1942 is one were very little detail is available on the individual *Kompanie*s and their respective commanders.

Eberhard Stehr: Platoon Leader in the 3. *Kompanie*

Date of birth: 17.01.21 SS number: 365 459

It is known that Eberhard Stehr served with the 3. *Kompanie* as a *Sturmmann* in January 1941. He next appears under the 3. *Kompanie* in April 1942, holding the rank of *Untersturmführer*, in the role listed above. It is also known that by April 1944 he was holding the rank of *Obersturmführer* and serving in the SS Panzer-grenadier Training and Replacement Battalion Nr. 1. By July of 1944 he was back with the 1st Panzergrenadier Regiment. He was killed in April 1945 in Hungary. His final rank was *Hauptsturmführer*.

CHAPTER EIGHT

REST AND EXPANSION

The *LAH* was re-structured up to two regiments. *Obersturmbannführer* Fritz Witt was given command of the 1st Regiment with *Sturmbannführer* Albert Frey gaining command of the I Battalion, within the 1st Regiment. On the 10th of July 1942 they were ordered to an area east of Paris for the refit to begin. The moves began two days later and were complete by the 26th. The *LAH* were subordinated to the LXXXI *Armeekorps* under General Kuntzen.

During July replacements were sent to the *LAH*. One man who was sent to the 3. *Kompanie* was Gerhard Dilling. He had joined the *LAH* on the 1st of April 1942 and was trained for the following three months as a radio operator/messenger. His links to the 3. *Kompanie* would last right up to the last days of the war – and beyond, but we will read more about him later.

On the 29th of July the *LAH* marched through Paris in a parade before von Rundstedt. They then moved to new billets west of Paris. During August intensive training was undertaken. On the 19th of August the attempted Allied landings at Dieppe took place. The 1st Regiment was ordered to stand ready. The alert was suspended the following day. On the 28th Dietrich and Albert Speer visited the landing sites. The training continued in this area until the start of October. Hitler then ordered the *LAH* to the Normandy region as it was considered the most likely point for the expected Allied landings. The I Battalion was billeted in the Canon area. At the start of November the Americans landed in North Africa. Once again the *LAH* were put on alert. At the end of this month the Vichy area of France was occupied.

One known addition to the 3. *Kompanie* at this stage was Günther Zaag. He had just come from Bad Tölz and had reached the rank of *Standartenoberjunker*, or officer cadet. He had fought with the *LAH* in the first Russian campaign and was present as the *LAH* battled through Rostov. He recalled the lack of ammunition and severe weather conditions during those days. His present surroundings were more agreeable and he recalled the beautiful Normandy countryside as he enjoyed the sights around Caen. Little did he, or the rest of the men of the *LAH*, know that they would all be fighting for their lives in this exact area during mid-1944.

Then at the end of December, the *LAH* were once again ordered east. The loading started in January 1943 and was complete in February. At this stage the 3. *Kompanie* were commanded by *Obersturmführer* Manfred Gessner. It is known that *Untersturmführer* Hans Flocke and *Untersturmführer* Hans-Gert Friese were the Platoon commanders, but no further information is available on these two officers.

Obersturmführer Manfred Gessner: Seventh Commander of the 3. _Kompanie_

Date of birth: 19.01.18 SS number: ?

It can be determined that Manfred Gessner joined the *LAH* during October-November 1936 and was assigned to the 1. *Kompanie*. By 1941 he was a Platoon Leader within the 1. *Kompanie* and was wounded during November of that year at the same time as Gerd Pleiss was mortally wounded. It is not known when he joined the 3. *Kompanie*, but he would have been with them during their period of rest and re-fit in France. He was about to lead the men of the 3. *Kompanie* into battle as they once again returned to Russia. There is no other information available on this officer.

Global Overview

Before we go further with the *LAH*, it is worth giving a brief overview of events elsewhere in the globe. The German soldier had been fighting for two and a half years up to this point and they had enjoyed many splendid victories over very worthy adversaries. Adolf Hitler had undertaken his gamble in the Soviet Union and the first few months had brought some promising signs that this campaign would lead to another victory. Events towards the end of 1941 had proved otherwise. The uncompromising Russian winter set in and brought all the fighting to a standstill. Moscow had not been taken, although the German troops got to within sight of the gates of the Russian capital. The objectives were then changed and the Ukraine was given precedence. In the south, the Caucasus region and Stalingrad were the objectives. There was no clear victory in the desert campaign as yet and the German cities were suffering increasingly heavy air raids. During 1942 the first 1000 bomber raids took place. Japan's attack on America at Pearl Harbor had brought the U.S. screaming into the war and changed the nature of the conflict to a truly global one. The U.S. wasted no time in gearing up for total war and during 1942 they destroyed some of the Japanese aircraft carriers at the Battle of Midway. Germany had declared war on the U.S. and they in turn began to make their presence felt in Europe. Their air raids over Germany were added to the existing British attacks.

What Hitler needed was a decisive blow in the east that would bring victory, and a good bargaining tool, to him. The Russian army had proved to be resolute and determined in the first year and a half of Operation Barbarossa. In the autumn of 1942 they had begun a major counter-offensive. They re-took areas around Moscow and they also made gains in the Stalingrad area. Any forthcoming battles would be vital.

CHAPTER NINE

EAST AGAIN: DESTINATION KHARKOV

After Stalingrad, the Russians wasted no time in capitalising on their gains. They pushed deeper and deeper into the positions of the German Army Group South and Army Group Centre. Their first main objective was the city of Kharkov. The Soviet Voronezh Front was positioned to the north of Kharkov and the Southwestern Front was to the south of the city. Together they had the objective of capturing this city and defeating the German troops in the area. There was also the objective of cutting Army Group South off in the Crimean region. The Germans would do all in their power to stop the extensive Russian advances. Strong German units were needed for this objective and the *LAH* would be one of the units designated for this area.

The main bulk of the *LAH* arrived in the train station at Tschugujew, southeast of Kharkov. This put the *LAH* northeast of the positions that they had been in on their previous battles in Russia. Their train journey had taken between 10-14 days. They were positioned around the large bend in the Donez River east of Kharkov. The I Battalion arrived on the 29th of January 1943 in the middle of a heavy snow storm. By the 2nd of February (around the time of the surrender of Stalingrad), they were positioned north of the station from Martowaja to Chotomlja. At this time the Donez was frozen solid. The enemy had massed seven divisions and was advancing towards Kharkov from the west at Dwuretschnaja. On the 4th of February the Russians began their attacks. Heinrich Springer, who was now the commander of the 1. *Kompanie*, used his men to stop the advances. They were using the MG42

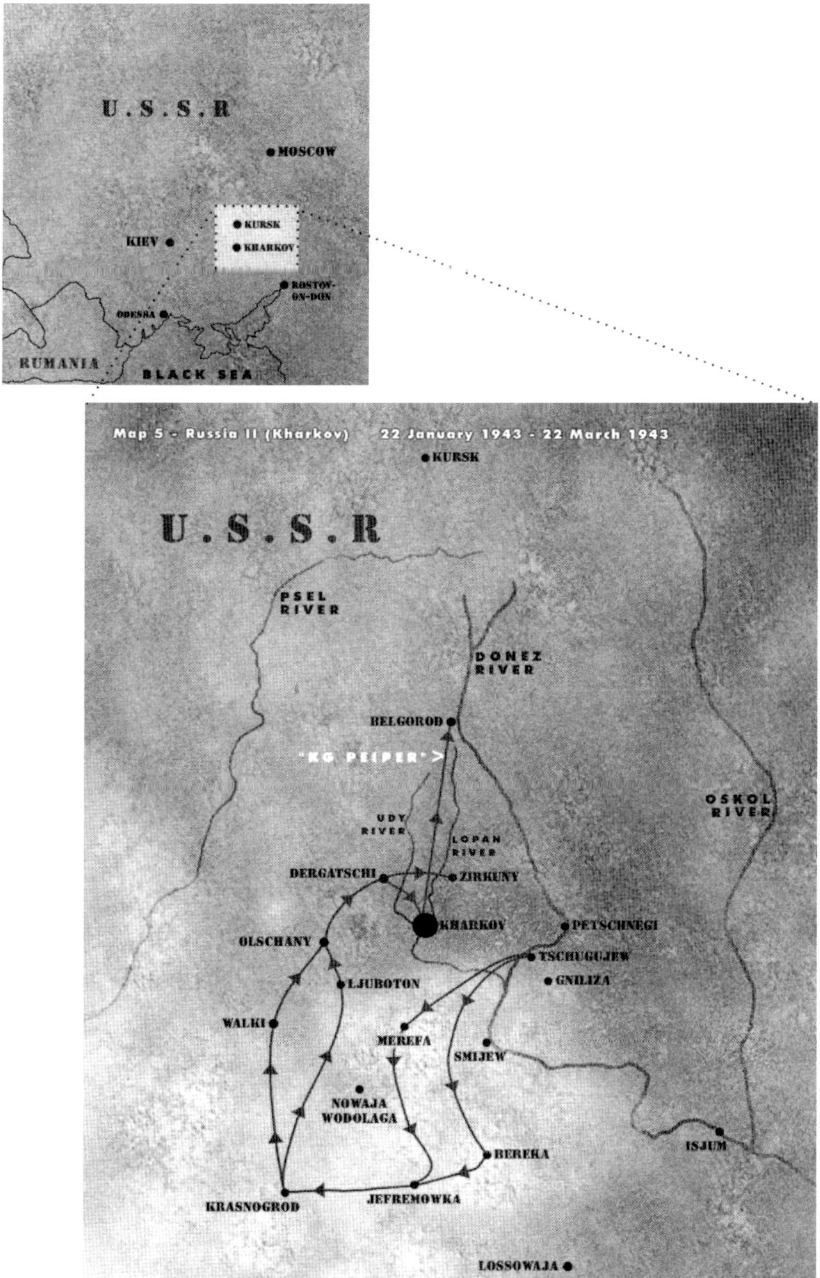

Map of Russia II: Kharkov

for the first time and were very impressed with its' awesome capabilities. On the 5th the enemy attacked along the whole front line. Hardest hit were the I and II Battalions of the 1st Reg. and the whole of the 2nd Reg.

The 3. *Kompanie* in Action Near Kharkov

Günther Zaag recalled that on the first day of February 1943, the 3. *Kompanie* were positioned south of Petschenigis. They had a small copse of woods in front of them and a mountain forest behind them. Their positions were widely dispersed and they did not have adequate men to cover their assigned area. They faced the strong possibility of the enemy being able to break into their positions. They did have one heavy mortar positioned on their left, but it had limited ammunition supplies, so it could only fire very infrequently. He did recall that this sort of situation was not new to the men of the *LAH*. They had the task of capturing the hill in front of them, which was near Kizewka. The planned date for this attack was the 5th of February. Zaag recalled that they had the element of surprise and they were confident of victory. Besides the heavy mortar they also had one heavy machine gun to assist them. They moved closer to the enemy positions under darkness. The Russians sent up two flares to keep a watch on their own positions. The men of the 3. *Kompanie* got to within grenade throwing range of the enemy. They unscrewed the caps from the grenades and got them ready for use. At the agreed time they threw their grenades and then immediately got up and ran fast towards the enemy positions. Zaag recalled that they were firing their machine pistols whilst running. He also recalled that their advance was so rapid that they almost ran into the blast from their own grenades!

With this determined action they captured the objective. They then came under sniper fire from a very well concealed enemy sniper. They used the snow to help camouflage themselves against this fire. At this point, Zaag recalled that they could hear columns of vehicles moving far to the rear towards Kharkov. The Russians were in the process of trying to capture this important city from the Germans. The 3. *Kompanie* took up defensive positions over the next few days.

The Abandonment of Kharkov

On the 8th the enemy launched heavy attacks in the Gniliza area, held by the 2nd Reg., and the Petschenegi area held by the 1st Reg., the attacks were pushed back.

It was around this time that the *Korps* realised that the city of Kharkov was in danger of being encircled. This would have resulted in the forces within being cut-off. With the memory of Stalingrad still very much in everyone's mind, the move to a better line began. The enemy was amassing ever-increasing forces in the area opposite the German positions. *Kampfgruppe* Peiper forced a link with the 320th Infantry Division who had been cut-off in the Wodjanoje area, south east of the city. The order to abandon Kharkov and move to an area behind the Udy River came on the 14th of February. The order was given by 'Papa' Hausser, at that time commanding the SS *Panzerkorps* containing the 1st, 2nd and 3rd SS-Divisions, and was in direct contradiction to an order given from Hitler to hold the city. At this time the *Das Reich* and *Großdeutschland* divisions were receiving heavy blows to the north of the city.

The 3. *Kompanie* Pull Back

Over the previous week the 3. *Kompanie* had played their part in helping the 1st Regiment hold the Petschenegi sector. They then received the order to pull out of their present positions late in the afternoon of the 14th of February. The order was passed from position to position, but not everyone got to hear this order as the enemy sniper had taken his toll upon the men of the 3. *Kompanie*. Not all of the casualties are listed, but it is known that *Untersturmführer* Hans-Gert Friese and *SS-Mann* Alois Hauser were two of the 3. *Kompanie* killed. The both of them died on the 12th of February 1943. Günther Zaag himself almost became a casualty. He recalled that a burst of enemy machine gun fire hit one of his 3. *Kompanie Kameraden* standing beside him. He escaped with a bread bag full of holes! This was done whilst moving to another position.

The 3. *Kompanie* Attack Upon Nowo Bereka

The following day the 3. *Kompanie* reported to Fritz Witt. They were ordered to attack the village of Bereka, which is east of Krasnograd. The village stretched lengthways across the positions held by the 3. *Kompanie*. Zaag recalled that at that stage there was sixty men in the 3. *Kompanie*. He also recalled the extreme weather conditions, which presented temperatures of twenty-five degrees below zero and snow that was at times waist deep. The attack itself began at 10:00 a.m. and the advance was made through the deep snow and to add to this, they had to contend with a howling snowstorm. The advance continued however, towards the bigger problem, that of the enemy.

Gerhard Dilling, who was now holding the rank of *Sturmmann*, was also present during this attack. He had his camera with him and he recorded some of the images from this time. He was ordered by Battalion leader Albert Frey to advance to the head of the *LAH*'s positions. On the way he passed a Sturmgeschütz, this was one of two StuGs that were assisting the 3. *Kompanie* in this attack. When Dilling got to the end of the road, he asked where he was to set-up. Albert Frey told him to carry on towards the crossroads up ahead and set-up there. This was the furthest point of the I Battalion positions and Dilling found himself alone at this stage, not a good position to be in with the Russians close by. The attack commenced and as the advance proceeded the machine guns jammed due to the extreme cold. The StuGs also made very slow progress in the deep snow. The maps showed that the various squads had to move up a hill so that they could reach the correct positions for the attack. The snow and wind deadened all of the noise. A reconnaissance was sent out to try to get a better idea of what they were up against. Günther Zaag recalled that this was soon found to be a mistake.

A shot rang out and the first man fell dead. This man was Platoon Leader *Untersturmführer* Hans Flocke and he had been shot through the head. Flocke had been trudging through the snow next to Günther Zaag a few moments earlier. The enemy mortar shells began to fall upon the positions of the 3. *Kompanie*. The StuGs replied by firing high explosive shells into the village. This succeeded in forcing the enemy to start withdrawing. The fire from both sides intensified and at this point the StuGs pulled back and moved around the back of the hill. There was a lot of confusion and the men of the 3. *Kompanie* were trying to take cover in the snow, whilst firing against the enemy. The 3. *Kompanie* commander, *Obersturmführer* Manfred Gessner was killed during this early stage of the attack. Günther Zaag recalled how horrible the whole thing was as he watched his *Kameraden* being hit very hard by the enemy. Amongst this confusion, *Oberscharführer* Hermann Dahlke took control of the remainder of the 3. *Kompanie*, assisted by Günther Zaag. They succeeded in taking the village and holding it against repeated enemy attacks. The wounded were tended to under the relative safe cover of the StuGs. The names of the wounded or other possible dead are not known.

The following day the remnants of the 3. *Kompanie* were relieved. Dahlke and Zaag reported to the I Battalion commander, *Sturmbannführer* Albert Frey.

They gave an account of the previous days' fighting and how they witnessed the demise of the 3. *Kompanie*. Günther Zaag recalled that Albert Frey was visibly pale whilst listening to these reports. He also recalled that both Dahlke and himself did not find it easy to recount the previous day's actions.

Hermann Dahlke: Eighth Commander of the 3. *Kompanie*

Date of Birth: 11.02.17 SS Number: ?

Hermann Dahlke was born in Greifswald, Pomerania. He joined the SS during mid-1934 and was posted to the *LAH*. After a period of four years with the *LAH*, he left his military service and took up an office job. When the political situation deteriorated in September 1939, he was recalled to the *LAH*, where he found himself in the 3. *Kompanie*. Dahlke fought during the campaign in the west and was awarded the Second Class Iron Cross on the 8th of July 1940. He also received the Black Wound Badge. He went on to fight in the Balkans and Greece with the 3. *Kompanie* and by the time of the end of the campaign in Greece he was holding the rank of *Scharführer*.

The start of the Russian campaign would make great demands of many German soldiers, with the first winter providing a few unwelcome surprises for them. Many of them displayed great courage and Hermann Dahlke of the 3. *Kompanie* would be one of these individuals. He was awarded the First Class Iron Cross on the 3rd of December 1941 and he also moved up to the rank of *Oberscharführer*; he was also given command of a *Zug* within the much depleted 3. *Kompanie*. The defensive fighting of early 1942 and the subsequent refit in France during the latter half of 1942, gave people like Hermann Dahlke the chance to pass on to new recruits the lessons they had learned up to now. These experiences would serve them well in the forthcoming second visit to the Russian Front. Hermann Dahlke certainly put his experiences to good use on the 15th of February 1943 when he took temporary command of the *Kompanie*.

Defensive Fighting on the Udy River: February 1943

Due to the increasing enemy pressure a new defensive line was ordered to be established behind the Udy River; these positions were reached on the 16th of February. Along with the I Battalion the 3. *Kompanie* fell back to the Taranowka-Jefremowka area on the 17th. They had helped to destroy the VI Russian Cavalry

Korps. Hitler revisited the front on this day and on the 18th new orders were issued. The recapture of Kharkov was not possible at this stage. Therefore, the *LAH* pulled back slightly to the line from Beresowka to the hills south of Borki. Over the next few days, attacks were conducted towards Jeremejewka by Kurt Meyer's men. This was south west of the I Battalion positions at Beresowka.

A further move back was ordered. The Pioneer Battalion had been surrounded and cut-off. The 1st Reg. were to reach them and free them, other *LAH* elements would conduct limited attacks to prevent the Russians from advancing further; the I Battalion was fighting in Borki. To shorten the line further, the *LAH* moved further back to the south west with the I Battalion being positioned near Jelenowka. By the 27th the new line held was in a horseshoe shape running from Karlowka to Nikolskoje to Krassnograd. It was on the 27th of February that the 3. *Kompanie* added the names of *Untersturmführer* Erwin Froese, *Untersturmführer* Karl Hogela and *SS-Mann* Claus Gronenberg to their list of dead. *Untersturmführer*'s Froese and Hogela are not listed as commanding the 3. *Kompanie* at any stage. It is known that Hermann Dahlke took temporary command on the 15th of February. It is possible that these two officers were assigned temporarily whilst a suitable officer was found to replace *Obersturmführer* Manfred Gessner. Their deaths would have made a bad situation even worse. Bearing in mind the fact that the 3. *Kompanie* can list the deaths of five officers within a two-week period this can without doubt be regarded as a very difficult time for the 3. *Kompanie*, and the *LAH* as a whole. *Obergrenadier* Walter Ockel was also wounded on the 27th of February. The following day the town of Olchowatka was taken after a brief but heavy fight, this was beside the I Battalion positions. The enemy had attempted a breakthrough, but had paid a heavy price.

Recognition for the I Battalion and the 3. *Kompanie*

The recent heavy battles had exacted a great toll on the men of the *LAH*. It had also however, gave some of them the chance to display great courage. This courage was recognised at higher levels. On the 28th of February 1943, Günther Zaag was awarded the First Class Iron Cross. At the start of March, *Sturmbannführer* Albert Frey was awarded the Knight's Cross for the constant successes of the of the I Battalion reconnaissance patrols. On the 6th of March, Hermann Dahlke was promoted to *Untersturmführer* and given command of the 3. *Kompanie*. He was also awarded the Knight's Cross to the Iron Cross for his actions on the 15th of

February at Bereka. He therefore became the 3. *Kompanie*'s second and final holder of the Knight's Cross. He had taken control at a critical moment and succeeded in defeating the enemy. His bravery was rewarded and he would continue to show bravery in the difficult battles that lay ahead. Last, but not least, Günther Zaag was also promoted to *Untersturmführer* on the 10th of March, thereby becoming one of Dahlke's platoon leaders.

The Advance to, and Recapture of Kharkov

It was during the start of March 1943 that orders were issued for attacks towards Ochotschaje and Taranowka. These were changed after the Russians began to move forces through the positions of the *LAH*, *Das Reich* and *Totenkopf* divisions, and their IV *Panzerarmee* neighbours. The *LAH* were sent to the Krassnograd area, they would be attacking directly north towards Walki. The *LAH* took the left flank with *Das Reich* on the right; they had to reach the Msha River that ran through Walki. The I Battalion had the objective of Minkowka, southeast of Walki. Walki itself fell on the 7th of March with the town of Ljubotin being reached the next day. This town is west of Kharkov, the attack then resumed towards the north of Kharkov.

For this new attack on Kharkov, the *LAH* were ordered to attack from the north, *Das Reich* were advancing from the west. On the 10th of March the 1st Reg (*Kampfgruppe* Witt) had captured Dergatschi north of Kharkov with the help of the *Totenkopf* Division, the advance continued east towards Zirkuny. On the 11th of March, *SS-Mann* Heinrich Kauth and *Sturmmann* Ernst Ruckner, from the 3. *Kompanie*, were both killed.

On the 12th of March the recapture of Kharkov began in earnest. The *LAH* were to the northeast of the city, with *Das Reich* to the north and northwest; *Totenkopf* were providing flank cover. The I Battalion was advancing from the north around Tscherkaskoje. By mid-morning they had linked up with *Kampfgruppe* Peiper. *Das Reich* had also worked into the southeast of the city. The following day the I Battalion was ordered to move to the southeast near the airstrip, they had to move back to the northeast and clear the area of the enemy. The fighting in all parts of the city was intense with the enemy putting up stiff resistance. On the 13th of March the I Battalion was on the Woltschansk Road. The following day would see them fighting in the northeast of Kharkov. It was on the 14th of March that the city of Kharkov fell to the combined efforts of the *LAH*, *Das Reich* and *Totenkopf*

SS divisions. Sepp Dietrich received the Swords to the Knight's Cross for the actions of his troops. On this day the I Battalion was fighting in the northeast of Kharkov.

The 3. *Kompanie*'s Actions in Kharkov

We will at this stage return to the recollections of *Untersturmführer* Günther Zaag in order to gain an insight into the 3. *Kompanie*'s part in the recapture of the city of Kharkov. He recalled fighting through difficult street battles with the remnants of the 3. *Kompanie*. They moved through the multi-story buildings, which were mostly only shells due to the intensity of the fighting and its' accompanying destruction. As always the Russian marksmen were making life hazardous for the men of the 3. *Kompanie*. They moved from house to house with their pockets full of ammunition and weapons always ready to fire. He also recalls the presence of the charismatic Kurt 'Panzer' Meyer.

Enemy T-34s moved closer to a building that the 3. *Kompanie* were in. Two of the enemy tanks fired shells into the attic of the house, but the 3. *Kompanie* defended itself well. The enemy tried to rush the cellar, but failed in the withering fire

This photograph was taken by Gerhard Dilling as the 3. Kompanie were preparing for their attack at Bereka. This StuG was one of two that assisted the 3. Kompanie at this time. (Gerhard Dilling)

This second photograph shows the position that Dilling had to advance to – alone! The main road can be seen on the right and the woods on the left were known to contain enemy soldiers. The crossroads were situated close to the small patch of woods on the right. (Gerhard Dilling)

This photograph was taken around the same time as the previous two. Gerhard Dilling's job as a radio operator meant that he spent a lot of his time with the Battalion headquarters. On one such occasion an Opel Blitz belonging to the I Battalion fell into enemy hands. A rescue mission was sent out and the truck was promptly re-taken! This photograph was taken just after the truck was returned to its rightful owners. (G. Dilling)

Above: This photograph was taken later in 1943 and shows the radio operators from the 3. Kompanie. From left to right are Hornlein, Nickol, Rttf. Holgemann, Fuhring, Dick, Unknown, Hubner. (Gerhard Dilling)

Right: Hermann Dahlke photographed in March 1943 after the award of the Knight's Cross and his promotion to *Untersturmführer*. The fact that he received a field commission is evident in his collar insignia. They are a converted set of other-ranks collar patches, without the customary silver braid around the edges. (Justin Horgan)

dispensed from the weapons belonging to the 3. *Kompanie*. This position became increasingly difficult and the men positioned themselves at all vantage points. One T-34 came to within fifty-feet of the house and continued to bombard it, assisted by enemy infantry. There were also enemy troops in the house opposite and due to the heavy pressure that they were exerting upon the *LAH* positions, the neighbouring troops next to the 3. *Kompanie* had to pull out. The 3. *Kompanie* however, stayed in their cellar and prepared for things to get even more difficult.

The day turned to evening and the enemy tank moved closer to the house, finally stopping right next to the house itself. Zaag informed his *Kameraden* of this and they all listened in anticipation for the next move. The next move would come from the men of the 3. *Kompanie* themselves. They removed bricks from the wall of the house so that they could get a clear view of the tank. Once they were ready, they fired two shots in quick succession. The T-34 caught fire and with this the immediate threat was removed. The nearby enemy infantry were still close by and they continued to put the 3. *Kompanie* positions under pressure. This intense pressure would last for a total of ten hours, before relief came! During this time, losses of five-dead and four wounded were incurred, their names are not known. Zaag himself was remembered for his bravery and the example he set for the men with him. The 3. *Kompanie* had certainly played their part in the capture of the city of Kharkov, a superb and important SS victory.

When the fighting was over, Zaag recalled spending some very happy times with an elderly Russian family in the apartments of the city, not far from the main square. The family had two daughters and Zaag got to return to one of his pre-war passions, that of music. One of the daughters played on the family piano and they all enjoyed the delights of the great Mozart and Beethoven. In these pleasant surroundings, it was hard to imagine that they had been staring death in the face a few days earlier.

No Time for Rest: A Move to the North: Belgorod

The fighting did not end with the capture of Kharkov. The danger from the strong Soviet forces to the north still existed. The German objective was to push the enemy back across the Donez River and use this river as a natural defensive barrier. The Russians, who were confident after their stunning victory at Stalingrad, had allowed their over-confidence to work against them. The excellent strategist, von Manstein, had pulled off another important victory for the German forces. It was one that could be counted as a true SS victory, a fact that did not go unnoticed by Adolf Hitler. The expectation placed on the troops of the Waffen-SS was increased significantly after the Kharkov victory and failure on their part was not a quality that Hitler was about to allow them.

The next immediate objective was Belgorod, to the north. The advance began on the 16th of March with the *LAH* on the left and *Das Reich* and *Totenkopf* on their right. *Kampfgruppe* Peiper advanced towards the objective over the next two days. They succeeded in racing through the enemy lines and right into Belgorod, this feat earned Peiper the Knight's Cross. Contact was established with the *Das Reich* and *Großdeutschland* divisions. The next week was spent in defensive positions. Hitler sent a congratulatory telegram to the forces involved in the capture of Kharkov and Belgorod. These successes had effectively smashed the Soviet winter offensive, a period of rest followed. In the clear up operation the bodies of fallen comrades were discovered, they had been badly mutilated by the enemy. The fear of capture by the Russians was a growing worry for the men. The end result of the battles around Kharkov and Belgorod was that another potential Stalingrad was avoided and the Russian offensive was stopped. This victory gave the German troops a much-needed boost at a time of extreme difficulties. The cost to the *LAH* alone had been 4500 casualties. The importance of this victory should be remembered for what it was; it showed the brilliance of Hausser and von Manstein and the capabilities of the men under them. The *LAH* were to spend the next three months in this area.

Josef 'Sepp' Dietrich: First Commander of the *LAH*

Date of birth: 28.05.1892 SS Number: 1 177

Sepp Dietrich was born in Hawangen, Bavaria. His military experiences go back to the First World War where he fought first as an artilleryman and then as a tank crewman in one of Germany's first tank units. He ended the war as an NCO and holder of the First and Second Class Iron Crosses. He was one of the inter-war year supporters of Adolf Hitler and the fledgling Nazi Party. He became a member of Hitler's bodyguard in 1932. In June of that year he became head of that bodyguard. The forming of *LAH* was done under the control of Sepp Dietrich in March 1933. The following year his loyalty to Adolf Hitler was put to the test when he took part in the "Night of the Long Knives". He acted as ordered in what was a critical time for the Nazi Party. The importance of the SS rose significantly after this event and

This photograph shows *Sturmbannführer* Kurt Meyer as he orders the artillery to get into position during the attack to re-take Kharkov. (Gerhard Dilling)

This second photograph was taken a short while later and shows the SiG33 (Schweres Infanterie Geschütz – heavy infantry gun) in position. Sturmbannführer Meyer orders the artillery to fire upon the retreating Russians to prevent their escape. (Gerhard Dilling)

the loyalty of Dietrich and his *LAH* was assured. The transformation of the *LAH* from a bodyguard unit to a potential military unit was carried out under the watchful eye of Dietrich in the years leading up to the outbreak of the Second World War. When the fighting started, Dietrich could be assured that his men were ready to stand on the front line and fight for Germany.

He led the *Leibstandarte Adolf Hitler* into battle in Poland during September 1939. On the 25th of September he received the Clasp to the Second Class Iron Cross. Just over a month later he received the Clasp to the First Class Iron Cross. The opening of the western campaign would see Dietrich lead the expanded *LAH* through the successful and difficult battles that followed. He is well remembered for his decision to ignore a Führer Order and attack the Wattenburg Heights in 1940 – a feat that earned him the Knight's Cross to the Iron Cross. The *LAH* were sent east into the depths of Russia and the Oakleaves to the Knight's Cross followed at the end of 1941 for the *LAH*'s successful battles as part of Army Group South. The fortunes of war would alternate between good and bad for the *LAH*, but in March 1943 they would play their part in the excellent victory at Kharkov. This

This photograph shows *Sturmbannführer* Meyer outside one of the buildings in the city of Kharkov itself. He is seen together with *Sturmbannführer* Albert Frey, who was at that time the commander of the I Battalion. Also shown are *Untersturmführer* Pfeiffer and *Untersturmführer* Rust, who were the I Battalion's ordnance officers at that time. They are all observing the breakout attempts of some Russian soldiers. (G. Dilling)

This photograph shows the same group a few minutes later, this time with a number of grenadiers moving around. (Gerhard Dilling)

This photograph shows some officers of the LAH enjoying a short rest after the fighting for Kharkov. Among the officers that can be seen are *Hauptsturmführer* Wiesemann of the Sturmgeschütz Abteilung I, and *Obersturmführer* Peinemann who commanded the 2. Kompanie/1st Regiment of the LAH. There were still a considerable amount of enemy troops in the city at this stage. (Gerhard Dilling)

earned Dietrich the Swords to the Knight's Cross. It was at this point that Sepp Dietrich handed the command of the *LAH* over to Theodore Wisch. He had commanded the unit for ten years and seen them develop into a first class fighting formation. His links with the *LAH* were not over yet though.

He was ordered to form the I SS *Panzerkorps*, which would contain the *LAH* and the new 12th SS Panzer Division *Hitlerjugend*. These two divisions would fight side-by-side in the Normandy battles during the summer of 1944. For the successful delaying actions of the 1st SS *Panzerkorps*, Dietrich received the Diamonds to the Knight's Cross, he was one of only twenty seven people to receive this high award. He continued to lead his divisions during the Ardennes Offensive and Hungary as commander of the 6th SS Panzer Army. He ended the war with the rank of *Oberstgruppenführer* und *Generaloberst der Waffen-SS*. He always regarded the *LAH* as 'his boys' and he would witness their rise to an elite fighting formation and their death at the hands of Germany's enemies during late 1944 and 1945. The history of the *LAH* owes much to this influential man.

Fritz Witt: I Battalion and 1st Regiment Commander

Date of birth: 27.05.08 SS Number: 21 518

Fritz Witt was born in Hohenlimburg, Westfalia. At the age of 23 he joined the SS and entered into service with the 1. *Sturm*, II *Sturmbann*, *SS-Standarte* 30. This was the *Standarte* for the Hagen/Westfalia area. His career in the *LAH* began on the 17th of March 1933 when he was one of the first 117 men hand-picked to form the protection squad. He held the rank of *Scharführer* (*Unterscharführer*) at that stage, but this would quickly change. By the 1st of April 1933 he had been promoted to *Truppführer* (*Oberscharführer*). This was changed again on the 15th of September 1933 when he rose to the rank of *Haupttruppführer* (*Hauptscharführer*). On the 1st of October 1933 he was promoted again to the rank of *Sturmführer* (*Untersturmführer*) and the following day he became a Platoon Leader in the 2. *Kompanie* of the *LAH*. Judging by these rapid promotions, it can be determined that Fritz Witt's leadership qualities were evident even in these early days. On the 9th of May 1934 he was promoted again, this time to the rank of *Obersturmführer*. On the 12th of January 1935 he moved to the Deutschland Standarte and by the 17th of May the same year he was in command of the 3. *Kompanie* within this Standarte. On the 1st of June 1935 he was promoted to *Hauptsturmführer* and during the following month he attended a course at the infantry training school at Doberitz.

The LAH's first commander Sepp Dietrich photographed in May 1944 alongside Fritz Witt. There are not many photographs showing Dietrich in the black panzer uniform. (Peter Witt)

It was as a *Kompanie* Commander that he entered into the first battles of what became the Second World War. He was awarded the Second Class Iron Cross on the 19th of September 1939. This was followed on the 26th of September with the award of the 1st Class Iron Cross. After the successful campaign in Poland, it was becoming evident that his leadership abilities were suitable to higher responsibilities. During December 1939 he attended a Battalion Leaders course at Erfurt. On the 25th of May 1940 he was promoted to *Sturmbannführer* and on the same day became the I Battalion Commander within the *Deutschland Standarte*. He was able to take part in the campaign in the west during 1940 and he successfully led the I Battalion through various engagements. The battles in France especially, provided excellent examples of this man's ability and after the campaign was concluded, he became one of only five SS soldiers to be awarded the Knight's Cross of the Iron Cross during 1940. This award was made on the 4th of September 1940.

The following month he returned to the *LAH* where he led the III Battalion . On the 26th March 1941 he assumed command of the *LAH*'s I Battalion and he led this Battalion during the campaign in the Balkans. It was during this campaign that he would suffer the loss of his brother Franz, then serving as a Platoon Commander in the 3. *Kompanie*, within the I Battalion. He was promoted further on the 27th of June 1941 to the rank of *Obersturmbannführer* and he continued to lead the I Battalion during the first difficult battles in Russia. In further recognition of his leadership skills he was awarded the German Cross in Gold on the 8th of February 1942. During February 1942 he was also awarded the Infantry Assault Badge in Bronze (23rd Feb.), and the Royal Bulgarian Bravery Medal IV Class, 1st Grade (27th Feb.). On the 1st of July 1942 he was given command of the entire *LAH*'s Infantry Regiment. During the *LAH*'s refit in France 1942, he was awarded the Star of Romania Medal with Swords and the Eastern Front Medal. The *LAH* returned to Russia in early 1943 and by that stage Fritz Witt was holding the rank of *Standartenführer*. On the 1st of March 1943 he was awarded the Oakleaves to the Knight's Cross for the Infantry Regiment's successes in the battle for Kharkov.

The *LAH* went through another major change after the battle for Kharkov when a number of its' key commanders were sent back to Germany to form what became the 12th Panzer-Grenadier Division *Hitlerjugend*, later the 12th SS Panzer Division *Hitlerjugend*. Fritz Witt was given the task of leading this new formation and the wealth of ability and experience that he had gained up to now would be passed onto his men within the HJ Division. He passed the command of the *LAH*'s

1st Infantry Regiment to Albert Frey. Fritz Witt was promoted to *Oberführer* on the 1st of July 1943 and further promoted to *Brigadeführer* und *Generalmajor* on the 20th of April 1944, not long before the Allied invasion of France in June 1944. It was during this Allied invasion that Fritz Witt was killed on the 14th of June 1944. Off shore naval guns were shelling the area and he was killed by a direct hit before he could reach the safety of the slit trenches. His remains were to see no less than three different graves. The final one is to be found in cemetery in St. Andre, near Evraux, France. With his death, the *HJ* Division, the SS and the German Army as a whole lost a very capable and experienced commander. The I Battalion, the 1st Regiment and the *LAH* definitely benefited from the leadership abilities of this very competent commander.

CHAPTER TEN

PREPARATION AND EXECUTION OF THE KURSK OFFENSIVE

Towards the end of March Dietrich went to Hitler to receive the Swords to his Knight's Cross. When he returned, he brought the news of the forming of the 12th SS Panzer Division *Hitlerjugend* and the forming of the I SS *Panzerkorps*. This new division was formed using the experienced men of the *LAH* as the officers and NCO's. The *LAH* lost people such as Sepp Dietrich, Kurt Meyer, Fritz Witt, Heinrich Springer, Max Wünsche and Hubert Meyer. These people had a wealth of experience that had been earned as leaders within the *LAH*. To make up for the losses, many Luftwaffe troops were transferred to the *LAH*, replacement vehicles also began to arrive. There were changes to the command of some of the units within the *LAH*. Albert Frey took over the command of the 1st Regiment with *Sturmbannführer* Hans-Joachim Schiller taking over the I Battalion.

The period of rest immediately after Kharkov was a welcome move for the men of the German and Russian forces. They both adopted defensive positions whilst the next moves were being planned at the highest level of command. During late April 1943, the *LAH* were moved to the west and north west of Kharkov. Extensive training was conducted as the recent additions to the division had to be quickly incorporated into the ranks.

The advances into Kharkov and Belgorod by the 4th Army in the south and the advances made by the 9th Army in the north had created a bulge or salient in the front line. The centre of this bulge was around the town of Kursk, which up to the start of the battle was a little known Russian town. The bulge itself was about

Left: This early photograph dating from 1935 shows Fritz Witt while serving with the "Deutschland" Standarte. Of special interest is the early 'number' cufftitle. The edging on this cufftitle would have been green as Witt was in the 3. Kompanie of the I Battalion of this Standarte. (different battalions had different colours). (Peter Witt) Right: Fritz Witt seen here as a *Brigadeführer* and wearing some of the many awards he received in recognition of his skills and bravery. This photograph was taken not long before he was killed in France in June 1944. (Peter Witt)

120 miles wide and eighty miles deep. Plans were drawn up to deal with this threat during May. The plans were to cut-off the bulge and destroy the enemy forces inside. This would shorten the front line and free up sizeable forces that could be used as a reserve for the long awaited Allied landings in the west. Von Manstein wanted to use a similar plan to that of Kharkov, but Hitler wanted to build on the recent success and he was determined to regain the decisive initiative in the east.

Stalin had been furious at the loss of Kharkov and he wanted to smash any further German advances. His generals persuaded him to adopt a defensive posture instead. The Russians had been receiving information from the 'Lucy' spy ring, based at Bletchley Park in England. This information gave the expected start date for the next German attack. In the two months prior to the start of the Kursk offensive, the Russians set about constructing extensive defensive positions within the bulge. Formidable defensive belts were built with the objective of blunting the German attacks. When the Germans had been sufficiently weakened, a counter attack would be launched with strong Russian reserves.

Strong armoured forces were assembled by both sides, along with formidable aerial formations. The Russians would have no fewer than four Air Armies on tap with the Germans having two Air Groups. On the ground there were no less than eighteen Russian Armies in the area bringing a total of around 1.3 million soldiers up to the start date. In the north of the salient was the Central Front with the Voronezh Front being positioned in the south; The Steppe Front was in reserve. The Russian Divisions contained within the above Army Groups would out number the German Divisions by at least 6:1, with the strongest Russian forces being placed in the north of the salient.

On the German side there were eleven *Korps* with a total of 900,000 men. The 4th Army was positioned in the south and would use Belgorod as their jump off

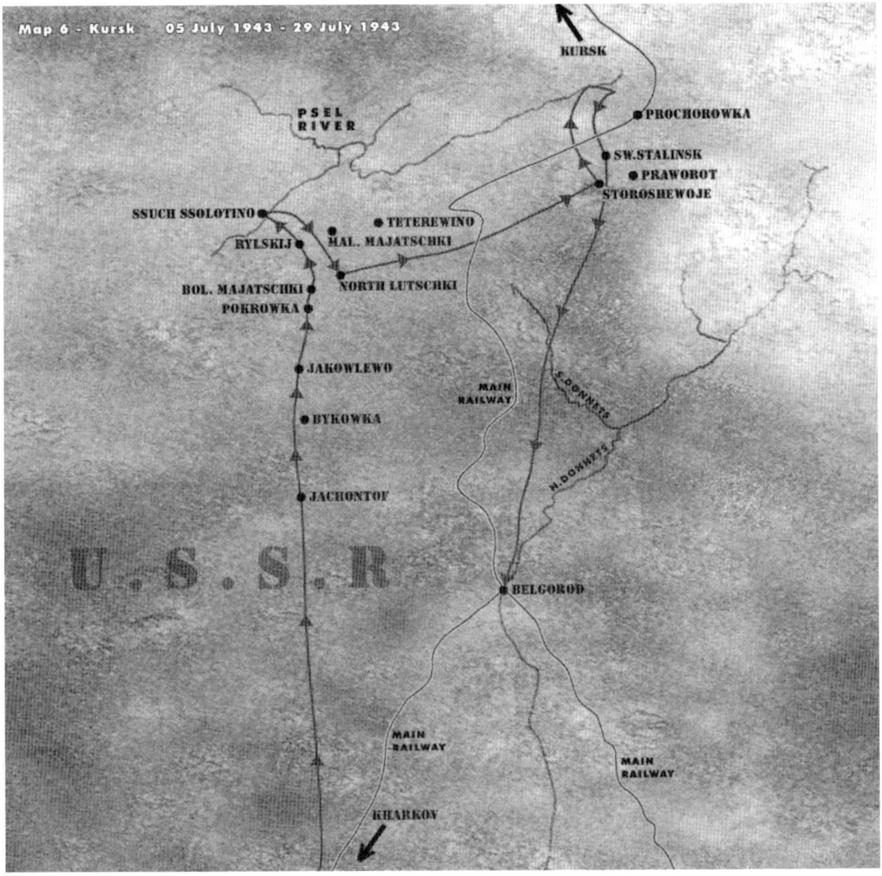

Kursk Map

point. The 9th Army was positioned near Orel in the north. There would be plenty of the new Panthers in use during the forthcoming battle, a fact that helped to delay the start date until these new Panther tanks were ready for use. Tiger Is and Ferdinands would also be used in larger numbers. The strongest German forces were placed in the south. Much was expected of the new German tanks. One other important factor that would not favor the Germans was the fact that they did not have any reserves to call upon; the recent losses made this an impossibility.

Operation *Zitadelle*: The Mighty Clash of Steel

In the last days of June, the orders were given for the move from the west of Kharkov to the jumping off areas. The start date for the forthcoming Operation *Zitadelle* was finally given as the 5th of July 1943. The day before this, *Standartenführer* Theodor Wisch took over command of the *LAH* from Dietrich. The *LAH*'s role in this battle involved them moving north to take the town of Jakowlewo. They were also to force a crossing over the Psel River which was northeast. They were in position by the 4th of July. The positions of the men were as follows, the 2nd Reg. were on the left with the 1st Reg. beside them, the *Das Reich* and *Totenkopf* divisions were to the right of these positions. The 1st Reg. had responsibility for the area from Jachontof to Jakowlewo.

The 3. *Kompanie*'s Participation in the Kursk Offensive

We return to the recollections of *Untersturmführer* Günther Zaag, serving as a Platoon Leader in the 3. *Kompanie*. During the evening of the 4th of July 1943, the *Stabscharführer*, or Spiess (person's name not known), had gone and organised food and ammunition supplies for the men of the 3. *Kompanie*. The men sat around in the dusty soil, the dry climate at this time of year and the advance to these positions had created a lot of dust. This dust had settled on the men of the *Kompanie* and left them looking like Moroccans! All of the weapons were cleaned, checked and readied for action. Sentries were posted to guard against possible enemy incursions. Only then did the rest of the exhausted men go to sleep. Zaag remembered the star filled clear sky above them and it was a peaceful night, except for an enemy machine gun firing in the distance. One or two flares were sent up during the night, also.

During the early hours of the 5th of July, everyone had some bread and a drink. The activity was increasing with tanks and Pak guns moving forward, close to the positions of the 3. *Kompanie*. It was during this activity that Russian artillery started to shell their position. Zaag recalled that there was an artillery observation officer nearby and he went to him and asked him to engage the enemy artillery. The men of the 3. *Kompanie* watched as the German artillery engaged the enemy and silenced it. At one stage one of the German shells must have hit an ammunition dump as they witnessed a huge explosion. Two Stuka dive-bombers flew overhead and began to engage T-34s. These planes belonged to Hans-Ulrich Rudel and had been modified to carry the 3.7cm anti tank guns under their wings.

During the previous days the 3. *Kompanie* had captured Russian soldiers. Through an interpreter the prisoners were offered the chance to fight alongside the men of the 3. *Kompanie* as Hiwis. After much discussion, around twenty former enemy soldiers agreed to join the *Kompanie*. The remainder were taken to a rear collection area, accompanied by four men from the 3. *Kompanie*. After this, the supplies were distributed among the men. The *Kompanie* Commander, *Untersturmführer* Hermann Dahlke, gave a speech to the men. With this the *Kompanie* began their advance.

Left: *Untersturmführer* Günther Zaag photographed on the 4th of July 1943 while talking to an *Unterscharführer* of the 3. Kompanie. The original photograph is of poor quality, but it is one of only a few photographs of the 3. Kompanie during the war. (The late Günther Zaag via James Mcleod) Right: This photograph shows Günther Zaag during the 3. Kompanie's first attack on the 5th of July 1943. It is, as far as is known, the only photograph of the 3. Kompanie 'in action'. (The late Günther Zaag via J. Mcleod)

They moved through a small village and here they came across a destroyed enemy anti-tank gun. Beside the gun was a dead enemy soldier and it was evident that he had taken the full force of a German tank shell. Zaag recalled that the advance got more and more difficult. They had the task of having to overrun Russian anti-tank emplacements, which were numerous. German tanks were advancing alongside them. There was also enemy infantry nearby and he recalls the constant danger of imprisonment, regarded more frightening than death itself! He also recalled the uncomfortable feeling of being next to friendly tanks as they were hit by enemy shells. The men would hit the ground and if they were lucky they would only receive a shower of hot metal splinters all around them.

The advance continued and they sought cover place after cover place. They also found enemy supplies such as ammunition and weapons in a barn. Some of these weapons were from America. Also in the barn was a brand new American Willys Jeep hidden under some straw; it was taken away after a few days for evaluation.

The 3. *Kompanie* Reach Jakowlewo and Count the Cost

By the end of the 5th of July the 3. *Kompanie*, who were the lead *Kompanie* for the I Battalion, had fought through numerous obstacles. These included mine filled forests, anti-tank emplacements, barbed wire obstacles and one or two small villages. They had fought at close range with enemy tanks, infantry and been subjected to enemy artillery fire, but had succeeded in pushing forwards. Their casualties were light, but significant. During one of the heavy enemy bombardments, the 3. *Kompanie* Commander, *Untersturmführer* Hermann Dahlke, was killed. Dahlke's bravery was without question. He had served with the *LAH* from before the war and had gained a wealth of experience. He had risen through the ranks to reach the rank of Second Lieutenant and of course he had recently been awarded the Knight's Cross to the Iron Cross. His level of experience and ability would not be easily replaced. Zaag also mentions the death of another *Kameraden* from the 3. *Kompanie* on this day, but his name is not listed. Gerhard Dilling was advancing very close to Dahlke when he was killed. Dilling himself managed to get through this first day un-scathed.

After the death of *Untersturmführer* Dahlke, *Untersturmführer* Günther Zaag assumed command of the 3. *Kompanie*. During the evening and night of this first day of the Kursk offensive he assessed the situation so far for the men now under his command. He recalled looking at the men as they ate their emergency rations, the strain of this first day was showing upon their tired faces.

The 3. *Kompanie* Capture of Jakowlewo

Throughout the next day, they attempted to consolidate their hold upon the eastern part of this village. They had to contend with an enemy tank and infantry incursion. The official reports state that around fifty enemy tanks broke into the western part of the village and moved towards the 3. *Kompanie* positions. The enemy artillery kept up its' death song and Zaag witnessed the German field kitchen position receiving a direct hit. He'd seen one motorcycle messenger being blown to pieces with this shell.

The 3. *Kompanie* received orders to advance further west into the village. To help them they were given three Pak 40 anti-tank guns. Their current positions were on the edge of a wooded area that did not provide good protection or cover. Zaag ordered the men to dig in as best they could. He had a discussion with the accompanying anti-tank gun commander and together they witnessed the advance of some enemy tanks. Directly in front of them was a field and they also witnessed some enemy infantry trying to use the field as cover to get closer to their positions. At the right time they opened fire, the Paks immediately destroyed two T-34s with a third T-34 being knocked out shortly after this. The men of the 3. *Kompanie* engaged the enemy infantry and succeeded in stopping the enemy advance.

During the evening of the 6th of July the order to move into the rest of the village was given. For this part of the advance the *Kompanie* was given four StuGs to assist them. The *LAH*'s 1. *Kompanie* would also attack the village. Zaag travelled forward into the attack on the back of one of the StuGs. They came under immediate enemy tank fire as they advanced over the difficult terrain. They pushed into the western part of the village as the men of the *Kompanie* engaged the enemy with determination. With help from the supporting StuGs, the enemy was persuaded to retreat further back. During the rest of this day and throughout the 7th of July the village of Jakowlewo was taken by the 3. *Kompanie*. They also managed a link with their 1. *Kompanie* neighbours. It was through perseverance and good leadership that this objective was taken and secured.

The 3. *Kompanie* Advance to Bol. Majatschki

From this village the 3. *Kompanie* and the I Battalion moved slightly northwest through Pokrowka. The objective for the 8th of July was Bol. Majatschki, positioned north of Pokrowka. Reconnaissance had revealed the presence of enemy tanks and infantry. Once again the 3. *Kompanie* were chosen as the lead *Kompanie*. This time they were given five StuGs to assist them. Their orders were to attack Bol. Majatschki from the west. Without delay, Zaag led the 3. *Kompanie* into the attack. They hit the first houses in the village, which surprised the Russians. An intense house-to-house fight ensued, during which *Untersturmführer* Zaag received a wound. The StuGs were on hand to help in this attack. The enemy put T-34s and American built tanks, along with infantry, against the *Kompanie*. The men kept up the pressure though and succeeded in knocking out five tanks and defeating the enemy infantry. As before, the objective was secured and held. The rest of the I Battalion were positioned to either side of the 3. *Kompanie* to help hold this area. *Untersturmführer* Zaag's continued bravery and excellent leadership was not going unnoticed at higher levels.

The Advance Continues

On the 9th of July the I Battalion were ordered to Rylskij and Ssuch Ssoltino, which were north east. They reached the crossing over the Ssoltino River in Ssuch Ssoltino only to find that the crossing had been destroyed by the Russians. The line now held by the *LAH* was from here to Teterewino. Many enemy tank attacks had been put in against the positions of the *LAH* in these first few days of the campaign. The 3. *Kompanie* itself had fought well and had achieved all of their objectives. The fact that they were repeatedly chosen to lead the attacks was a testament to their abilities, reliability and of course to the leadership of *Untersturmführer* Günther Zaag.

The next objective was the town of Prochorowka. The main railway line ran through this town and it was therefore very important for both sides to gain control of this area. For this the 3. *Kompanie* and the rest of the I Battalion had to advance back towards the northeast. This advance was started on the 10th of July. The *LAH*'s 2nd Regiment was nearby and their advance had left them with an exposed right flank. It was critical to secure the eastern area. There was a large forest positioned to the east, which had the potential to endanger the 2nd Regiment's right flank. It was this wooded area that the I Battalion had to secure. The reliable

3. *Kompanie* was given the order to attack the southern part of the forest. They were to push further into the forest and thereby secure the southeastern and southern parts of the woods. This would protect the 2nd Regiment's right flank.

The 3. *Kompanie* went into the attack with their usual vigour. They immediately ran into heavy defensive fire. The enemy positions were well concealed and well constructed. This was not about to stop the 3. *Kompanie* however, as they pushed further into the forest. They advanced eastwards and after heavy fighting, succeeded in reaching their objective. They were given some Pak 40s and ordered to dig them in immediately, so that any enemy attack from the left would be stopped. The 2. *Kompanie* had been advancing on the left of the 3. *Kompanie* and they ran into well-defended enemy positions. They were surrounded for a time, but were then relieved. The enemy numbers had been reduced significantly in this area due to the attack of the I Battalion. They held their positions and awaited the arrival of the 12th of July.

Prochorowka: The Steel Whirlwind

It is worth taking an overall view of the Kursk Offensive up to the night of the 11th of July, before going further. Model's 9th Army in the north had quickly discovered that the strength of the Russian forces facing them in this area were too strong for them to break through. His troops fought well, but the Russians had placed their strongest forces in the north, which blunted any attempts by the Germans to advance. The full extent of the advance by the Germans in the north during the Kursk Offensive amounted to a mere twelve miles. The progress in the south had been steady, if slower than expected. The Russians were growing increasingly worried and they pushed their all-important reserves, which included the 5th Guards Army and the 5th Guards Tank Army, into the southern sector around Prochorowka. The destruction of the German armoured threat was paramount to the Russians.

In place around Prochorowka for the 12th of July 1943 were around 850 Russian tanks. The Germans had around 300 tanks in the immediate area with a further 230 tanks fighting nearby. The Russians were aware of the enemy forces moving towards them, but the Germans were not aware that a huge enemy armoured force stood in their path.

The titanic armoured battle that developed during the 12th of July was unprecedented. The fight that developed was an intensive and very close range struggle, where both sides went to extreme measures to seize the initiative. Any hopes of the artillery or the aircraft overhead helping out in the battle were removed due to the close range nature of the fighting. An exhaustive clash raged throughout the whole day with no real decisive outcome. Darkness brought a lull to the battlefield. The Russian reserves had managed to contain the German threat, but both sides in Prochorowka were in a poor state at the end of the 12th. We will now return to the advances of the 3. *Kompanie* fighting within the 1st Regiment *LSSAH*.

The 3. *Kompanie*'s Actions During the 12th of July 1943

During this day the 3. *Kompanie* were in their positions in the large forest. A full enemy regiment hit their position during the day, supported by at least twenty T-34s. Enemy artillery also lent its weight to the attack upon the 3. *Kompanie* and the I Battalion. Heavy fighting ensued during the next few hours. The Russians penetrated the positions of the 2. *Kompanie* to the left with the strength of around two companies. *Untersturmführer* Zaag ordered his men onto the attack. This was not an easy task as they themselves were under attack from their flank and rear areas, they also put their accompanying Paks to good use. Whilst under attack from three sides they succeeded in assisting the attack against the numerically stronger enemy forces. The 3. *Kompanie* could not be dislodged from their positions, despite repeated and heavy enemy attacks. No less than three T-34s fell victim to the Pak guns. Zaag was wounded again during this day, but he stayed with his men and his leadership was an example to them. They successfully defeated this large enemy incursion and held their positions throughout the rest of the 12th of July.

The *LAH* infantry were fighting in more of a defensive role at this time. The Division was making no headway against the deep defensive positions of the enemy. The 3rd SS Division *Totenkopf*, fighting further northeast, were making some progress; but not enough to change the outcome of the campaign. Army Group Kempf, who had been battling towards the SS positions, could not reach them. It was against this background that Adolf Hitler suspended Operation *Zitadelle* on the 13th of July 1943. The main reason however, was the Allied landings that had been made in southern Italy.

Preparations to Withdraw: The Russian Counter-Stroke

Over the next few days the Russians launched infantry attacks against the right flank of the *LAH*'s positions. The order was given for the removal of the Division from its' current positions to an area back towards Belgorod and further south. These moves were conducted under the cover of darkness and with radio silence. The *LAH* were in their new positions by the 20th of July. Orders were then issued for new attacks, but these were subsequently cancelled. Finally on the 25th of July 1943 orders were given for the *LAH* to prepare for railway transportation. At this stage the men of the 3. *Kompanie* or the rest of the Division were not aware of their next destination.

The Russians had launched their main counter-attack between the 13th and the 16th of July. The northern sector received the blow first, followed by the southern sector. Quick, if costly, progress was made by the Russians in the northern sector. By the time the *LAH* left the Russian Front for the second time, the northern sector was under severe pressure and the southern sector was not in a favorable position either. The *LSSAH* were not able to change these developments in any way. They boarded their trains and began their new journey south. Behind them lay almost 500 dead and 2000 wounded *Kameraden*. The Russians had suffered around 4000 dead and 6500 casualties, together with 1000 tank and 1100 anti-tank gun losses. Back at the 3. *Kompanie*, *Untersturmführer* Günther Zaag was about to move to a new role and the 3. *Kompanie* were about to receive a new commander. This new commander however, was no stranger to this *Kompanie*.

Günther Zaag: Ninth Commander of the 3. *Kompanie*

Date of birth: 22.03.20 SS Number: 320 498

Günther Zaag was born in Dresden. Like many of his *Kameraden* he was raised in a Germany that was undergoing immense changes. It is known that during 1936, at the age of 16, he spent time in London as part of his studies. Like any tourist he enjoyed the many sights and sounds of the city. He recalled travelling on the Underground, listening to speakers in Hyde Park and visiting Horse Guards Parade. He took many photographs and enjoyed his time there. He stayed at Number 20, Fairfax Road. The following year, 1937, he entered into service with the Allgemeine-SS and joined the 46. *Standarte* in Dresden. From the 1st of April 1939 to the 10th of September 1939 he served with the R.A.D., or Reichs Labour Service. It was straight after this that he volunteered for war service.

He joined the *LAH* on the 15th of September 1939 and was assigned to the 1. *Kompanie*. After training he served with the Wach Battalion in Berlin. He spent time at the front also and during October 1941 he was in battle at Taganrog. He was by this stage serving with the *LAH*'s 12. *Kompanie* as part of a machine-gun squad and holding the rank of *Sturmmann*. He also took part in the battle for Rostov and he distinctly recalled the very poor weather, the shortage of ammunition and the lack of heavy weapons. As he put it, 'this was good enough reason to dig in'. At the end of 1941 he suffered a severe case of jaundice that involved him being transported back to Germany. This journey took him via Mariupol, Prague and then Karlsbad. On the 31st of December 1941 he was awarded the Second Class Iron Cross. This was quickly followed in January 1942 by his promotion to *Rottenführer*. He had a long convalescence in hospital and when he was released he spent time with the *LAH*'s Replacement Battalion. It was from here that he went to Bad Tölz.

He joined the 3. *Kompanie* straight from Bad Tölz with the rank of *Standartenoberjunker*. His experiences with the 3. *Kompanie* are recorded in the preceding pages and there is no need to repeat them here. When the *LAH* got to Italy in August 1943, Zaag was moved to the post of Ordnance Officer for the *LAH*'s I Battalion. Whilst in Italy he took part in the surrender negotiations for the city of Milan. He accompanied Albert Frey as they met with the local Italian commander General Rugero. He recalled his amazement the he, an *Untersturmführer*, was present at such a politically important occurrence. They succeeded in gaining the surrender of Milan without a shot being fired. This fact was celebrated with his fellow officers when he returned to the *LAH*!

He was awarded the Close Combat Clasp in Bronze and the Black Wound Badge in October 1943; this was for his actions with the 3. *Kompanie* during the preceding months. Towards the end of 1943 the *LAH* were once again sent eastwards and during this time he took part in the rescue mission to open the Tscherkassy Pocket. Just prior to the start of the Allied invasion of Normandy, Günther Zaag received the German Cross in Gold on the 23rd of May 1944. This was for frequent bravery and the official award recommendation mentions his actions and bravery whilst with the 3. *Kompanie* at Kharkov and Kursk during 1943. He fought with the *LAH* throughout the Normandy battles and he even succeeded in escaping the encirclement around Falaise. He found himself fighting around Aachen in the latter part of 1944 where he received a serious wound. He was captured by the Americans and transported to Arkansas in the U.S. He was kept as a prisoner of war until 1947.

In addition to the award of the German Cross in Gold, he also received the Second Class Iron Cross, the First Class Iron Cross, the Russian Front Medal, the

The photograph on the left shows Günther Zaag holding the rank of *Oberscharführer*, whilst attending his Officer's training course at Bad Tölz. (Justin Horgan) The photograph on the right shows Zaag after his promotion to *Untersturmführer*, whilst serving with the 3. Kompanie. His 1st and 2nd Class Iron Crosses can be clearly seen. (Erwin Bartmann)

Günther Zaag photographed alongside his wife Christel in 1944, after he left the 3. Kompanie. His 1st and 2nd Class Iron Crosses, the Black Wound Badge, Infantry Assault Badge, Close Combat Clasp and the ribbon for the Russian Front Medal can also be seen. (The late Günther Zaag via James Mcleod)

Black Wound Badge and the Close Combat Clasp in Bronze. He joined the 3. *Kompanie* at a critical time, when they were enduring heavy losses. He stayed with them throughout the fighting at Kharkov and Kursk. This brave and competent Officer left a good impression upon the 3. *Kompanie*. He survived the war and kept in close contact with the former *Kameraden* of the 3. *Kompanie*. He died in June 1999. His recollections have helped immensely in tracing the history of the 3. *Kompanie*.

CHAPTER ELEVEN

THE SOFT UNDERBELLY OF EUROPE: ITALY

Whilst the *LAH* were fighting in the inferno at Kursk, other events were taking place that would decide their next objectives. The Allies had made a successful landing on the island of Sicily, off the southwest coast of Italy. By the time of the huge armoured battle at Prochorowka, the Allies had landed around 150,000 men. This presented the very real possibility that the Italians would defect to the Allied side. The *LAH* were ordered to this area in anticipation of this move. On the 31st of July 1943, *Standartenführer* Theodor Wisch and *Sturmbannführer* Rudolf Lehmann met with Sepp Dietrich and *Feldmarschall* Erwin Rommel near Munich. The *LAH* moved first to Innsbruck and then onto northern Italy between the 26th of July and the 1st of August. In the first few days of August 1943 the *LAH* were in positions from Bozen to Verona. The Brenner Pass was in this area and it was of particular concern to the Germans. The Italians were observed moving two divisions into this area.

The first half of August was spent on intensive reconnaissance activity for the men of the *LAH* in order for them to familiarise themselves with the area. This was broken slightly on the 14th of August when various members of the *Kompanie*s of the 1st Reg. were ordered to provide personnel for a ceremonial honour guard for *Feldmarschall* Erwin Rommel. This was to take place at Bologna during a meeting between Rommel and his Italian counter-part. Some reports indicate that the plan was to kidnap Rommel, but this was changed when the *LAH* turned up. An honour guard did not carry ammunition, but whether the Italians knew this fact is unknown!

A few days later a secret order was issued to prepare the troops for disarming the Italians. The rest of August was spent on training exercises. The troops however, were kept on a three-hour readiness.

The *LAH*'s Part in the Disarmament of the Italian Army

The *LAH* extended their area further south towards the Reggio area. On the 3rd of September notification of the code word to be used for the disarmament was forwarded, the code word was Nordwind. On the 8th the expected peace between Italy and the Allies was announced; the following day the disarmament order was issued. The *LAH* moved to strategic areas and began to disarm the Italian troops. The I Battalion was in the Parma area and were witness to the only attempted resistance. It did not take much to break the will of the Italians; they were no match for the seasoned veterans of the *LAH*. The *LAH* did suffer over fifty casualties but on this day alone over 18,000 prisoners were taken, 750 of these were English. Over the next three days the disarmament continued. The 1st Reg. moved to Milan, and the 2nd Reg. moved towards Turin. Some minor resistance took place but nothing significant. The disarmament netted over 110,000 prisoners, almost 8000 were English, and vast quantities of material.

By the 13th of September the I Battalion was in Varese. The following day they were to be found in the areas of Gallarate, Busto, Arsicio and Legnano on disarmament duties. From the 15th to the 19th extensive reconnaissance was carried out, there were reports of sizeable forces in the Cuneo area. A split in the Division was ordered on the 20th of September. The bulk of the *LAH* were to stay in northern Italy, but the 1st Regiment was on the move to Croatia.

The *LAH*'s 1st Regiment's Participation in Anti-Partisan Duties: Croatia

The march route for the 1st Regiment was east to Udine, this town was reached on the 22nd. Three main operational areas were identified; they were Gurz, the Istria Peninsula and an area south of Laibach. Preparations were made and on the 25th the operation began. The I Battalion was in the Sistiane area moving east, the partisans were moving east and northeast. On the 27th the I Battalion had moved towards Cossovello and Copriva; with the towns of S. Vito and Pochrai being reached over the next few days. By the 2nd of October the I Battalion had made it to Cernova; these areas were all south of Trieste. Two days later they were

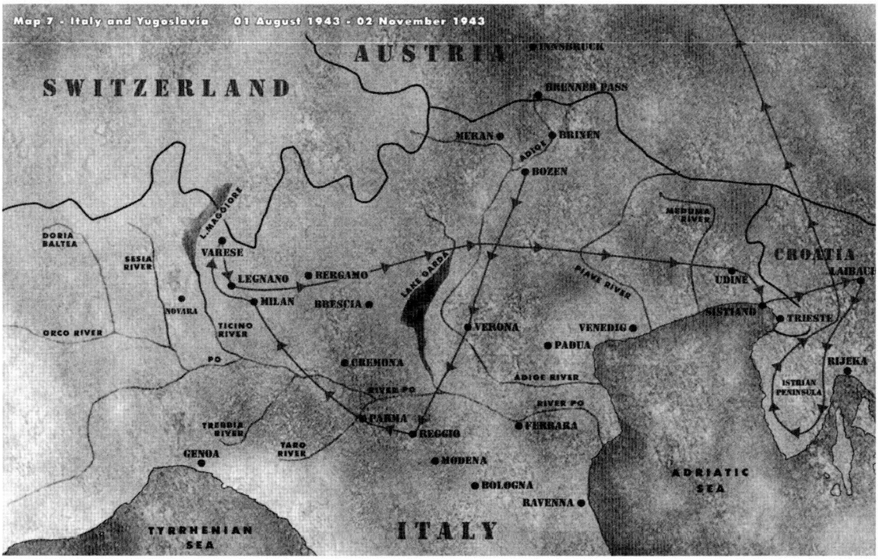

Italy Map

responsible for securing the north-south connection in the Visinada to Caroiba area. They were moving in a southerly direction and the towns of Cittanova and Montana were reached by the 6th; moving to Caraiba and Pisino sector quickly followed this. Pisino was where the guerilla leader Tito had been only a few days prior to this. The I Battalion then moved onto the Istrian Peninsula and proceeded to sweep through this area during the rest of October 1943. Towards the end of the month new orders were received that detailed a new move for the *LAH*. Their short stay in Italy was ended due to the worsening situation on the Russian Front. They were going east once more.

CHAPTER TWELVE

THE RUSSIAN FRONT PART THREE: SHITOMIR AND TSCHERKASSY

After Kursk the Russians went over to the attack with the full weight of their forces. They recaptured large parts of land and pushed the Germans back over the Dneiper River, Kiev was also retaken. There was a danger that Army Group Centre and South would have a wedge driven between them and that Army Group South would be cut-off. The enemy forces in this area consisted of Vatutin's 1st Ukrainian Front and Koniev's 2nd Ukrainian Front. Russian tanks had reached Shitomir by the 13th of November 1943. It was into this situation that the *LAH* would be placed. It was hoped that the Führer's Fire Brigade would help stem the Russian steamroller.

For their new objective, the *LSSAH* would be placed under the XXXXVIII *Panzerkorps*. They moved from their positions to the St. Polten and Innsbruck areas and then onto the Ukraine between the 28th of October and the 7th of November. The artillery had been sent first, followed by the bulk of the division who were in Italy. The 1st Reg., still in Croatia, was sent later. The designated area was around Shitomir, south of Kiev. They would be fighting in the northern sector of Army Group South's area of responsibility. The lead elements arrived in Kirowograd on the 2nd of November where they were placed with the 8th Army. Due to enemy action, the Division was detrained in different areas. They finally linked up southwest of Fastow around the 7th. The enemy in this area was the 1st Ukrainian Front and they were advancing from Kiev in the east towards Shitomir, northeast of Fastow. Strong enemy forces were also moving on both sides of Fastow.

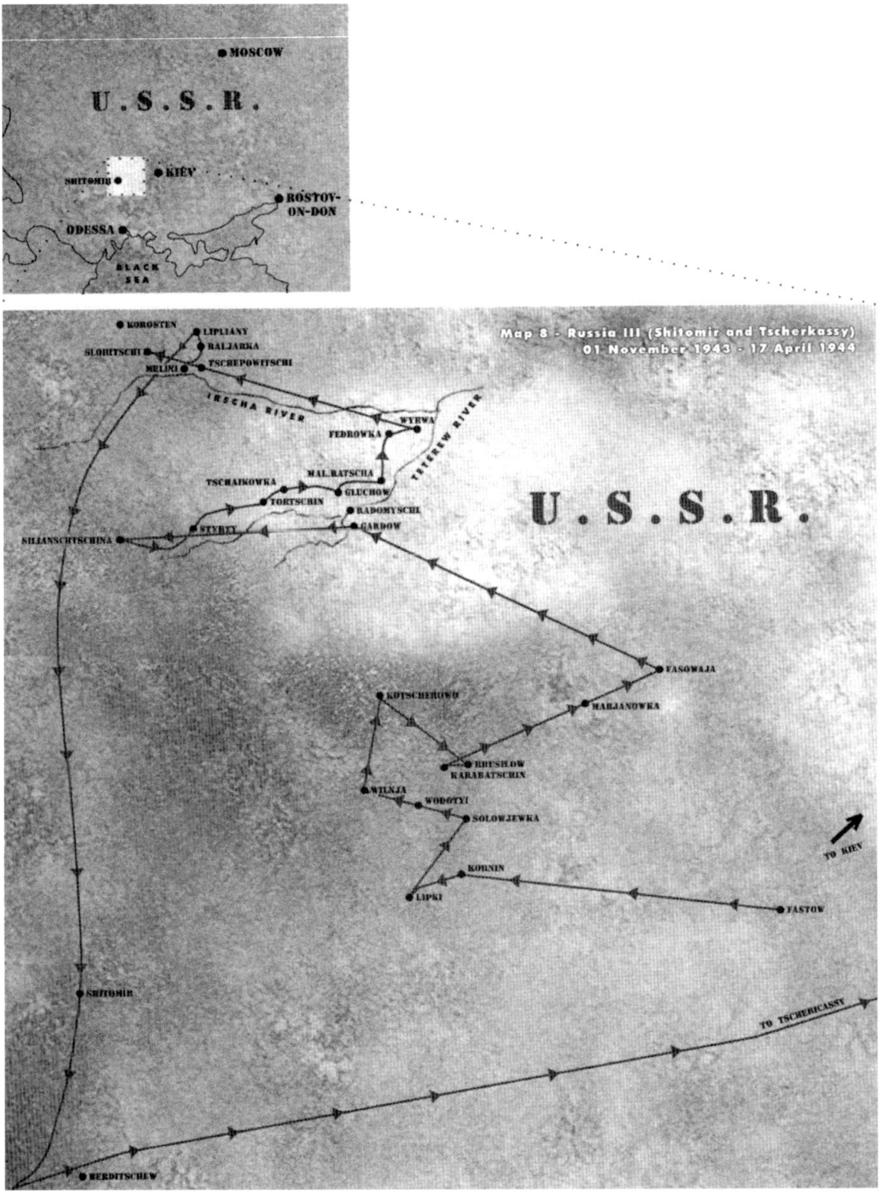

Russia III: Shitomir and Tscherkassy

Some elements of the division were still in other areas; immense difficulties were resulting from the decision to move the division in piecemeal fashion from the Italian theatre.

Ferdinand Huser: Tenth Commander of the 3. *Kompanie*

At this stage the 3. *Kompanie* were commanded by *Untersturmführer* Ferdinand 'Ferdi' Huser. Ferdi Huser had been the 3. *Kompanie*'s *Spiess*, or *Stabscharführer*, during the 1940 campaign in the west and on into late 1941, during the first campaign in Russia. He was replaced as the *Spiess* during the early part of 1942 by *Sturmscharführer* Bruhn. He was present at the post mortem of the six 3. *Kompanie* soldiers discovered in Taganrog in early 1942. What he done between then and assuming command of the 3. *Kompanie* is not known. He replaced *Untersturmführer* Zaag during October. It cannot be determined when he was promoted to *Untersturmführer* or what awards he received.

Off the Trains and into the Attack: The Fastowez Area – November 1943

The I Battalion was detrained in the Berditschew-Kasatin area on the 8th of November. They were then moved to Rozyn, where they took up defensive positions. On the 10th of November they had moved to Fastowez and they were fighting north against heavy attacks, on the following day they captured Klechowka. The

This photograph was taken in May 1940 as the LAH prepared for the advance west. It shows Heinz Kirsch on the left and Ferdinand Huser on the right. At that time Huser was the 3. Kompanie *Stabscharführer* or 'Spiess'. He was killed in April 1944 in Russia as commander of the 3. Kompanie. This is the only known photograph of 'Ferdi' Huser. (Heinz Kirsch)

enemy was massing east of Fastow for an attack, where the plan was to assault them in their northern flank. The move was to the north towards the Shitomir to Kiev road. By the 12th the 1st Reg. were in the Dunajka area south of the railway line. The 2nd Reg. moved towards Kornin further north. Over the next two days the advance continued. The 1st Reg. moved to the left of the 2nd Reg. and reached Lipki, which was occupied by the I Battalion on the 14th of November. All of these advances were done under attack. On the 15th new orders arrived that required the XXXXVIII *Panzerkorps* to advance on Kiev from the west in a frontal attack. General Balck, who is widely recognised as one of the best commanders that the Germans had, was given command of the XXXXVIII *Panzerkorps* around this time. Other Divisions were attached to this Korps for the attack. Amongst these were Das Reich, 7th Panzer Division, 1st Panzer Division, 19th Panzer Division and the 25th Panzer Division.

Further North: Kotscherowo and the Surrounding of the 1st Regiment

On the 15th the 1st Reg. reached and took Solowjewka to the north, the I Battalion were on the right flank. They continued west and captured Wodotyi; strong enemy forces were seen in this area. The following day they moved further west and took Wilnja southeast of Solowjewka. On the 17th the 1st Reg. reached Kotscherowo next to the main Shitomir to Kiev road; this advance was done against heavy enemy attacks. *Obersturmbannführer* Frey was awarded the Oakleaves to the Knight's Cross. The 18th saw the 1st Reg. surrounded and cut-off in Kotscherowo; they fought off many strong enemy attacks. A *Rottenführer* from the 11. *Kompanie* was awarded the Knight's Cross for helping to beat off these attacks. At the time there were only a handful of men left in his area. He took control and effectively organised the survivors into a squad who prevented the Russians from breaking into the town. On this day the 3. *Kompanie* suffered the death of *Scharführer* Willy Liebig in Kotscherowo.

On the 19th orders were issued for the attack on Brussilow, this was southeast of the 1st Reg.'s current position. They were to attack from the north, the 2nd Reg. were to attack from the south. The 1st Reg. was relieved on the 20th at Kotscherowo and they began to prepare for the attack. The attacks got under way over the next two days but had to be abandoned due to heavy enemy defensive fire. A shift in position was called for, the 1st Reg. would now attack from the northwest with the 2nd Reg. attacking from the east, but this too proved unsuccessful. On the 23rd the

1st Panzer Division penetrated Brussilow, the I Battalion of the *LAH* were fighting near Karabatschin west of Brussilow.

Radomyschl and the Balka River

Orders were sent through that shifted the emphasis of the attack northeast towards Marjanowka and Fasowaja. The objective was the enemy bridgehead on the Dneiper River near Kiev. Under heavy enemy fire the attack was suspended on the 25th of November and defensive positions were ordered to be held. The *LAH* were to move north across the Shitomir to Kiev road and assemble around Radomyschl, they were to engage the enemy who were moving south. The positions were reached by the 26th, they were in the Sabelotschje area south of Radomyschl. The next day they launched an attack from here and succeeded in forcing a crossing of the Balka River, north east of their positions. The I Battalion captured a bridge near Point .170. On the 29th the town of Gardow had been taken, these advances towards Radomyschl had been done against strong enemy forces. They had also managed to advance towards the Teterew River, the losses were mounting with the Division suffering 1500 casualties, The I Battalion was down to 174 men. It was on the 29th of November 1943 that *Unterscharführer* Rudi Mahlkuch of the 3. *Kompanie* was killed.

The Thrust Towards the Teterew and Irscha Rivers

On the 30th, the *LAH* was relieved by Army and *Fallschirmjäger* forces. They were moved approximately forty-five kilometers west to the Silianschtschina area, they firstly moved slightly to the southeast to throw the enemy off their real intentions. The objective was reached by the 2nd of December. New orders were issued for the *LAH* to move east towards the Korosten to Shitomir road. Their advance was between the Teterew and Irscha Rivers. They had the 1st and 7th Panzer Divisions as their neighbours along the way. The attack began on the 6th in an easterly direction, towards the junction of the two above-mentioned rivers.

On the first day of this attack, *Obersturmführer* Kurt Kleist, *Sturmmann* Waldemar Richert and *SS-Mann* Walter Schuld of the 3. *Kompanie* were all killed. Bearing in mind that *Untersturmführer* Ferdi Huser is listed as the 3. *Kompanie*'s Commander during this time, the question is where does *Obersturmführer* Kurt Kleist fit into the picture? It is impossible to answer this question with the information currently available. The facts are as stated over the last few pages, but the author would be grateful if anyone could shed some light on this question.

The 3. *Kompanie*, together with the rest of the 1st Regiment, moved from Silianschtschina to Styrty on the 6th. The towns of Tortschin and Tschaikowka were reached on the 7th. At Tortschin the 3. *Kompanie*'s *Oberscharführer* Erich Ambrolat was killed and at Tschaikowka, *Unterscharführer* Hans Pospiech was killed.

The attacks continued against enemy resistance and the town of Gluchow was reached on the 8th of December. The *LAH* were then ordered to shift southeast and cross the Teterew River. The 1st Reg. were to cross close to Radomyschl, the 2nd Reg. were to cross further north at Tschudin. By the morning of the 9th the 2nd Reg. were in the Meshiritschka area, the 1st Regiment's attack was suspended due to enemy pressure. The 68th Division had managed to break through to Radomyschl so later that day the 1st Reg. were ordered to assist them.

Over the next two days the 2nd Reg. suffered many counter-attacks; they moved southwest towards Mal. Ratscha. Orders followed from *Korps* level that required all forces to assemble for the destruction of the enemy on the west-side of the Teterew River. The *LAH* were ordered to move to the Irscha River and the Kiev to Korosten railway line on the 14th. This attack progressed as far as Fedrowka, approximately four kilometres south of the rail line. The 1st Panzer Division were ordered to take over whilst the *LAH* were moved back to deal with the enemy who had broken through in the Mal. Ratscha and Litowka areas. On this day the 1st Regiment were involved in hard fighting on their way towards Wyrwa.

A Move to the North: Tschepowitschi

On the 16th they were ordered to move to the Tschepowitschi sector approximately forty kilometers northeast. The move began on the 17th and they were ready two days later to begin the attack. The initial advances were good and the enemy was taken by surprise, the thick bushy terrain offered as many problems as the enemy. The jumping off point was halfway between Slobitschi and Meleni, with the line of advance being in a northerly to northeasterly direction. The fighting raged around Tschepowitschi, Baljarka and Lipliany area over the next five days. On the 21st of December, the 3. *Kompanie* suffered the deaths of *Unterscharführer* Helmut Schlag and *SS-Mann* Harald Schminke near Baljarka. On the 23rd, *Sturmmann* Adam Zimmermann was wounded in Peremoga and on the following day, *Sturmmann* Rolf Franke was killed near Dolgie-Polja.

The 1st Reg. was fighting from the east, the 2nd Reg. from the south. The enemy had sizeable forces in this area and the *LAH* were in danger of being outflanked, it appeared that the *LAH*'s attack had pre-empted the enemy attack to the south. Enemy reinforcements were arriving constantly from the east. The number of battle ready tanks was becoming a problem, at one stage in this fight the Division was down to thirteen tanks. Due to enemy pressure the advances could go no further. The positions just captured were first ordered to be held; this was changed after the danger of encirclement developed.

Crisis Near Berditschew: New Year 1944

On the 24th of December 1943 the *LAH* were ordered to move south of Shitomir, into the area west of Berditschew. This move began on Christmas Day via Shitomir, the congestion in this city presented immense problems. The Division fought through various towns including Woliza and Ljassokwa, the fighting in these towns surrounding Shitomir lasted for the next four days. The *LAH* were ordered to continue south, a gap had developed between the XIII and XXXXVIII *Armeekorps*, which the *LAH* had to close. By New Years Eve the *LAH* were on the outskirts of Berditschew, they were ordered to withdraw due to strong enemy pressure. They were moved back across the Gnilopjat River and moved south, they were subordinated to the XIII *Armeekorps*. Around this time the entire 1st Regiment had a fighting strength of less than 450 men.

The *LAH* fought through Demtschin and Ratschki over the 4th and 5th of January 1944. This was a time of heavy strains on the German forces. The *LAH* found itself unable to prepare for proper offensive operations due to constant enemy attacks. The move west continued with the *LAH* having to fight their way through many towns. They reached the area south west of Januschpol on the 7th, they were holding a line from here to Ssmela. The 1st Reg. was on the Sherebki to Ssmela road, the enemy was trying to push through and force a gap in the lines. The following day Peiper destroyed an enemy tank attack between the positions of the 1st and 2nd Regiments; the tank attacks continued for the rest of this day and the next. The 10th saw a slight withdrawal of the *LAH* line to the southwest, the enemy pressure died down also. The enemy was observed moving equipment west in preparation for a large attack. On the 11th the 1st Reg. were near Ssmela, at this stage the 1st Reg. slightly improved their fighting strength with 560 men being available, the 2nd Reg. were worse off with only 380 men, tank strength was at twenty. This is an example of the losses that the *LAH* had suffered in the recent fighting, they were a mere shadow of their once mighty selves. The attacks began again on the 12th. Counter-attacks were waged to close the gaps. The following day Peiper's force destroyed over thirty tanks. Wittmann and his gunner received the Knight's Cross for destroying their 88th tank – a long overdue award.

On the 14th the pressure eased off slightly and Peiper used this opportunity to launch an attack. They advanced to the northwest from Ssmela and by the late afternoon were in Krassnopol ten kilometers away, the enemy had fled in panic. The following day he received the Oakleaves to his Knight's Cross. The sector quieted down over the next few days, one noticeable action was the successful artillery attack on the known location of an enemy officer conference in Sherebki. On the 19th the *LAH* were relieved and sent south to the Chmelnik-Ssandraki area. The move to the new area took place over the next few days.

On the Move Again: The Bila Sector

Once in the new area the *LAH* were given the objective of assisting in the surrounding of eight Russian Divisions in the Bila sector and annihilating them. The attack started on the 24th, but the *LAH* were not up to the start line so they had to follow up. The enemy had amassed strong forces west of Berditschew and was expected to move south. The orders were to stop this enemy advance as the situation was becoming critical. The *LAH* were subordinated to the XXXXVI *Armeekorps* and they joined the attack on the 25th. Moving southeast the 1st Reg. had to take the Lipowez station. As they advanced the enemy tried to break through, the fighting was very intense. They took their objective on the 27th of January against enemy tank attacks and the added problem of non-existent roads, due to the rains. They continued their advance southeast and ended this day in Napadowka.

On the following day there was heavy fighting around the Lipowez station. Enemy forces from the Wladimirowka area were trying to break through to their comrades who had been cut-off in Gaissin (north of Lipowez). The I Battalion was situated approximately halfway between these two places. The station was ordered to be abandoned and the attacks continued southeast. On the 29th the enemy broke out of Gaissin. The *LAH* were further south. Wittmann destroyed his 114th tank on this day. The attack continued to Oratoff and some elements reached Frankowka, the fighting died down slightly. On the 1st of February 1944 the *LAH* were relieved by the 1st Infantry Division and moved to the Kischschenzy-Nesterowka area, this move was completed the next day.

The *LAH*'s Part in the Relief of the Tscherkassy Pocket: February 1944

At the start of February 1944, sizeable Russian forces made up of nine Armies and one Corps had succeeded in surrounding over 50,000 German soldiers in the Tscherkassy area. The German forces inside this pocket were the XI and XXXXII *Armeekorps*, five different Infantry Divisions, 5th SS Division *Wiking* and the SS Brigade *Wallonian*. The *LAH* were assigned to the III *Panzerkorps* made up of the 1st Panzer Division, 16th Panzer Division, 198th Infantry Division, and 17th Infantry Division. They had orders to break the encirclement west of Tscherkassy and free the troops inside. The move towards this area was a difficult one due to thick muddy road conditions. The Division moved in piecemeal fashion and by the 6th of February elements were in Tinowka. The *LAH* were to the rear of the III *Panzerkorps* covering the flanks, at this stage breakdowns had left the *LAH* with twelve combat ready tanks. All of the forces in this area were being hit hard by enemy attacks assisted by T-34s. On the 8th the surrender ultimatum was given to the forces inside the pocket, they had until 11:00 a.m. on the 9th to decide.

The *LAH* moved further northeast towards Tatjanowka and east to Repki. By the 11th of February the Division had less than 130 men ready to attack, the combat ready tank strength was standing at seven. This was a period were one or two men were fighting off odds of 30:1 or 40:1 along with tank attacks. Extreme enemy pressure was bearing down on the *LAH* in the flanking positions, and they continually repulsed enemy attacks. The 14th saw the *LAH* moving east to Frankowka, they were relieved by the 34th Infantry Division. They moved as far as Oktjabr and linked with the 1st Panzer Division, this was a small force of 120 men. Inside the pocket itself, which covered an area of only five kilometres, preparations were made to fight out on the 16th. These moves from the inside linked with the forces moving towards them from the outside on the 18th, although the link was made south of the intended point. The first elements out belonged to the 5th SS Division *Wiking*; they met with the 1st Regiment of the *LAH*. Once the link had been made the forces inside the pocket poured out. They suffered enemy attacks on the way but in all 32,000 men escaped. This was done against huge enemy forces, frost and mud; the both groups of Germans involved had been pushed beyond the limit. They could congratulate themselves on a job well done.

Fighting Near the Pripet Marshes: Tarnopol: March 1944

From the 19th of February the Division was around Lissjanka and Oktjabr, they moved onto the defensive along with the 1st Panzer Division. A move to the southwest was ordered and this was carried out towards Kutschowka, this move was done whilst under enemy attacks. By the 27th the *LAH* were ordered to the Proskuroff area. This chapter in the *LAH*'s history was a difficult one with a huge strain being placed on the men and machines. At the point of the move most of the elements of the Division were down to 35% of their usual mobility, the number of tanks that were ready for action was sitting at a mere three.

While the relief action was taking place a serious situation had developed south of the Pripet Marshes (Army Group South). All panzer forces were to be moved to this area against expected heavy attacks, the forces already there had been pushed back. The *LAH*'s new position would place them back in the Tarnopol area that they held back in 1941; they would be under the XXXXVIII *Armeekorps*. By the 5th of March 1944 elements were in the Kupel area, battles raged around this area for the next five days. The Division had to pull back slightly to the southwest and hold a line from Klininy to Wojtowzy. On the 10th the *LAH* were issued with a new order that allowed for a certain freedom in their further operations. The general order was still to fight west to link with the 7th Panzer Division. The enemy was still trying to surround Tarnopol. The *LAH*'s mission was to hold the rail and road links between Proskuroff and Tarnopol. The fighting continued with heavy enemy pressure, *Major* Rudel's planes where overhead assisting these battles. The moves continued back to the Bowonez sector, south east of Tarnopol. On the 12th Rudolf Lehmann was appointed the temporary divisional commander, as Theodor Wisch was ill.

Over the next week small attacks were launched, the enemy seemed to be preparing for a new assault. The Division had suffered losses in these battles and around this time the combat strength of the Division was just over 1000 men. The 1st Regiment was holding the line from Widawa to Kurniki. On the 21st the enemy launched a major attack along the river, the focus of this attack was in the middle of the 1st Reg.'s area. Large tank incursions were observed.

Due to enemy pressure the *LAH* were joined together with the 7th Panzer Division and the 68th Infantry Division and formed into a new *Kampfgruppe* under *Oberst* Dr. Mauss. This battle group was ordered to the south to hold the main road open. The 1st Regiment ended up in the Kalinowka area on the eastern flank.

On the 15th of March the encirclement of Tarnopol by the Russians began, some men from the *LAH* were in the city at the time. A situation also developed around this time, were the Russians broke through the positions between the 8th Army and the 1st Panzer Army. The enemy incursions were aiming at an encirclement of the positions now held by the *LAH*. This was the point of breakdown in the German forces. The enemy was able to replace their numbers and had a vastly superior number of men. The German soldier had been battling continually for thirty-three months in this hell and was exhausted. At this point the *Panzerkorps* had a total of twenty-four tanks ready to fight any counter attacks.

For the next week the positions continued to be pushed back, by the 29th of March the *LAH* were in Andrejewka. Around this time they were part of *Kampf-gruppe* Mauss. Due to enemy pressure the *LAH* were ordered south east of their positions to the Losiacz area. This move took place during the first few days of April. The 2nd Reg. were west of the town around Dawidkowce; the 1st Reg. suffered many attacks in the Losiacz area. The enemy pressure continued and the moves further west followed up to the 13th of April. Contact was made with other units including the 10th SS Division Frundsberg. The *LAH* were in an area south of Buczacz around twenty-five kilometers west of Losiacz, they fought off counter-attacks in this area. They had succeeded in freeing themselves from the encirclement on the 14th. They were then relieved by the 7th Panzer Division and moved to Monasteryska. They were fed and cleaned and then mounted onto rail wagons. On the 15th of April Tarnopol fell to the Russians. The *LAH* were to move to the Flanders region in France, via Lemberg. This move took place between the 17th and the 25th of April 1944. The 3. *Kompanie* suffered the death of *Untersturmführer* Ferdi Huser during April 1944. It cannot be determined from the available sources how he died. He was succeeded by *Hauptsturmführer* Maurer.

Hauptsturmführer Paul Maurer: Eleventh Commander of the 3. *Kompanie*

Date of birth: 26.12.12   *SS number: 267 703*

There is very little information available on this officer. It is known that he was promoted to *Untersturmführer* on the 20th of July 1936 and by 1938 he was an *Obersturmführer* serving with the *Ordnungspolizei*. On the 30th of January 1940 he was promoted to *Hauptsturmführer*. After his service with the 3. *Kompanie* he would reach the rank of *Sturmbannführer* in January 1945.

Destination France: April 1944: Time for a Rest?

With this the *LAH*'s 1943-1944 winter struggle had come to an end. They had succeeded in denying the enemy the southern area of the eastern front. The cost had been high. The casualties were measurable in the thousands with the 2nd Regiment being particularly hard hit. The cost to the Russians was high also. They required a rest and this began towards the end of April 1944. The Germans had moved some of their key divisions out of this area for a much needed rest period. Overall, the Russian Front was not under the control of the Germans, and had not been since the battle of Kursk almost one year earlier. Hitler ordered that the 1st SS Panzer Division *LAH* were to be given priority for new vehicles and equipment. This is where the myth begins that the Waffen-SS were better equipped than the Army. Although this was the case in April 1944 it was definitely not the case in the previous five years. The division was now part of Dietrich's I SS *Panzerkorps*. From this time to the start of June 1944 the Division received men and machines to replace their heavy losses. The machines were easily incorporated; the men however had to be taught the tricks learned by the few survivors. This was an enormous task.

One of these few survivors was Gerhard Dilling, who was now holding the rank of *SS-Junker*, or officer candidate. He would however, not be helping the new 3. *Kompanie* replacements to become effective soldiers of the Waffen-SS. Instead he made his way to the SS-*Junkerschule* in Prague and here he started his officer training. This training would last until early 1945 and by the time he returned to the *LAH* many of his former *Kameraden* would be dead or wounded.

CHAPTER THIRTEEN

THE NORMANDY INVASION

The western Allies had been training and amassing a huge force of men and materials since early 1942. They had hit the German forces in many places such as North Africa, Sicily and southern Italy; they had sent extensive aid to the Russians also. It was no secret however, that they needed to strike at the Germans from the French coast. Adolf Hitler knew that this eventuality was growing ever nearer. His biggest problem was knowing where the Allies would land. The Allies had been employing an elaborate deception plan in the run up to the planned invasion and it was very successful in deceiving Hitler into thinking that the Pas de Calais area would be the target. Once Eisenhower issued his fateful order for the invasion to begin; the full weight and might of the western Allied war machine would land right at the door of Fortress Europe. It would land with a heavy blow in the Normandy region on the 6th of June 1944. One of the German Divisions situated in the west at the time of the Allied 'D-Day' invasion was the recently mauled and much depleted 1st SS Panzer Division *LAH*.

The Allied plan was as follows; five beaches were identified as being suitable for the planned attack. They were Utah Beach on the Allied right flank, assigned to the U.S. VII Corps. Next to this was Omaha Beach assigned to the U.S. V Corps. In the middle sector was Gold Beach assigned to the British XXX Corps. On the Allied left flank was Juno Beach assigned to the Canadian 3rd Infantry Division. On the extreme left flank was Sword Beach assigned to the British 3rd Infantry Division. The complete area detailed for the beach landings stretched from Ste.

Mére Eglise on the Contentin Peninsula all the way up to Caen, which was earmarked to be reached on the first day.

On 'D-Day' around 130,000 Allied soldiers poured out of some 6000 ships in the English Channel towards the various beaches detailed above. The French countryside and the beach area had been 'softened-up' during the preceding weeks by extensive bombing from the air. It was essential that the Allies established a firm footing on the beaches in the first few hours. This would provide the springboard for the subsequent attacks towards the heart of the Third Reich. The Allies would only have one chance to get this right. Facing the Allies on the morning of the 6th of June would be around 50,000 German soldiers. The first few hours

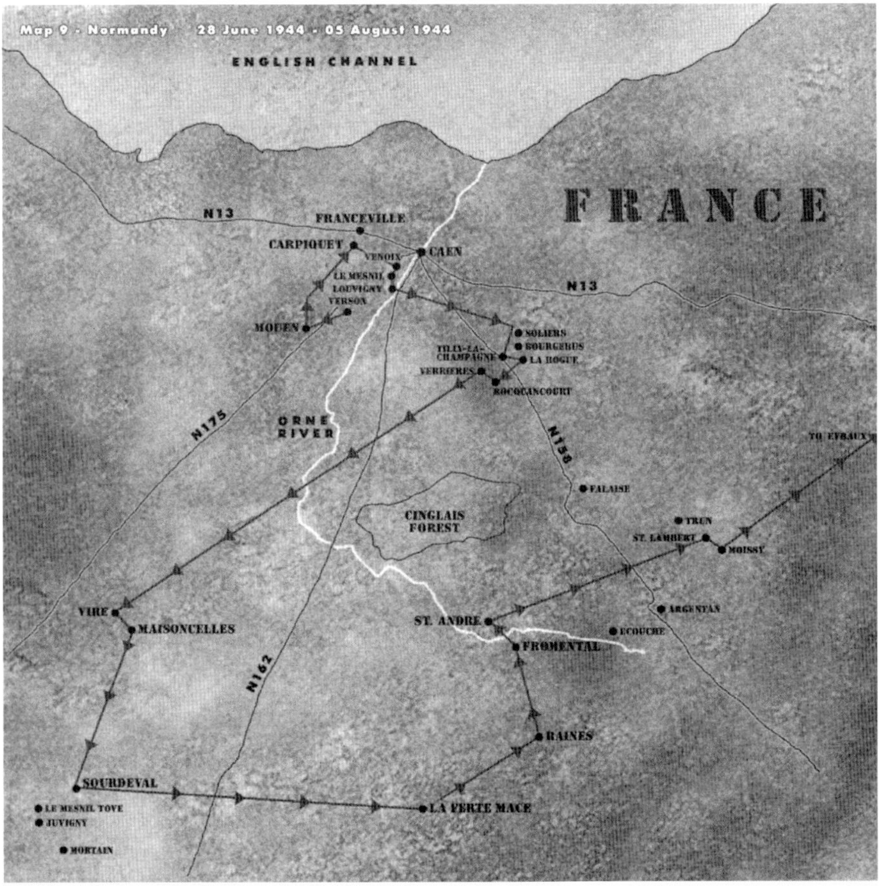

Normandy Map

would be critical to both sides. Hitler's much feared two main-front war was about to occur.

The *LAH* Prepares to Engage the Western Allies

On the 6th of June the *LAH* were put on a two-and-a-half hour march notice. They were detailed to make themselves as combat ready as possible and to use vehicles that would assist them to this end. For the next two days the *LAH* moved from Tournhout to the Schelde Estuary. The Allied deception plan had led the German High Command to believe that there would be a second landing in the Belgium area on the 10th of June; the *LAH* were to counter this expected landing. The 1st Regiment were in the Ursel-Aardenburg area.

On the 12th Hitler ordered the *LAH* to join the 12th SS Panzer Division around the Caen area in France. Two days later Fritz Witt, who was commanding the 12th SS Panzer Division, was killed by off-shore artillery fire. He had been the Commander of the *LAH*'s 1st Regiment during the decisive battles in Russia during the early part of 1943. The *LAH*'s move to France began on the 17th of June. The destination was not reached until the 6th of July due to enemy air attacks, the destruction of the rail system and the destruction of all of the crossings over the river Seine. The *LAH* was massed south of Caen and were being monitored by the Allied High Command. The 12th SS were to their left, with the 9th and 10th SS Divisions positioned to the left of 12th SS. The 9th and 10th SS Divisions had only arrived at the end of June.

The Allied landing in Normandy was not the only worry that Hitler had to contend with. During June 1944 the Russians launched their Summer Offensive. The main target was Army Group Centre. The Russians had gathered around three million men and vast quantities of equipment for this offensive and when it was launched, huge gaps were torn in the German positions. By the first week of July 1944, almost twenty German Divisions had been destroyed. Replacing this sort of manpower and material was impossible for the Germans at this stage of World War II.

Containment of the Allies at Caen: June 1944

By the end of June the Allies had established a firm bridgehead with ample help from the ships and planes. They were then faced with the problem of breaking out of this bridgehead, they began to launch operations with this objective in mind. On the 27th of June the first Allied attempts to capture Caen began with Operation Epsom. The I Battalion of the *LAH*, under *Hauptsturmführer* Lotter, joined the 12th SS in an attack against British forces moving towards the Odon River. The route was along National Highway 175, southwest of Caen. The attack objective for the 28th was Mouen, the I Battalion was positioned on the right. They were to cut-off the Allied advance towards Caen; the I Battalion met the Allies at Verson.

The 3. *Kompanie* fights at Verson: Late June 1944

The 3. *Kompanie* were fighting around the railway line on this day. One member of the 3. *Kompanie* serving at this time was Gerhard Franz. He had joined the *LAH* during March 1944 when he was only 17 years old. He was first sent to Unna and then onto the Arnhem-Turnhout area. All of the new recruits were sent to different *Kompanies*, with Gerhard being sent to the 3. *Kompanie*. They went through intensive and difficult training. Gerhard recalled that although this was a difficult period for them, many good friendships were formed. He then accompanied the rest of the *LAH* to the Normandy region. He found himself in the Verson area on the 28th of June 1944. His main function during this period was to be a messenger for the 3. *Kompanie*.

He recalled that the 3. *Kompanie* were fighting on the right flank for this attack. They had managed to gain the addition of three panzer IVs from the Heer's 21st Panzer Division. The tanks and the men were finding the Normandy bocage hedgerows a problem as they restricted the visibility. Gerhard was part of a *Zug* under *Unterscharführer* Ziegenhart. They were approaching the town along the main road, which also ran alongside the railway line. On the left was a small wooded area. Three British tanks emerged from this wooded area. The enemy tanks began to fire once they noticed the accompanying panzers. One of the enemy tank shells hit the ground close to where Gerhard and *Unterscharführer* Zeigenhart were situated; a fragment of this shell hit Zeigenhart's steel helmet and left a dent in it. They had some cover from a hedge on the railway embankment. One of the panzers began firing on the three British tanks and succeeded in destroying all three of them. Some of the enemy crews bailed out and along with the supporting enemy soldiers, they took cover in a small ditch. The 3. *Kompanie* were responsible for capturing ten enemy soldiers along with two light machine guns. The action was not over yet and the advance continued. Further enemy soldiers were moving back towards Verson and the 3. *Kompanie* gave chase. The supporting panzers could not advance any further because of the destroyed enemy tanks and debris on the railway. The IV *Zug* of the 3. *Kompanie* began to lay a mortar barrage upon the enemy positions, but due to increasing pressure they began to take heavy casualties. An enemy tank attack was launched with supporting infantry but this moved away from the 3. *Kompanie*'s positions. Verson was taken the same day by the Germans. Mouen was also reached, but a stalemate situation developed during the night and following day.

Caen: The Thorn in the Side of the Allies

A situation report on the 30th of June asked for a straightening of the line and a clear plan. The 12th SS was near exhaustion. The Contentin peninsula had fallen to the Allies and their ships and planes were hammering hard against the German forces in the Normandy area. However, they had still not managed to break out of the vital Caen area. The *LAH* had helped to check the Allied plans. The II SS *Panzerkorps* had even managed to retake some ground, including the all-important Hill 112.

At the start of July the British and Canadian forces continued their attacks to gain ground. The resistance put up by the *LAH* and the 12th SS was giving them plenty to think about. The 1st Reg. shifted northeast of their positions towards Caen. The objective was to retake Carpiquet. The 3. *Kompanie*, along with the 2. *Kompanie*, advanced along the Franqueville road as far as the rail line northeast of Carpiquet. They then moved onto the defensive due to enemy pressure. The bulk of the Division was in the assembly area in the Cinglais forest eight to ten kilometers south of Caen.

At this stage the Allies had landed considerable amounts of men and materials on the beaches of France. Over 850,000 men, 148,000 vehicles and 500,000 tonnes of supplies had reached the area. In the American sector the fall of Cherbourg allowed them to free up considerable forces and continue their advance. In the British-Canadian sector, the failure to capture Caen was becoming an embarrassment. American officers were expressing dissatisfaction with the failure of their English friends to open the eastern flank. To answer these criticisms Operation Charnwood was launched with the sole objective of capturing Caen. For the first time in history bombers were used to assist a ground attack. In addition to this the Allies had help from the fighter planes, heavy guns from four ships, artillery fire from three separate units, two Tank Brigades plus engineer tanks such as the flail tank and the flame-throwing Crocodiles, the ground forces were made up of three British-Canadian Divisions.

A 3. *Kompanie Kameraden*'s Recollections of the Allied Material Superiority

Before we continue with the Allied attack, it is worth mentioning the recollections of the 3. *Kompanie*'s Gerhard Franz from this time. He recalled that the enemy artillery, naval gunfire and aerial attacks were exacting a heavy toll on the German forces. The feelings of the *Kameraden* of the 3. *Kompanie* were one of frustration. How could men armed with only rifles and machine pistols defeat these types of weapons. The Allied material might was certainly making its' presence felt on the ground. On the 5th of July 1944 Gerhard was wounded, as was the *Kompanie* Commander *Hauptsturmführer* Maurer. They were both placed side by side in the field hospital. Due to the nature of their wounds they were then moved to Paris on the 25th of July. Shortly after this they were both sent back to Germany by hospital train for a period of recuperation. Gerhard recalled that he has never been on a more enjoyable train ride before or since that journey! *Hauptsturmführer* Maurer was succeeded by *Hauptsturmführer* Harrer as the *Kompanie* Commander.

Hauptsturmführer Karl Harrer: Twelfth Commander of the 3. *Kompanie*

Date of birth: 28.12.15   SS number: ?

There is no information on this officer.

The Allied Destruction of Caen

The Allies were to move on Caen from the northwest, north and northeast. The aerial attack began on the evening of the 7th of July. The spectacle was impressive to see but its only result was the destruction of Caen and the death of hundreds of civilians. The German defenders suffered some losses, but these were light. The artillery fired upon the positions held by the *LAH* also. There was amazement on the part of the defenders that the Allies did not follow up this aerial attack with immediate ground attacks. It was apparent that the Allies had a lot of lessons to learn. At this time the expectation of the second landing in the Pas de Calais area kept twenty-three divisions tied up in that region. If the handful of German divisions in the Normandy area could cause the problems they did, it is worth considering what difference an additional twenty-three divisions would have made. The Allied deception plan together with the German High Command's evaluation proved decisive in the long run.

During the 8th of July the 12th SS pulled back slightly and the bulk of the *LAH* moved closer to Caen. The area held was now between the Odon and Orne Rivers. The moves took place over the next two days under constant aerial attacks. By the 10th the 3. *Kompanie* were holding Venoix. The Allies continued their push into Caen, the *LAH* and the 12th SS pulled back slowly. On this day the British captured the banks of the Odon and Orne Rivers during hard fighting, they did not however attempt a crossing of the Orne at this stage. The great prize of Caen came over one month late for Montgomery. The *LAH* were now in positions between Le Mesnil and Louvigny. Operation Jupiter was launched in an attempt to take Hill 112 and Maltot, fighting also took place around Eterville. The losses to both sides were heavy and the Germans did give up some ground. The Operation did not achieve its' aim. By the 12th of July the *LAH* were in positions south of Caen, between Maltot and the Caen to Falaise road.

On the 15th the *LAH* were relieved by the 272nd Infantry Division, they moved east to positions along National Route 158 – the Caen to Falaise road. At this time the Allies were preparing a new operation to open this precise area. The British/ Canadian attack would use extensive artillery and bomber support. The attack was drawn up after Eisenhower complained to Montgomery about the lack of progress in his sector. The attack would be launched with the help of the British VIII Corps, comprised of three divisions. The bulk of the attack would be from the south and east of Caen. The preparations began on the 15th of July and lasted for the next two days.

The attacks for Operation Goodwood began on the 18th. One thousand Allied bombers flew over and carpet-bombed the area. This was followed by naval and artillery fire, then the medium bombers flew over and delivered some more death and carnage. The ground forces began to move forward behind the cover of a rolling artillery barrage. One veteran of the *LAH* recalled the tactics employed by the Allies during this time. He stated that they would select an area as a target. This area would then be subjected to complete and extensive artillery fire. He personally witnessed the death of a farmer tending his crops in the field and a woman who was pushing a pram along a dirt road. He did not view this 'non-precision' bombing as warfare, but mere murder.

The *LAH* at Bras and Bourgebus Ridge

Under this type of attack the Allies made advances up to the town of Cagny where the 21st Panzer Division stopped them. At Bourguebus Ridge the men of the *LAH* brought the Allies to a standstill, but they exhausted themselves by doing so. In the ensuing pause, the *LAH* and 12th SS forces were moved up. When the Allies reached the ground before Bras and Bourguebus, they ran into the *LAH* forces that had a commanding view over the whole area. In a short space of time the Panthers of the *LAH* began to knock out Sherman after Sherman. By the end of the first day over 120 Allied tanks were out of action. The experienced soldiers of the Waffen-SS were teaching the inexperienced Allied soldiers some very valuable lessons. At this stage the 3. *Kompanie* were just north of Soliers. Tank battles raged for the following day as the Allies tried to push through the positions held by the Germans. Due to Allied pressure the *LAH* moved back to Tilly la Campagne and la Hogue. The 3. *Kompanie* were placed alongside the 7. *Kompanie* of the *LAH*'s Panzer Regiment in Tilly la Campagne, where they were then ordered to prepare defensive positions. The Allies took some areas including Bras and Hubert-Folie, the cost to both sides was mounting. The pressure continued on the 21st of July when the Allies took Bourguebus Ridge itself.

This operation, despite all of its support, can be considered a failure. The defenders took the weight of the aerial and artillery attacks on top of the frontal attacks by three complete divisions. They brought these attacks to a standstill and inflicted losses of over 250 tanks on the enemy. The defenders retreated slowly and did not let the situation develop into a rout. The whole operation gained the Allies seven miles of ground. What gains would the German forces have made given these same resources? Montgomery received immense criticism for this operation with some people even calling for his removal. The *LAH* even managed some localised counter-attacks on the 21st. Meanwhile, in the south the Americans had taken St. Lô.

The Allied Push Towards Tilly la Campagne

Over the next two days the fighting died down, the Allies could be seen preparing for a new attack. The line held by the *LAH* was from Tilly la Campagne to Verrieres, the 3. *Kompanie* were placed as part of the reserve forces in Rocquancourt, they then moved back towards Verrieres. On the 25th of July the Canadians launched Operation Spring. The objectives were to take Tilly, Verrieres and la Hogue. The bulk of the fighting was on both sides of Route N.158. The I Battalion were fighting on the left of the road. Verrieres was lost to the Allies, but their advances were stopped from going any further. This operation was suspended on the 26th. This proved to be the Canadian's second bloodiest operation during the Second World War, the attempted landings at Dieppe being the worst. The Canadians did mount some attacks over the following days and into August. The thorn in the Allies' side was the small and relatively insignificant town of Tilly la Campagne. On the 2nd of August a massive bombardment of the town took place. Planes, artillery and then some more planes reduced this town to a pile of rubble. But each time the Allies tried to take the town, the defenders of the *LAH* appeared from under the rubble and stopped each attack. The attacks continued in other areas also. In Tilly, a grenadier of the 6. *Kompanie* was part of an MG team, two enemy battalions attacked with strong artillery support. The Grenadier was soon alone as his comrades suffered injuries and death. He himself lost one eye, but kept firing. He lost the other eye but still kept firing wherever he heard the sounds of the enemy. He only stopped firing when his MG took a direct hit and injured his hand. He was rescued by his own side and managed to survive the war. *Grenadier* Göstl was awarded the Knight's Cross for these actions and was the only Grenadier in the Waffen-SS to receive this award. This is an excellent example of the fighting spirit of the Waffen-SS and the sort of problems the Allies had to overcome.

The *LAH*'s Participation in Operation Lüttich: August 1944

On the 4th of August the *LAH* were relieved by the 89th Infantry Division and moved south. The Americans had been making good progress in that sector. The new orders were to move via Vire and onto Mortain. The *LAH* were to cut the Allied forces off from their supply routes and to force an opening to the coast. The operation was titled Lüttich and was due to start on the 7th of August; not all of the *LAH* were in position by this time. The attack had the 116th Panzer Division attacking from Sourdeval, the 2nd Panzer Division and the *LAH* attacking Juvigny and the 2nd SS and 17th SS attacking Mortain. Over the next two days the attacks received intense aerial bombardment, the rocket-firing Typhoon aircraft were well organised and any movement brought immediate attack. The Allies had known of the impending German attack in advance through intercepted radio traffic and had prepared well. The *LAH* and 2nd Panzer Division did advance as far as le Mesnil-Tove, they were against the U.S. 9th Division. The 116th made little progress, whilst the 2nd SS pushed through Mortain and onto Romagny. The attack was coming under increasing defense, on top of this the Americans were breaking through with large forces to the south. In the north the British were breaking into the area south of Caen. The orders arrived to suspend the attack.

The 3. *Kompanie* Remain in the North: *Kampfgruppe* Schiller

As mentioned earlier, not all of the *LAH* took part in this operation. The forces that were held back became part of *Kampfgruppe* Schiller; these forces included the 3. *Kompanie*. They were placed under the 84th Infantry Division and sent to the area south of Vire, they were facing mixed Allied forces. They succeeded in repulsing strong Allied incursions near Maisocelles. They were moved back to the rest of the Division on the 10th of August. They joined the Division's fight on the 11th helping the 116th Panzer Division, the 3. *Kompanie* fought near Sourdeval. As this was happening, the Allied encirclement began to take shape with the U.S. 3rd Army in the south, the Canadian 1st and British 2nd Army in the north, and the U.S. 1st Army in the west. As the attack towards Avranches could not be continued, the *LAH* were pulled out on the 11th of August 1944 and sent to la Ferte Mace, south of Argentan.

The Death of the German Forces in France: The Falaise Pocket

The moves by the three Allied armies was causing a pocket to be formed. The opening of this pocket was at the town of Falaise. Inside the pocket were the *LAH*, 2nd SS Panzer Division, and the 85th Division. Over the 14th and 15th of August the forces inside this encirclement were battling under hellish conditions. La Ferte-Mace was abandoned and the units there moved back towards Ranes. This town was also under attack but the *LAH* held on. There was a lot of confusion in these areas, the Allies were moving at will and the sky was filled with the dreaded fighter-bombers. Anything that moved was destroyed. Falaise town fell to the Allies on the 16th of August. Under intense pressure the retreat continued north, by the 18th most of the Division was around Fromentel and St. Andre. Every soldier was trying to escape. The moves north were made through enemy lines and resulted in many dead, wounded and captured men, those who did make it through were extremely lucky. All forces inside the pocket were ordered to escape east over the Orne River. The fighter-bombers were flying repeatedly over the pocket and inflicting their

Left: This photograph shows two NCOs from the 3. Kompanie during the Normandy fighting. Unfortunately, their names are not known. (Patrick Agte) Right: Another photograph from mid-1944 showing a squad of soldiers from the 3. Kompanie being briefed by their platoon commander. Unfortunately, none of the names of these men are known. (Patrick Agte).

Below: This photograph also shows a group of 3. Kompanie soldiers atop one of their vehicles. This picture also dates from the Normandy fighting in mid-1944. The camouflage measures that the German army had to adopt during this time are very evident from this photograph. The front end of the vehicle is just visible. (Patrick Agte)

death and destruction. The Canadians had broken through to an area near Chambois, while the Americans were on the opposite side of this town. On the 19th of August orders were drawn up for the breakout attempt. This breakout was carried out by small groups of men who forced their way through wherever they could. The main breakout was near St. Lambert, situated halfway between the neck of the pocket. The I Battalion was near St. Lambert, they moved about within the pocket and finally pushed out to the southeast at Moissy. The 2nd SS Panzer Division was moving down and helping to keep a gap open for the escaping troops. The pocket was being continually shelled and fired on by artillery and fighter-bombers, confusion, death and fear rained inside the pocket. The pocket had been closed by the 19th of August 1944 around Chambois. For the next two days breakouts were accomplished by small groups of men consisting of mixed forces from the Army, *Fallschirmjäger* and Waffen-SS. By the time the pocket had been closed the *LAH* had effectively ceased to exist, from the 6th of June 1944 until the middle of August, their estimated casualties stood at around 5000.

After Falaise: The Race to the Seine River

After the breakout, the pursuit continued. The next objective was to get across the Seine River. The Allies did not relent and the forces south of Rouen gave chase. What was left of the *LAH* was pulled out and sent to the Pacy-Evreux area. On the way the *LAH* fought the enemy in Bonneville, le Neubourg and Mantes-Gassicourt. They were attempting to hold the Allies off as long as possible. As with the Falaise pocket the moves were made by small groups of soldiers. As the bridges had all been destroyed most crossings were done on makeshift rafts or hastily repaired bridges, usually only capable of taking men and light vehicles. By the 25th of August the remaining *LAH* forces were across, this was the day that Paris surrendered to the Allies. The retreat continued with elements of the Division moving through Muids, Gournay and Amiens. At some points the Allies had passed these units, who in turn had to pass through Allied held territory to escape. The movement was in a general northeast direction; Amiens fell to the British on the 31st of August. With this the Allies split.

The *LAH*'s Defensive Positions on the Westwall: Autumn 1944

Elements of the U.S. 1st Army moved north in an attempt to cut-off the German forces before they reached Holland, U.S. V Corps and U.S. VII Corps moved east.

Again under intense pressure, elements of the *LAH* moved east through Marle, la Copelle, Charleroi and Dinant. These moves were made whilst under attack. This carried on until the 4th of September 1944. The orders then arrived for the *LAH* to be moved to Germany for a rest. The following day von Rundstedt assumed command of the forces in the west. The moves east were towards the Westwall defenses, the move to German territory was through Huy, Houfalize, Bastogne and Nadrin. The main problem in these areas was the partisan attacks. By the 12th of September some *LAH* forces were behind the Westwall in Burg Reuland. The much talked about Westwall was in poor condition and the forces had to carry out a lot of work to get them combat ready. Other *LAH* forces fought near Keppenhausen on the 14th and Olzheim at the end of September. Also, at the start of October a *Kampfgruppe* of the *LAH* was fighting the Allies near Nijmegen, this was the tail-end of the Allied Market Garden Operation that had been destroyed by the 9th and 10th SS Divisions.

The main characteristics of the fighting from the Falaise pocket onward were the dissolution of many individual *Kompanie*s. It is hard to pinpoint precise *Kompanie*s or even if they survived. The 3. *Kompanie* are not mentioned in the period from mid-August, we can assume that they were so badly decimated that they failed to function as a recognisable *Kompanie*.

The *LAH*'s *Kampfgruppe* Rink's Defense of Aachen

Approximately six kilometres south of the main *LAH* forces, a *Kampfgruppe* was formed under *Hauptsturmführer* Diefenthal and fought with Army units in the area around Aachen. Within *KG* Diefenthal there was a second group under the command of *Obersturmführer* Rink. Between the 10th and 14th of October 1944 this *Kampfgruppe* fought in the Würselen area, just north of Aachen. American forces where on both sides of them. Hard battles were fought in this area as both sides tried to gain control. On the 12th of October *KG* Rink was removed and sent into Aachen to help defend the town, the Americans were already in parts of the town. This *Kampfgruppe* helped to repulse many attacks from the 13th. They even managed a successful counter-attack on the 15th. This was the day that the *Kampfgruppe* finally reached Aachen from their positions in Würselen. The U.S. 1st and 30th Infantry Divisions were almost completing their encirclement of Aachen; this was done by the 16th. *Kampfgruppe* Diefenthal was suffering extreme pressure to the northeast and was pushed back, the two *Kampfgruppe*s were only two kilometres apart at this stage.

The American circle grew steadily smaller with *KG* Rink refusing to give up the fight. The Army commander of Aachen, *Oberst* Wilck, finally surrendered on the 21st of October as American tanks stood outside his command bunker. *Kampfgruppe* Rink however, had not surrendered. He decided it was senseless to fight to the last man as he had been ordered. As the Aachen forces surrendered, the remnants of *KG* Rink (less than forty men) attempted their breakout back to the German lines. One of the men that surrendered was the former 3. *Kompanie* Commander Günther Zaag, who had been wounded during the battle. The *Kampfgruppe* split into small groups and made their own plans.

Those that made it out included *Obersturmführer* Rink who brought nine other men with him. He had hidden in a cellar for three days before moving out. They reached the German lines on the 25th of October 1944. They were sent onto the rest of the survivors of the *LAH* who were moved to the Lübbecke-Osnabrück area for a rest period.

Theodore 'Teddi' Wisch: Second Commander of the *LAH*

Date of birth: 13.12.07   SS Number: 4759

'Teddi' Wisch was born in Wesselburener Koog in the Holstein area of northern Germany. He was one of the original 117 men specially selected to form the Fuhrer's bodyguard squad during mid-March 1933. He would reach the rank of *Untersturmführer* on the 28th of July 1933 and followed this by assuming command of the 1st *Kompanie* on the 1st of October 1933. He would hold this position until the start of the war and on into the Polish campaign. His wartime experiences began during the campaign in Poland where he received the 2nd Class Iron Cross on the 24th of September 1939. This was followed in November when he was awarded the 1st Class Iron Cross. By the time of the start of the western campaign in 1940, he was commanding a battalion. He would continue to be a Battalion Commander during the fighting in the Balkans in early 1941. His bravery and leadership skills were noted and on the 27th of September 1941 he was awarded the Knight's Cross to the Iron Cross. He was also promoted to *Obersturmbannführer*. In the summer of 1942 he took command of the newly formed 2nd Regiment of the *LAH*, by this stage he was holding the rank of *Standartenführer*. Just over six months later, he received the German Cross in Gold with the *LAH* in Russia.

It was in March 1943 that he took over the command of the 1st SS Panzer Division *LAH* from Sepp Dietrich. He would lead the division during the intensive fighting at Kursk in the summer of 1943 and then on into Italy. It was whilst in Italy that he was promoted to *Oberführer*. The defensive battles in Russia during late 1943 and early 1944 placed a strain on the men of the *LAH*. The relative successes of the *LAH* during this period earned 'Teddi' Wisch the Oakleaves to the Knight's Cross. By the 30th of January 1944 he was holding the rank of *Brigadeführer* und Generalmajor der Waffen-SS. He would take the division into the decisive battleground of Normandy during the summer of 1944. He would see his division pushed back and virtually wiped out. He himself managed to escape the Allied encirclement at Falaise, but he did receive serious wounds to his legs. He ended his eleven-year service with the *LAH* towards the end of August 1944. He was awarded the Swords and Oakleaves to the Knight's Cross. Like Sepp Dietrich and Fritz Witt, 'Teddi' Wisch had been with the *LAH* since its' formation and he had risen through the ranks to become an effective and popular divisional commander. When he left the Division for the last time, the *LAH* lost a very experienced and competent man.

Albert Frey: I Battalion and 1st Regiment Commander

Date of birth: 16.02.13 SS Number: 111 913

Albert Frey was born in Heidelberg. He joined the SS on the 15th of December 1933 when he served with the *Deutschland Standarte*. He joined the *LAH* in 1938 after he had completed his officer-training course. He had reached the rank of *Obersturmführer* by the time of the Polish Campaign. During the fighting in Poland he received the 2nd Class Iron Cross on the 25th of September 1939. He then went on to win the 1st Class Iron Cross during the battles in France in 1940. By the time of the first Russian battles in 1941 Frey was the commander of the 11. *Kompanie*. He would be the I Battalion Commander by the end of 1941; he had succeeded Fritz Witt in this role. He was awarded the German Cross in Gold for the Battalion's actions at Taganrog in late 1941. 1943 would be a good year for Albert Frey. By that stage he was holding the rank of *Sturmbannführer* and on the 3rd of March he was awarded the Knight's Cross to the Iron Cross, again for the successes of the I Battalion. He was then promoted to *Obersturmbannführer* during March and given the command of the 1st Regiment of the *LAH*, succeeding Fritz Witt who left the *LAH* to help form the 12th SS Panzer Division. Albert Frey led the 1st Regiment through the heavy fighting at Kursk and then into Italy. The defensive battles in Russia at the end of 1943 would earn him the Oakleaves to the Knight's Cross; he received them on the 20th of December. He moved with the division to France in the summer of 1944. It was here that he was wounded and left the command of the 1st Regiment. He ended the war with the rank of *Standartenführer*. He was regarded as a very able and brave commander who kept his head in the heat of battle. He is still alive at the time of the writing of this book.

Hans-Joachim Schiller: I Battalion Commander

Very little is known about Joachim Schiller's early days in the SS. As far as can be determined, he served in the 6. *Kompanie* in the inter-war years and by 1939 he was the commander of the *LAH*'s training *Kompanie*. He then led the 3. *Kompanie*,

Left: This photograph shows *Brigadeführer* Theodore 'Teddi' Wisch during 1944. He served as the LAH's second commander from 1943 until autumn 1944 when he was badly wounded. He is seen wearing the Oakleaves to the Knight's Cross, but he also received the Swords and Oakleaves to the Knight's Cross on the August 28, 1944. (Author's collection) Right: Albert Frey pictured holding the rank of *Standartenführer* and wearing his Oakleaves to the Knight's Cross. Frey survived the war and helped to form the Truppenkameradschaft (Veterans Association) of the I SS Panzerkorps (1st and 12th SS Divisions). (Albert Frey)

Hans-Joachim Schiller, on the extreme right, photographed while serving as the LAH's Adjutant after his service with the 3. Kompanie. He went on to hold the rank of *Obersturmbannführer* and was awarded the German Cross in Gold. (Mark Yerger)

Another photograph showing *Sturmbannführer* Schiller, on extreme right, while serving as the LAH's adjutant, IIa. Also in the photograph is the LAH's Ia, *Hauptsturmführer* Rudolf Lehmann. They are both seen talking to the LAH's commander, Sepp Dietrich. (Ralf Tiemann)

with the rank of *Hauptsturmführer*, through the early stages of the Second World war up until the end of August 1941, when he was badly wounded. He was replaced by Heinrich Springer, and then when Springer was injured in late 1941, Schiller assumed temporary command of the 3. *Kompanie* until mid-1942. His next post was that of Divisional Adjutant; a post he held until July 1943. He had reached the rank of *Sturmbannführer* by early 1943. He then took over the command of the I Battalion in July 1943 from Albert Frey and he stayed with this Battalion until late 1943 or early 1944. In July of 1944, Schiller was once again back in command of the I Battalion, only this time he was holding the rank of *Obersturmbannführer*. He led the I Battalion during the fighting in Normandy in July of 1944 and at one stage he had his own *Kampfgruppe*, which also contained the 3. *Kompanie*. He left the I Battalion during July and it can be assumed that he was injured at this point. No further information is available on Joachim Schiller other than that of former 3. *Kompanie Kameraden*, Max Schmidt, who stated that Schiller was wounded during the final battles in Berlin in 1945. The history of the 3. *Kompanie* cannot be mentioned without the name of Joachim Schiller. He was a popular *Kompanie* Commander, and it is known by the author that he was given a book as a Christmas present by the men of the 3. *Kompanie* at the end of 1940. It is also known that he survived the war and helped to form the East German Army. He held the rank of Colonel in this army and lived up until 1991.

CHAPTER FOURTEEN

SITUATION AFTER THE NORMANDY BATTLES

The Normandy landings were a vital part of the Allied strategy to defeat the Germans during the Second World War. They had successfully cleared France of the enemy by the end of August and the French capital had been liberated. The Allied plan had come up against some unforeseen difficulties, however. The successful delaying actions by the mainly SS troops in the northern sector had delayed Field Marshall Montgomery's plans by a month. The more rapid advance in the south by the Americans had started to bring planning differences to the fore. As the Allied advance continued, an apparent rift appeared between the British and the Americans. The efforts put in by the Allies in their attempt to close the Falaise Gap had not only inflicted a serious blow upon the Germans, but it also ground the offensive capabilities of the Allies to a temporary halt. There was criticism that almost half of the enemy troops had managed to evade capture and live to fight another day. Before the Allies could go any further they had to re-supply and replace their losses sustained in the recent battles.

Overall, things were going well for the combined forces of the Allied armies. The Italian capital of Rome had been liberated on the 5th of June 1944. Successful landings had been made in the south of France. The Soviets had started their main summer campaign, which succeeded in tearing a huge gap in Army Group Centre. The land under the control of Hitler's troops was growing less and less each day. The Allies could feel confident that the war would soon be over. Montgomery was critical of the American plans and he began to push for his 'single thrust' plan, designed to punch into the heart of the Reich. This brought him into direct conflict with his boss, Eisenhower. The Americans had favoured a 'broad-front' approach, which would send probes towards the enemy lines at various points. Montgomery got his chance however, and during September 1944, the Allies attempted the capture of a series of bridges, running through Holland, that lead to the German border during the Market Garden operation. This failed in its' final objective and gave a graphic example of what lay in wait for the advancing Allies.

The much-vaunted 'West-Wall' defenses would prove a deadly killing ground for many Allied troops in late 1944. The Reichswald and Hürtgen Forests would be amongst some of the hardest fought battles that the Allies would have to endure during the war. The German soldiers were proving that they were far from defeated and worse was to come for the Allies. The Germans were fighting closer to home with shorter supply lines and they were fighting for their homeland. They believed in their struggle and they were not about to give up just yet. Adolf Hitler had already started to make plans for his next big move even as the battles in Normandy were drawing to a close. This was the overall situation in the autumn of 1944.

The period from the end of September 1944 was the start of another rest and re-fit period for the 1st SS Panzer Division *LAH*. The 3. *Kompanie* had suffered a lot of losses during the battles in the Normandy region. These losses were replaced with new recruits and former injured *Kameraden* who were well enough to return to active duty.

One such 3. *Kompanie Kameraden* who had recovered from the wounds he received in Normandy was Gerhard Franz. He returned to the 3. *Kompanie* in September 1944 and was sent to an area near Berlin. He remembered that there were many new recruits who had transferred from the Luftwaffe or Kriegsmarine to the Waffen-SS and also a group of volunteers from various European countries. The poor manpower situation in Germany at this late stage in the war was becoming apparent also. Gerhard recalled that a group of Russians were assigned to the 3. *Kompanie*, despite the fact that not one of them could speak any German! Gerhard would take up his old function as *Kompanie* messenger.

One former member of the Kriegsmarine who transferred to the 3. *Kompanie* around this time was Günther Junker. He had initially joined the Kriegsmarine in January 1944 and went through the training period with them. The need for Navy personnel was becoming less and less necessary, so in April 1944, Günther volunteered for the Waffen-SS. He was attached to the Training and Replacement Battalion 1 (*LAH*). He was then sent to the 3. *Kompanie* in July 1944. He moved with the *Kompanie* from Ginsterheide to Waldbröhl, prior to the start of the Ardennes Offensive. Günther Junker and Gerhard Franz would fight together with the 3. *Kompanie* in Hitler's last great battle in the west. The 3. *Kompanie* were commanded by *Hauptsturmführer* Griese at the start of the Ardennes Offensive.

Hauptsturmführer Wilhelm Griese: Thirteenth Commander of the 3. _Kompanie_

Date of birth: 02.06.03 SS number: 391 981

There is no information available on this commander.

CHAPTER FIFTEEN

PREPARATION FOR THE ARDENNES OFFENSIVE

The summer of 1944 was a critical time for the armed forces under the control of Adolf Hitler. Not only had the armies in the west, and the east, received a severe mauling, elements of the German Officer Korps had decided that the time was right to send a clear signal to the enemies of Germany. The assassination attempt on the Fuhrer's life in July was a significant decline for the Army's reputation in Hitler's eyes and the increasing importance of the Waffen-SS. They had rightfully earned a reputation for steel hard devotion to duty, whether in the attack or on the defense. They had proved their worth at Kharkov, Kursk and in the recent battles in Normandy. Hitler would use the premier Waffen-SS divisions as the spearhead in the forthcoming offensive in the west during the winter of 1944. His namesake division would lead the attack under the overall control of Hitler's faithful Sepp Dietrich.

The 1st SS Panzer Division *Leibstandarte Adolf Hitler* was hastily rebuilt towards the end of 1944; as were many of the other divisions involved in the recent fighting. Sepp Dietrich would lead the newly created 6th Panzer Army, which would contain the 1st SS Panzer Division *LAH* and the 12th SS Panzer Division *Hitlerjugend*, among others. The *LAH* would receive the latest weapons and equipment. The expectations of their success were running very high at the higher echelons of command. What was to be their part in this massive attack?

The overall plan for the battle, which received the code-name 'Wacht am Rhein', was fairly straightforward. The Germans had gathered together a strong attacking force spread across three Armies. The 6th Panzer Army under *Obergruppenführer* 'Sepp' Dietrich had the northern most advance route. This consisted of the 1st SS Panzer Division *Leibstandarte Adolf Hitler*, 2nd SS Panzer Divison *Das Reich*, 9th SS Panzer Division *Hohenstaufen* and the 12th SS Panzer Divisions who were providing the armoured element. The 3rd Parachute Division together with four Volksgrenadier Divisions, the 12th, 246th, 277th and the 326th were supplying the infantry support. Their task was to advance along the route from their forming up area near Dahlem in Germany and into Belgium around the town of Losheim. Their objective was to cross the Meuse River, just below Liege and advance onto Antwerp. Alongside this was the 5th Panzer Army under the command of *Generalleutnant* Hasso von Manteuffel. He had the 2nd Panzer, 9th Panzer, 116th Panzer and the Panzer Lehr Divisions together with the 15th Panzer Grenadier Division. This armoured force had the 18th, 26th, 62nd and 560th Volksgrenadier Divisions providing the infantry element. Their objective was to move from Prüm in Germany and onto Antwerp via Brussels. The 7th Army under General Erich Brandenburger had the southern-most route into Luxembourg. This infantry only formation was made up of the 5th Parachute Division, 79th Infantry Division and the 212th, 276th and 352nd Volksgrenadier Divisions. They were to move from Bitburg in Germany and engage the U.S. 3rd Army, with the objective of tying down these forces. All of these forces were part of Army Group B commanded by *Feldmarschall* Model. They had some limited reserves made up of the 3rd Panzer Grenadier, 9th Volksgrenadier, Führer Begleit Brigade and the Führer Grenadier Brigade. This was an impressive line up to have assembled at this stage of the war. It totalled over 250,000 men and almost 1000 various armoured vehicles.

The Enemy Disposition

Facing this impressive line up would be a mixture of Allied forces. The 2nd and 99th Infantry Divisions were part of the U.S. V Corps under Major General Gerow. They were positioned opposite the 6th Panzer Army. Facing Manteuffel in the centre were the 28th and 106th Infantry Divisions who were part of Major General Troy Middleton's U.S. VIII Corps. In the south facing Brandenberger's men were the 9th Armoured and the 4th Infantry Divisions. All of these American units had recently been involved in heavy fighting and were in the area for a rest. These combined units totaled around 83,000 men, backed up with around 450 tanks and assault guns and around 400 artillery pieces. Most of them had already suffered at the hands of the enemy and the last thing they expected was to be the subject of an attack of this scale or intensity. Unlike the Germans, the Allies had many factors in their favor. Although initially outnumbered, the Allies had strong forces close by that could be called upon if needed. They included the battle tested U.S. 3rd Army, under the command of General George Patton. At this stage their supply lines had been established and when the weather permitted, they had complete domination of the sky. The British were also present on the northern flank and the part they would play would be significant in the latter stages of the German offensive.

Choosing the Target

The reason to attack in the west had been made because any new attack by the Germans at the end of 1944 needed the following ingredients. It needed to have a strong chance of success. The movement of the troops and the all-important panzers needed to be done in secrecy. These requirements ruled out a new offensive in the east. There were worries for the Germans that included the fact that the Allies dominated the skies, supplying the troops at the front would be difficult as they advanced further to the west and the routes of advance would be moving against the 'grain of the land'. Hitler had rightfully assessed that the Allies were working together under a strained relationship. He felt that a decisive blow would crack their alliance open. The necessary element of secrecy was achieved by telling only those people who needed to know and when they needed to know. It was not until the end of October 1944 that the three respective Army Commanders were told of the forthcoming tasks. They all agreed that the available forces were insufficient to achieve the objectives. The domination of the skies by the Allies would be countered by the very bad weather prevalent at this time of the year and the supply situation would be partly dealt with by capturing enemy supplies on route. It was into this situation, with these forces and against these enemy troops that Adolf Hitler launched his last great offensive in the west during World War II.

The *LAH*'s Situation and Movements Prior to the Offensive

By the end of October 1944 the bulk of the *LAH* were in the Lübbecke area. The division was estimated to be running at 25% of its' required strength in men and a poorly 20% of its required strength in vehicles and equipment. The replacements in men began to arrive and intensive training was begun. The new vehicles began to arrive also. It was however, easier to incorporate the new vehicles; the incorporation of the new recruits was a very difficult task.

On the 9th of November 1944 the *LAH* were moved to Cologne, a move that took nine days to complete. The various units were billeted in an area stretching from Jülich to Düren. It was at this stage that the division was placed under the direct control of Dietrich's 6th Panzer Army. It was known that the enemy would closely monitor the movements of the *LAH*, so they were therefore issued with false orders that gave them a reason for being in that area. There was no let up in the training programme and on the 10th of December, the *LAH* was considered combat ready.

The 3. *Kompanie*'s Objectives

Between the 12th and 13th of December the I Battalion were in Alendorf. By the following day the deployment of all of the troops in the assembly areas was complete. It was on this day that the regimental commanders briefed the individual *Kompanie* commanders on the mission ahead. There would be five main attack routes in the northern sector of the offensive. The *LAH* would be allocated two of these; March Routes D and E. There would be various *Kampfgruppes* set up within the *LAH* that included *Kampfgruppe* Peiper, *Kampfgruppe* Knittel and *Kampfgruppe* Hansen. The 3. *Kompanie*'s commander, *Hauptsturmführer* Griese, was told that they would be part of *Kampfgruppe* Hansen and that this *Kampfgruppe* would advance along March Route E. This particular march route was closest to the boundary between the 6th Panzer Army and the 5th Panzer Army. *Kampfgruppe* Hansen would move towards Heppenbach, Amel, Recht and then establish a bridgehead near Huy.

Motivation for the troops

The afternoon of the 15th of December was when Sepp Dietrich issued his written appeal to each of the soldiers on the ground; this appeal highlighted the importance of the forthcoming battle and the need for rapid advance, without concern for the flanks. The change over to an offensive operation after months of defensive fighting is something that inspired the soldiers and gave them new hope. Just before midnight on the 15th of December the final moves were complete and every soldier stood ready to push towards their objectives and engage the enemy once more. They would not have long to wait as the start of the offensive was timed for 05:35 a.m. on the morning of the 16th of December 1944.

CHAPTER SIXTEEN

OPERATION 'WACHT AM RHEIN' PART ONE: THE PUSH TO THE WEST

The start of the attack was in the form of an artillery barrage that was designed to 'soften up' the front line enemy positions. Some reports from the enemy soldiers commented that they felt as though all hell had been let loose. The reality however, was that the damage inflicted was far less than expected. As the first German soldiers advanced, they quickly discovered how ineffective it had been.

Delays From the Start

The start of the advance itself was slow. On March Route E, west of Krewinkel, a German minefield was discovered that had been laid during the defensive actions a few months earlier. The clearing of a path through this obstacle was time consuming and severely delayed the German advance. It also allowed the enemy valuable time to get over the initial shock and make plans. These delays meant that the majority of *KG* Hansen remained in their deployment area on day one of the offensive. A path was finally cleared during the night and it was ensured that this clearing was wide enough to allow the panzers to pass.

Advance and Detour

Day two got of to a better start with the troops of the 3. *Kompanie* and the rest of *KG* Hansen moving through Manderfeld and on towards Medendorf and

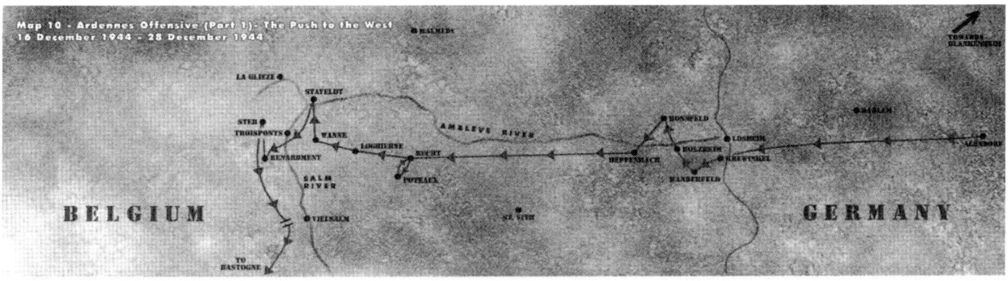

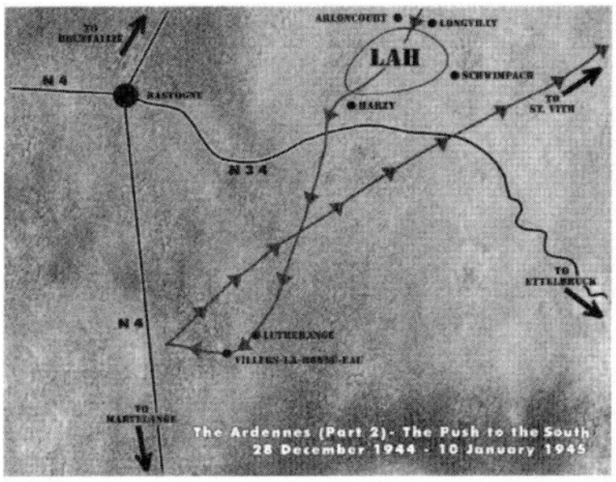

Ardennes Map

Heppenbach. The area between these latter two towns had been reduced to thick mud due to the weather, which not even the panzers could negotiate. Max Hansen ordered a detour north through Holzheim, Honsfeld and Büllingen and then back south towards Heppenbach. The I Battalion were accompanied by the tank destroyers of the I Panzerjäger Battalion. Recht was reached on the evening of the 17th of December and the grenadiers set up positions for the night. Behind the I Battalion, further elements of the III Battalion had run into enemy resistance. The enemy had crossed March Route E and temporarily severed it.

3. *Kompanie* Advance to the West

During the morning of the 18th of December the III Battalion pushed through the enemy positions and reached the I and II Battalions in Recht. Running southwest from Recht was the first major road along March Route E and this road led towards Vielsalm. The next main town along this road after Recht was Poteaux. This town had an important road junction running through it that not only contained the road to Vielsalm, further south west, but also the main road towards St. Vith to the south east. As the I Battalion moved from Recht, they clashed with American soldiers of the 14th Cavalry Group just before Poteaux. These enemy soldiers had intended to take Recht and were in the process of advancing on that town from Poteaux.

The 3. *Kompanie* Lose *Hauptsturmführer* Griese

Günther Junker from the 3. *Kompanie* recalled that they wanted to attack Poteaux direct. It was not known if Poteaux was clear of enemy forces as the men of the 3. *Kompanie*, and the I Battalion were being fired on by enemy tanks from a nearby hill. It was probably one of these enemy tank shells that severely wounded the 3. *Kompanie* commander *Hauptsturmführer* Griese. He had his arm blown off and luckily for him, a passing armoured ambulance picked him up. Before leaving his men, *Hauptsturmführer* Griese shouted out, 'on to Poteaux'. Günther mentioned that it was only at this stage that they knew what the objective was called! *Hauptsturmführer* Griese survived this wound. The battle continued with the 3. *Kompanie* suffering casualties. They were forced to entrench in the forward slope of their positions. They were then forced to withdraw shortly afterwards.

The Capture of Poteaux

The attack could only resume with the help of the accompanying Jagdpanzers. The men and machines pushed towards Poteaux and successfully took control of the town at around noon. The vital road junction was occupied and secured. The enemy had suffered quite a few losses in men and vehicles during this engagement. They withdrew towards Vielsalm. The aftermath of this attack was captured by accompanying war correspondents. The pictures that they took have been featured in countless books. They show various burning American vehicles with *KG* Hansen grenadiers moving between them. These grenadiers are officially stated as belonging to the 2. *Kompanie*. However, in a letter to the author, Günther Junker recalled that the 3. *Kompanie* were present, although he cannot identify anyone in the photographs.

Halt the Advance! A Move to the North

The advance past Poteaux was started, but in the afternoon orders were sent that would stop *KG* Hansen's advance along March Route E. They were ordered back to Recht for the night and their objective for the 19th of December would be Trois Ponts. March Route E would be taken over by troops of the 9th SS Panzer Division *Hohenstaufen*. This order was not popular with Max Hansen or any of his men. Defenses were set up in Recht during the night of the 18th.

The enemy was beginning to put their counter move plans into effect. Enemy tank, artillery and mortar fire was put in against the grenadiers at Recht. It was not until the afternoon of the 19th of December that the lead elements of the 9th SS Division arrived in Recht. *KG* Hansen's men moved out once it became dark. Their task was to help *KG* Peiper's men further to the northwest. The 3. *Kompanie* moved with *KG* Hansen from Recht towards Logbierme, which was north west of Recht. In their path was a patch of woods. This was a swampy area and it caused further delays. Günther Junker recalled that during the morning of the 20th of December, the 3. *Kompanie* and *KG* Hansen made contact with the 6th and 7th *Kompanie*s of the *LAH*'s Panzer Regiment.

During the 20th of December the advance of *KG* Hansen reached Wanne, around five kilometres south east of Trois Ponts. All round defense was set up in Wanne and preparations made for the following days' fighting. Further north, Peiper's men were under increasingly heavy enemy attacks and their fuel and ammunition situation prevented any moves on their part. They were relying on the infantry of *KG* Hansen reaching them.

The 3. *Kompanie* Move to the Ambleve River

On the morning of the 21st, *KG* Hansen moved out of Wanne and on towards the Ambleve River. The I Battalion was on the right hand side of the advance route, which brought them through Aisomont. They were moving against elements of the U.S. 82nd Airborne Division. The I Battalion moved onto Höhe Kinderheim and then moved further northwest, right up to the Ambleve River. Some elements of the I Battalion crossed the river three kilometres south west of Stavelot. These elements included the 1. *Kompanie*. The divisional commander *Oberführer* Wilhelm Mohnke, was watching the progress of *KG* Hansen as their success was essential to the relief operation of *KG* Peiper.

At this stage the 3. *Kompanie* were moving alongside the Jagdpanzers of the I *Panzerjäger* Battalion. Günther Junker recalled that they left the Jagdpanzers and moved out in combat formation towards a nearby farmhouse. At the farmhouse the 3. *Kompanie* came under enemy artillery fire. There was a bridge that had already been crossed by the 1. *Kompanie*, situated near the farmhouse. The Jagdpanzers moved up to the bridge and under the direct orders of *Oberführer* Mohnke, they began to cross the bridge. The *Panzerjäger Abteilung* commander, *Hauptsturmführer* Karl Rettlinger, felt that the bridge was not strong enough for the twenty-six

These two photographs show Hansen's Kampfgruppe just after their attack upon the town of Poteuax. Günther Junker and Gerhard Franz of the 3. Kompanie participated in this attack along with their 3. Kompanie Kameraden. (Patrick Agte)

The above photographs show the Jagdpanzer IV's of the Panzerjäger-Abteilung 1, LAH, who accompanied the I Battalion during their moves west in December 1944. (P. Agte)

ton Jagdpanzer IV/70 (Lang). He watched as the first vehicle, containing *Obersturmführer* Holst of the 1. Batterie, started to go over the bridge. This vehicle tried to steer whilst on the bridge, a maneouvre that brought the bridge crashing down and the armoured vehicle straight into the Ambleve River! The crew survived and the engineers were called to erect a new crossing.

A Cold Crossing and a Halt for the 3. *Kompanie*

The advance could not stall however, and Günther Junker recalled that the 3. *Kompanie* men tried various methods to cross the river including the use of ladders. Most of the men of the 3. *Kompanie* got an unscheduled bath during these attempts. They did eventually get across and they began to move up the riverbank. On the way they passed a knocked out enemy tank. In the town below the hill, the lead elements of *KG* Hansen were engaged in heavy fighting. The 3. *Kompanie* could not assist at this stage due to the very unfavourable terrain.

The engineers had arrived and they began their work on erecting the new crossing. This was done under enemy artillery fire that inflicted heavy losses on them. The work progressed slowly but the crossing was built. However, just after this work was completed, the force of the ever rising river washed the new crossing away! With this the 3. *Kompanie* had no chance of immediate help from the other side of the river and they could advance no further, the 3. *Kompanie* attack stalled at this point.

Further Advances and the Death of the I Battalion Commander

During the night of the 21st of December, the I Battalion moved up to a line running from Renardmont to Ster. It was from here that they attacked towards La Gleize on the morning of the 22nd. Günther Junker of the 3. *Kompanie* was close to the I Battalion Commander, *Sturmbannführer* Emil Karst. Günther was observing enemy movements at the other side of the woods they were occupying. He also noticed a machine gun position being set up that faced towards the 3. *Kompanie* men. He could not determine if this machine gun position was friend or foe. A messenger delivered Günther's report to the Battalion Headquarters and then returned with *Sturmbannführer* Karst and another officer. They both advanced into the woods and it was here that *Sturmbannführer* Karst was killed. An attempt to relieve him resulted in a second death; the bodies were recovered later. In a follow-up reconnaissance operation, Günther was wounded, although not heavily. *Hauptsturmführer* Herbert Rink took over the command of the I Battalion.

The Advance Grounds to a Halt

Hauptsturmführer Rink pushed the I Battalion forward against increasing enemy resistance. They reached as far as Ster, which was around 3.5 kilometres north east of Trois Ponts. The enemy troops consisted of elements of the U.S. 3rd Armoured Division known as Task Force Lovelady. The enemy had strong tank and artillery support and against this the *LAH*'s I Battalion could advance no further. The *LAH*'s supporting heavy weapons and armour were unable to assist due to the loss of the vital bridges. Before the end of the 22nd of December 1944, *Obersturmbannführer* Max Hansen called a halt to the advances of his *Kampfgruppe*. Not only did this end the advances of the 3. *Kompanie*, contained within the I Battalion, but it also ended the last remaining chance of relief for the men of *Kampfgruppe* Peiper who were trapped in the La Gleize area.

This photograph shows the Jagdpanzer IV belonging to *Obersturmführer* Holst in the Ambleve River after its unsuccessful attempt to cross the bridge. The remains of the German pioneer bridge can be seen in the background. (U.S. Army Military History Institute)

Overview of the First Week of the Ardennes Offensive

It is worth having a look at the overall advances of all of the German troops in the Ardennes Offensive up to this point. *Obersturmbannführer* Peiper's men had made slow progress on day one and they had also run into friendly mine fields that caused losses to the vital armour. This first day of the German offensive was one of confusion for the Allies, but day two was when they began to move strong forces towards the German positions. The 17th of December also witnessed the infamous clash between Peiper's men and American troops near Malmedy; Stavelot was reached the same day. Delays occurred at Stavelot that resulted in the crossing of the bridge over the Ambleve taking place on the 18th of December.

The next target for *KG* Peiper was Trois Ponts. The delays on the previous day allowed the enemy a vital breathing space. The bridges near Trois Ponts that crossed the Ambleve and Salm Rivers were destroyed. This forced Peiper to detour to the north towards La Gleize. They continued through La Gleize and on through Cheneux. There was a bridge nearby, but this was destroyed as Peiper's men got close to it. This removed Peiper's options for further advances and they therefore moved back to La Gleize. Throughout the 18th and into the 19th of December was when the Americans strengthened their positions, especially around Stoumont, which was Peiper's objective; No further moves could be achieved by Peiper and they were even forced to withdraw back to a smaller perimeter centered on La Gleize.

Further south, the 5th Panzer Army pushed towards Namur. They faced the U.S. 106th Infantry Division who suffered heavy blows. The town of St. Vith was on the route and this formed one of the main American defensive areas. This town fell to the Germans on the evening of the 21st of December. Advances had also been made past Bastogne, which became another enemy pocket of resistance. La Roche was occupied. South of this, the 7th Army had made very slow progress, but by the end of the 21st of December elements were assisting in the encirclement of Bastogne on the southern flank.

The 22nd of December was the start of the end for the German offensive. The 6th Panzer Army had stalled in its' advances and was coming under increasing pressure in its' positions on the northern flank. In addition they were suffering a shortage of ammunition and fuel for their vehicles. Within this area Peiper had been informed of the failure of *KG* Hansen and he began to contemplate the withdrawal and breakout of his remaining men. The southern flank, which was the responsibility of the 7th Army, was being hit hard also. The 5th Panzer Army was still making advances, but Bastogne was proving an increasingly difficult problem for the Germans.

The Enemy Counter Stroke Begins

The 23rd of December brought a clearing in the weather situation. The enemy wasted no time in sending large numbers of sorties towards the German rear areas. These aerial attacks made the already critical supply situation even worse. Peiper's men awaited the order to breakout and further south, the American General McAuliffe issued his much publicised 'nuts!' reply to the request for surrender of Bastogne. The enemy was beginning to call the shots.

The 23rd of December was not a good day for Gerhard Franz of the 3. *Kompanie*. The I Battalion had been ordered to move back over the Ambleve crossing and set up defensive positions on the south bank. During the day Gerhard was severely wounded and he had to be evacuated. The medical personnel began to move Gerhard in an armoured ambulance, but this came under enemy attack and it got stuck in a riverbed. Gerhard's *Kameraden* from the 3. *Kompanie* came to his aid and took him across the river in a dingy. This was the end of Gerhard Franz's war and the start of a twenty-two month period spent in various hospitals. Seventeen of these months were spent as a prisoner of war. In captivity all of his possessions were lost, including his soldbuch, which meant that he was nameless. A very dangerous position to be in after the surrender!

The defensive positions were maintained throughout the 23rd and 24th of December against enemy artillery fire. It was on the 25th of December that Peiper's men reached the lines of *KG* Hansen. They had spent the last two days moving through enemy lines. The 5th Panzer Army continued their pushes westwards, but Bastogne was becoming the focus of concern as the German advance slowed. The 7th Army's advance all but stopped on this day.

A Change in Orders for the 3. *Kompanie*

The 26th saw heavier attacks by the enemy on the ground and in the air. The I Battalion of the *LAH* suffered heavy assaults, which were fended off with the help of the Jagdpanzers. The 5th Panzer Army began to be pushed back as did the 7th Army. Orders were received that would send the *LAH* to the south to assist in the defeat of the enemy at Bastogne. Patton's U.S. 3rd Army had punched a path through to Bastogne during this day and the threat that this presented for the Germans had to be dealt with.

Over the following two days the forces of the *LAH* had to disengage from the enemy and get ready for the moves south. The infantry elements of the division assembled east of Vielsalm where they were relieved by Volksgrenadier divisions. All movement had to be done during the hours of darkness.

As the disengagement was taking place, the 3. *Kompanie*'s Günther Junker received a further more serious wound. He suffered a severe bullet wound in one of his lungs. He was moved to a rear area field hospital. It was whilst in this hospital that the Americans arrived and took the occupants prisoner. There were, however, twelve German soldiers who were too badly wounded to be moved. Günther Junker witnessed the shooting of these twelve wounded German soldiers by the Americans! In captivity, Günther had all of his personal effects stolen. He stated that the Germans expected this sort of behaviour from the Russian soldiers, but they were surprised to be robbed by American soldiers. Countless German veterans recount having their possessions stolen by the Americans and nothing was sacred; everything from pens to watches and wedding rings were taken. As one German Veteran recalled, 'we were at war with gangsters'!

CHAPTER SEVENTEEN

OPERATION 'WACHT AM RHEIN' PART TWO: THE PUSH SOUTH

The 28th of December would see most of the *LAH*, including the 1st Regiment, leave the Vielsalm area and transfer to Bastogne. The new area stretched from Arloncourt, Longvilly, Schimpach and Harzy. This area was roughly three to five kilometres east of Bastogne. By this stage in the German offensive, Bastogne had become the central key town for both sides. This town controlled a major road junction and it was sucking in ever increasing numbers of German and American soldiers. The fighting was intensive with the Germans trying to sever the American corridor that had been opened up from the southwest. The lack of German reserves was showing and the decision to move the *LAH* was not taken lightly. The fact that the decision was taken is an indication of the importance of Bastogne to the Germans.

On the 29th of December the *LAH* were divided into two separate *Kampfgruppes* and placed under a newly formed Army Group Lüttwitz. One *Kampfgruppe* was commanded by *Sturmbannführer* Werner Poetschke and was ordered to attack in the northern part of their area. *Obersturmbannführer* Max Hansen had command of the second *Kampfgruppe*, which still contained the 3. *Kompanie*. This *Kampfgruppe* would fight in the southern part of the *LAH*'s area. *Kampfgruppe* Hansen had the task of forming up in Lutremange, south east of Bastogne. They were then to move on Villers La Bonne Eau, slightly southwest and then reach the main Bastogne to Martelange road. *Kampfgruppe* Poetschke would also have to attack the main road, only they would be fighting to the north. The purpose of these actions was to push westwards and link with elements of the 3rd Panzer Grenadier Division and the Führer Begleit Brigade, thereby cutting the American corridor to Bastogne. The attack would start the following day.

The *LAH* Pushes Towards Bastogne

The attack was timed for 06:25 a.m. on the 30th of December, but whilst the men waited to jump-off, some of their targets were occupied by elements of American Infantry Regiments. Villers La Bonne Eau was taken by the U.S. 134th Infantry Regiment. The attack did move out at the planned time with very little artillery support. Later that day Villers La Bonne Eau was taken by the Germans against fierce enemy resistance. The advance pushed on but finally stalled just short of the main Bastogne to Martelange road. Extensive enemy artillery fire and an infantry attack prevented any further movements westwards. The captured positions were held during the night.

A renewed push was put in on the 31st of December and for a short period the main road was reached. However, elements of four different U.S. Divisions counter attacked and regained the area lost to the Germans. Both sides maintained the ferocity of the fighting in this area. The Americans tried further pushes on the first day of January 1945, but the *LAH* held firm. The troops on the ground were witness to the massive commitment of Luftwaffe planes during the day, but the only result was limited losses for the Allies and at least 20% losses for the Luftwaffe. The positions on the ground were held throughout the 2nd and 3rd of January 1945.

The 4th of January saw a further attempted push by *Kampfgruppe* Hansen and Poetschke towards the Bastogne to Martelange road. They were facing the U.S. 6th Armoured Division and a fierce armoured battle ensued. The Americans came out of this engagement worse off and knocked out enemy tanks littered the area. The U.S. General Patton issued a notable statement on this day, commenting that, 'we can still lose the war'. The 12th SS and 9th SS Panzer Divisions had been moved into the Bastogne area and they began their attempts to hit the enemy held positions from the northeast.

The End of the *LAH*'s Participation in the Ardennes Offensive

The 5th and 6th of January would see further attempts to sever the main road, but with no success. Elsewhere however, the combined efforts of the American and

British forces were making significant gains in the northern and southern flanks of the German held area. The 7th and 8th would see strong enemy attacks as they started their moves to encircle and cut-off the German forces in various areas. Against this backdrop, the *LAH* and other divisions were ordered to withdraw. The *LAH* were to start withdrawing on the 10th of January 1945 and move to an area near St. Vith. This disengagement took place between the 10th-12th of January.

From the 12th to the 14th of January, the bulk of the *LAH*, along with other German divisions, were moved from the St. Vith area towards Blankenheim. Some elements remained behind and formed a new *Kampfgruppe*. This *Kampfgruppe* fought a short unsuccessful engagement. Back with the main *LAH* forces the situation was assessed. Around the middle of January 1945, the 1st Panzergrenadier Regiment *LAH* had 120 men left. A normal fully established German *Kompanie* would have 150 men in its' ranks! This situation gives an excellent example of the ferocity of the recent fighting and the toll that this fighting took upon the German armed forces. The total losses during this operation were put at around 68,000 for the Allies and 80,000 for the Germans. The Allies had the ability to replace their losses, but the Germans had all but exhausted their available manpower and equipment, and also oil and ammunition for the artillery.

Why had the Offensive Failed

An assessment of the objectives in the aftermath can draw the following conclusions. The relevant army commanders expressed severe reservations with their allotted tasks. They felt that the objectives were not achievable given the present state of the German Army and the strength of the Allies. Adolf Hitler had assembled a huge number of men and materials, but this had been compressed into a relatively small area. This presented heavy congestion that would slow the rate of advance, speed was one of the key parts of the plan. The domination of the air by the Allies was removed due to the bad weather, but that quickly changed and the Allies succeeded in damaging the vital German supply lines. Once the Allies got over the initial surprise they quickly initiated a response that ultimately stopped the German offensive. The final assessment of the offensive was summed up quite well by the *LAH*'s old commander, Sepp Dietrich. In 1946 he stated, 'I had merely to cross a river, capture Brussels and then go on and take the port of Antwerp; And all this in the worst months of the year – December, January, February – through countryside where snow was waist deep and there wasn't room to deploy four tanks abreast, let alone six armoured divisions; when it didn't get light until eight in the morning and was dark again at four in the afternoon; with divisions that had just been reformed and contained chiefly raw, untried recruits; and at Christmas time!'

The offensive had used the only reserves available to Germany. After this there was nothing left to counter the Allies in the west or to stand in the way of the Soviets in the east. That fact however, would not stop the *LAH* taking part in one final offensive. This time it was a return to the east.

Wilhelm Mohnke: Third Commander of the *LAH*

Date of birth: 15.03.11 SS Number: 15 541

Wilhelm Mohnke was born in Lübeck. He was one of the original 117 men sent to Berlin on the 17th of March 1933 to form the *Leibstandarte*. Within three months he had gained the rank of *Untersturmführer* and he was given command of the 3. *Kompanie* within the new formation, taking over from Emil Sator. When the *LAH* were expanded further in October 1933, he moved to the command of the 5. *Kompanie*, but he now held the rank of *Hauptsturmführer*. He remained with this *Kompanie* until July 1935 when he assumed command of the training *Kompanie* for an interim period.

During the opening stages of World War II, Mohnke took part in the Polish Campaign. He was awarded the Iron Cross Second Class on the 29th of September 1939, and the First Class Iron Cross on the 8th of November 1939. During the campaign in the west in 1940, he assumed command of the II Battalion on the 28th of May 1940. He held the rank of *Sturmbannführer* at this stage. It was during the Balkan Campaign in early 1941 that Mohnke had a brush with death. He was severely wounded as the *LAH* moved through Bulgaria on the 6th of April. This wound removed him from front line service for over two years. During this time he was responsible for creating the *LAH*'s Panzer Abteilung, commanding the *LAH*'s Replacement Battalion and he also took part in a Regimental Commander's course in mid-1943. He also received the German Cross in Gold on the 26th of December 1941 and promotion to *Obersturmbannführer* on the 26th of June 1943.

The 15th of September 1943 seen Wilhelm Mohnke back in front line service as commander of the 26th SS Regiment within the newly formed 12th SS Panzer Division *Hitlerjugend*. He led this regiment during the intensive and costly Normandy battles in mid-1944. His 26th Regiment was all but annihilated during this fighting. It was also during this fighting that he was promoted to *Standarten-*

führer on the 31st of June 1944. He quickly followed this with the award of the Knight's Cross to the Iron Cross on the 11th of July 1944.

Mohnke was given command of the entire *LAH* on the 30th of August 1944 after 'Teddi' Wisch was wounded. Just prior to the Ardennes Offensive he was promoted to *Oberführer*. He led the *LAH* during the difficult battles in the west at the end of 1944. His recurrent illness would appear once more and during mid-January 1945 he was posted to the Führer Reserve and given the rank of *Brigadeführer* und *Generalmajor der Waffen-SS*. His replacement was Otto Kumm.

Wilhelm Mohnke would end the Second World War in Berlin as commander of the Reichs Chancellery. He was captured by the Russians and spent a difficult eleven-year spell of captivity in Russia until 1956. He survived his wartime wounds and also the difficulties of Russian captivity and managed to live up to August 2001.

CHAPTER EIGHTEEN

EASTWARDS AGAIN - HUNGARY PART ONE: THE GRAN BRIDGEHEAD

As mentioned previously, as the German Army began its fighting with the western Allies in Normandy in mid-1944, the Russians launched their summer offensive in the east. This offensive was targeted mainly against Army Group Centre and it succeeded in virtually destroying the central part of the German front line in the east during the remainder of 1944. With this success the Soviets forged further westwards and this worsening situation led to some of the German Allies changing sides. The first to go were the Rumanians and their departure further weakened the front line. The Hungarians were set to do the same, but a daring mission by Skorzeny and his men prevented this. Budapest itself however, was later surrounded and cut-off by the Russians.

This capital city was highly regarded by the Germans and a relief mission was ordered. Initially the 3rd and 5th SS Panzer Divisions took part in this during the first half of January 1945. Their thrusts met with little success however, against the massive Soviet forces. To add to this the Russians launched another major offensive overall. This was the start of the push towards Berlin and the Russians reached the southeast shore of Lake Balaton, which was south west of Budapest. It was determined that a counter-stroke was needed and the 6th SS Panzer Army was sent east to this area as part of these plans.

The LAH's third commander, Wilhelm Mohnke with the rank of *Standartenführer* and holder of the Knight's Cross. He would finish the war with the rank of *Brigadeführer und Generalmajor der Waffen-SS*. He was also the 3. Kompanie's second commander. (Author's collection)

Deception Plan and the Removal of the Cufftitles

In order to deceive the Soviets, an elaborate deception plan was set-up that showed the 1st SS Panzer Division moving throughout Germany. They first had to disengage from their positions in the west and regroup in Germany. This movement took place between mid-January and the early part of February 1945. The assembly area in Germany was around the Bonn and Cologne areas. From here the elements of the Division were sent south through Germany and then onto Austria and finally onto Raab in northern Hungary, situated around 100 kilometres south east of Vienna. Part of the deception plan stated that the men of the *LAH* had to remove their cufftitles from their tunics.

They began arriving at the start of January and no time was wasted in training for the forthcoming action. The replacements at this stage were not of the quality that the Waffen-SS were used to. Very little is known about the 3. *Kompanie* at this stage other than the fact that they were rebuilt after the Ardennes in preparation for the operation in Hungary.

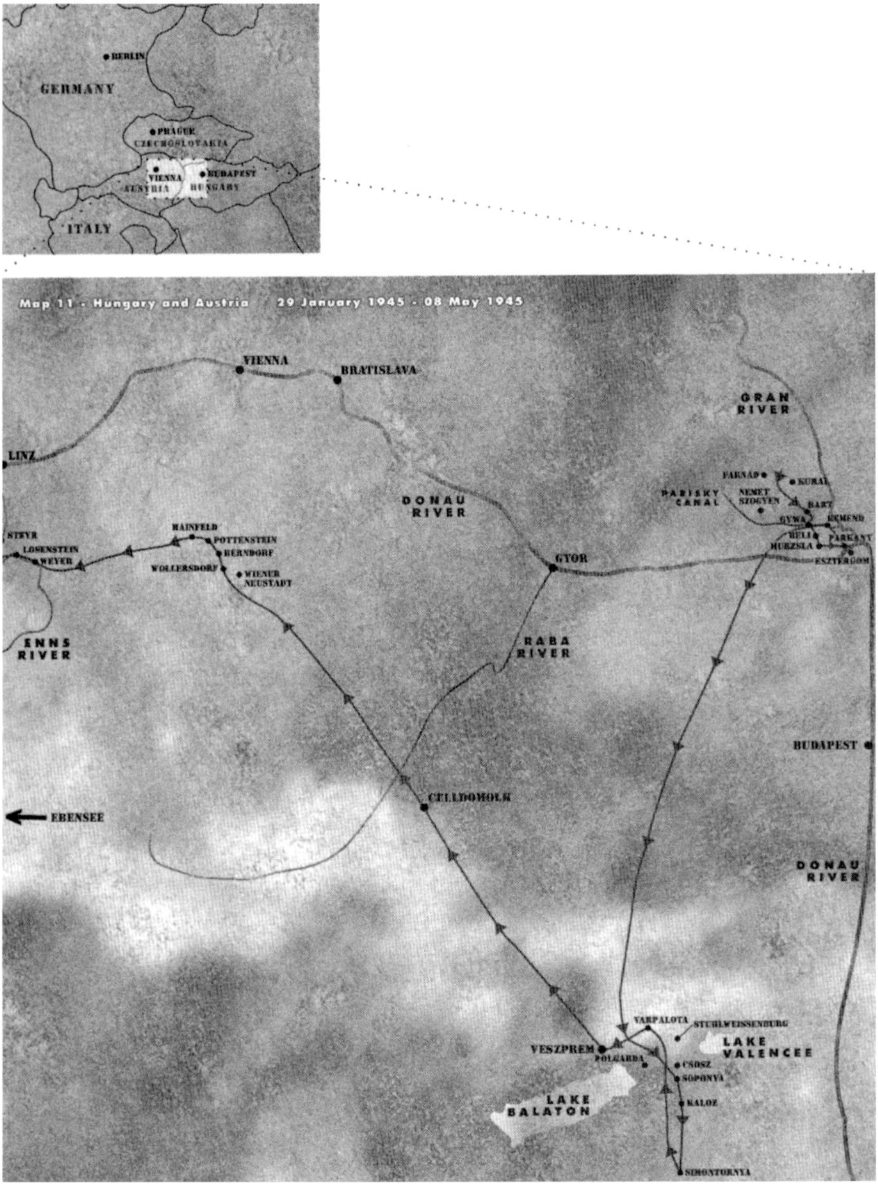
BERLIN
GERMANY
PRAGUE
CZECHOSLOVAKIA
VIENNA
BUDAPEST
AUSTRIA
HUNGARY
ITALY
Map 11 - Hungary and Austria 29 January 1945 - 08 May 1945
VIENNA
BRATISLAVA
LINZ
GRAN RIVER
FARNAD
KURAL
PARISKY CANAL
NEMET SZOGYEN
BART
GYWA
KEMEND
BELI
PARKANY
HURZSLA
ESZTERGOM
DONAU RIVER
STEYR
LOSENSTEIN
WEYER
HAINFELD
POTTENSTEIN
BERNDORF
WOLLERSDORF
WIENER NEUSTADT
GYOR
ENNS RIVER
RABA RIVER
BUDAPEST
CELLDOMOLK
EBENSEE
DONAU RIVER
VARPALOTA
STUHLWEISSENBURG
VESZPREM
POLGARDA
LAKE VALENCEE
CSOSZ
SOPONYA
KALOZ
LAKE BALATON
SIMONTORNYA

Hungary Map

The Enemy Positions in Hungary

As the *LAH* were conducting their moves and training, the Soviet pushes had been temporarily checked. The Russians held an area running from Karva on the Danube, through Kurt on the Parizsky Canal up to Bart and ending at Csata on the Gran River. These positions were north west of Budapest and became known as the Gran Bridgehead. It was into this area that the *LAH* would attack. Their area of responsibility was between Bart and Nemet Szogyen. They faced the Russian 7th Guards Army. The *LAH*'s line of attack was over the Parizsky Canal at Gwya, swing to the southeast and move into Parkany on the Danube River.

The 3. *Kompanie*'s Situation: February 1945

For this attack the *LAH* was divided into two groups. The bulk of the infantry, including the 3. *Kompanie*, were once again under the overall command of *Standartenführer* Max Hansen. The second group consisted of the armoured elements of the *LAH* and they were placed under the command of *Obersturmbannführer* Jochen Peiper. On the 16th of February 1945 Infantry Group Hansen assembled north of Kural. An early thaw had arrived which reduced the area to a muddy terrain. The attack began the following day with the *LAH* moving out behind the 46th Infantry Division. The 3. *Kompanie* Commander at this stage was *Oberscharführer* Reichel.

The Move to the Parizsky Canal

The attack began at 04:45 a.m. on the 17th of February and Peiper's group led the way. They ran into stiff Russian defenses. Peiper sent out the Tiger II Bs (King Tigers) against these defenses and throughout the day they pushed forwards. Infantry Group Hansen supported these moves. By early evening the *LAH* had reached Gywa on the Parizsky Canal where Infantry Group Hansen managed to set up a crossing and a small bridgehead later that night. This bridgehead was expanded during the morning of the 18th of February and with this Peiper's tanks crossed the canal and pushed to the south. By the end of the day advances had reached Murzsla, about eight kilometres south of Gywa. The positions were held and the push would resume the following day to the east towards Parkany, close to where the Gran and Danube Rivers meet.

Objective: Parkany

The push into Parkany and Nana, which is situated slightly to the north west of Parkany, began in earnest during the 19th of February. The panzers moved towards the town against stiff resistance, including aerial attacks by fighter-bombers. Infantry Group Hansen sent some elements of the infantry into Beli. It is not detailed in the *LAH*'s official history as to what individual *Kompanie*s attacked Beli. They succeeded in taking the town against enemy infantry supported by T-34s. Parkany was captured during the 19th of February.

A Move Slightly North to the Gran River

With the capture of Parkany, together with the attacks of other German divisions, the enemy held territory had been constricted into an area running from Kemend through to Csata. Up to this point the *LAH*, together with other divisions, had successfully moved out of their jumping off points and in two days they had crossed the Parizsky Canal and swept into Parkany. All that was left to do was to push to the north along the Gran River and eliminate the remaining enemy forces. This part of the attack ran into heavy Soviet defenses during the 20th of February. Kemend was reached, but a stop was ordered. The enemy moved strong forces into the Gran River area in order to halt the German successes. This situation remained throughout the 20th and 21st of February.

The push into these enemy positions made slow progress, when it did begin, as the *LAH*'s positions were pounded by Soviet artillery, tank and aerial attacks. Losses mounted, but by the end of the 23rd of February the town of Kemend was reached. The capture of this town was conducted during the 24th and included the men of Infantry Group Hansen. The fighting was hard with house-to-house fighting enduring for most of the day. By the end of the day the town was in German hands. With this, the operation to clear the Gran Bridgehead was complete.

Although the *LAH* and the 12th SS Panzer Division *HJ* had been successful, the use of them in this attack was criticised by the *LAH*'s new commander, *Brigadeführer* Otto Kumm. He knew that the *LAH* had not been given sufficient time to recover from the Ardennes fighting. The replacements sent before the Ardennes were poorly trained and their incorporation only helped to weaken the combat effectiveness of the 1st SS Panzer Division. The replacements sent after the Ardennes made this situation even worse. This new attack resulted in further losses of more than one thousand men. The situation for the *LAH* was growing bleak. They were a mere fraction of their usual quality. To add to their problems the Russians now knew of their presence in the area. The enemy anticipated their next moves and they prepared defenses accordingly.

CHAPTER NINETEEN

HUNGARY PART TWO: THE PLATTENSEE OFFENSIVE

The *LAH* were pulled out of the Gran area on the 25th of February 1945 and sent southwest, towards Lake Plattensee. Their new objective was to thrust to the south between Plattensee and Velenczesee. They would have the I *Kavalleriekorps* to their right and the II and III SS *Panzerkorps* to their left. The I SS *Panzerkorps* were in between these two formations, with the *LAH* responsible for the easterly most flank. The *LAH* themselves would be moving alongside the Sarviz Canal. The objective was an area of high ground close to Funfkirchen. They would be fighting against elements of the 3rd Ukrainian Front. The *LAH* were assembled into an area between Veszprem and Varpalota. These moves were conducted during the first five days of March 1945. Although the situation was far from favourable, in all respects, orders had to be followed. The attack was to start on the 6th of March 1945.

The weather situation in the few days before the attack was another factor that added to the worries for the men of the *LAH*. The temperature had risen enough for a thaw to begin. This reduced the area to a sea of 'bottomless roads'. This severely delayed the deployment of the entire 6th SS Panzer Army so that by the time of the start of the attack, only some elements were in place. It was known that the enemy facing them was strong. But there was no time to wait on the rest of the Divisions, the men of the *LAH* moved into the attack against a strong opponent, without adequate support.

The jumping off area was halfway between Polgardi and Csosz. The troops moved out at 04:30 a.m. with no covering artillery fire due to a shortage of ammunition. The first target was the town of Soponya, situated to the south of Csosz. This town was reached and portions of it were captured by the evening of the 6th of March 1945. The attack had been made against very strong enemy resistance. A brief lull ensued during the night, but on the 7th of March the push continued. By the end of this second day the town of Kaloz was captured. The remaining sectors of Soponya were also captured.

During the 8th and 9th of March, the forward moves continued towards the city of Simontornya situated on the Sio River. The enemy were putting up ever increasing resistance and the *LAH* were subjected to artillery, tank and mortar fire on route. The main Simontornya to Kaloz road was the *LAH*'s supply route and this was also under Russian artillery fire. The casualties for the *LAH* rose steadily. Simontornya was important to the Russians as a staging point for a counter-stroke against the advancing Germans. They defended it accordingly and many losses to the infantry and the vital panzers were endured as the *LAH* inched towards this objective throughout the 10th of March.

On the 11th of March 1945 the main push into Simontornya was launched. It was met with heavy enemy artillery fire that decimated the infantry ranks. The *LAH* fought tenaciously, and with the help of the 23rd Panzer Division, bridgeheads were established over the Sio River and the Sarviz Canal. The city was captured during the 12th of March by the *LAH*, but the enemy remained in the southern side of the city. They continued to pound the *LAH*'s positions with artillery fire and aircraft attacks. Attempts to expand the Sio Bridgehead at the city were pursued during the 13th of March, but events elsewhere would dictate the next moves.

A Worsening Situation: The Russian Push Towards Vienna

A worrying development had occurred on the eastern side of the Sarviz Canal. The attack of the II SS *Panzerkorps*, which included the 2nd and 9th SS Panzer Divisions, had come up against very strong enemy defenses. These enemy defenses had been recently constructed and this defensive wall considerably slowed the progress of these units. This left the *LAH*'s eastern flank exposed. In addition to this, the Russians had broken through around the Velenczesee area. What loomed on the horizon for the entire 6th SS Panzer Army and the III *Panzerkorps* was encirclement as the Russians moved towards the Austrian capital of Vienna.

Adolf Hitler had ordered the continued pursuit of the German attack. However, the Army and Korps Commanders considered the halting of the attack as the only option. Local orders were drawn up that would see the *LAH*, together with the rest of the divisions, withdraw back north to the Stuhlweissenburg area. Whilst the options were being considered, the fighting continued over the 14th and 15th of March. Elements of the 1st Panzergrenadier Regiment *LAH* were on the southern bank engaging the Russian soldiers. It is not detailed what *Kompanie*s were on the southern bank during this time. Throughout the 15th, 16th and 17th of March 1945, the Soviets were pushing ever-increasing forces against the II SS *Panzerkorps* area. The enemy was held, but it was clear that this holding action could not be maintained. Higher up the chain of command orders were being drawn up that detailed a counter move against the Russians in that area!

Over the next two days the Soviet push continued and the withdrawal of the *LAH* began. The developments in the area north of Stuhlweissenburg actually removed the plans for the attack eastwards. Instead a new attack directly north into the lead Soviet forces was called for. It took two days for Hitler to authorise these moves. This two-day delay gave the enemy a further valuable advantage over the Germans. The withdrawal of the *LAH* north was conducted during the 18th and 19th of March. As this was taking place, the Soviets had captured Csar, east of Varpalota. They were getting closer to cutting the Germans off between the Plattensee and the Velenczesee. On the 19th of March elements of the 1st Panzergrenadier Regiment engaged in fighting as they reached their objectives, which were around Varpalota. Further elements of the *LAH* occupied Inota. Various attacks were conducted throughout the day. The overall situation can be regarded as confused and changing rapidly. *Oberscharführer* Reichel was replaced as the 3. *Kompanie* commander during March 1945 by *Untersturmführer* Leopold Ertl.

Oberscharführer Reichel: Fourteenth Commander of the 3. *Kompanie*

There is no information available on this commander, other than the fact that he was not killed. It can therefore be determined that he was wounded badly enough to be removed as the 3. *Kompanie*'s commander. The situation at this time must have been very bad if an *Oberscharführer* was in command of the *Kompanie*!

The Withdrawal of the *LAH* and the Moves Westwards

The Soviets pushed their 6th Guards Tank Army into the area held by the *LAH*. This not only blunted the *LAH*'s attack plans, but it put their positions under a severe threat. The orders for the 21st of March were to hold the Inota area against these attacks. This was impossible and the enemy not only occupied Inota, but they also took control of Varpalota. The remaining *LAH* forces fought through the Russians and onto the Veszprem area to the southwest. This was to avoid encirclement and it also signalled the beginning of the withdrawal movements by the *LAH*.

The 22nd of March saw elements of the 1st Panzergrenadier Regiment fighting on the right flank of the *LAH*'s positions. They were encircled near Osku, almost mid-way between Varpalota and Veszprem. *Brigadeführer* Otto Kumm was with this group. The rest of the *LAH* were fighting further north. These two separate groups had to fight through strong enemy tank and infantry forces in order to reach Veszprem. The group from the 1st Panzergrenadier Regiment moved from Veszprem, north towards Kislod. It was here that they temporarily stopped the local advances of the Russians. Renewed attacks by the Russians overwhelmed the *LAH* and the rest of the German forces. The enemy were pushing through in large numbers and attempting to cut-off the various elements of Germany's forces. This fate happened to the infantry group of the *LAH* on the 26th of March. They had to fight through the enemy held lines in order to reach their own lines. The situation was changing rapidly and not in the favour of the Germans. A request to withdraw to a better line was turned down. This period in the *LAH*'s history is noted for the severe weakening of the individual *Kompanie*s and Battalions. With this, it was impossible to mount effective resistance against the massive concentration of enemy forces. It is known that *Untersturmführer* Leopold Ertl was killed in March 1945 whilst serving with the 3. *Kompanie*. His replacement was *Untersturmführer* Heinz Scheifes.

Leopold Ertl: Fifteenth Commander of the 3. *Kompanie*

There is no information on this officer.

Hitler's 'Cufftitle Order'

With the rapidly worsening situation, Hitler became despondent with what he considered as the failure of the Waffen-SS Divisions in their duty. It was from this that the order was issued directly from Adolf Hilter for all of the Waffen-SS Divisions, within the 6th SS *Panzerarmee*, to remove their cufftitles. Dietrich received the order on the morning of the 27th of March 1945. After reading the message and taking some time to consider the order, Dietrich stated that not one cufftitle was to be removed and that the order was not to be passed down the line. It is worth remembering that the majority of the cufftitles had been removed whilst en route to Hungary as part of the German deception plan.

The Russian Tidal Wave Overwhelms the *LAH*

It was also during the 27th that the Soviets reached the Raab River and put several bridgeheads across it. On this day the remaining elements of the 1st Panzergrenadier Regiment were northwest of Celldomolk. They were pushed towards the Raab and they managed to hold a crossing at Kleinzell, where the rest of the *LAH* moved over the river. One report from this time states that the trench strength of the 1st Panzergrenadier Regiment was only ninety men!

The move westwards by the *LAH* continued over the next few days. The Russians succeeded in pushing towards the German border and they crossed it in some areas. Their rate of advance was fast and their lead elements were ahead of the retreating soldiers of the 1st SS Panzer Division and the rest of the 6th SS Panzer Army. The 1st Panzergrenadier Regiment group's route of withdrawal, up to the end of March 1945, was from Nikitsch to the south of Wiener Neustadt. It was at this location that the *LAH* found themselves at the start of April. They were forced out of this city by a relentless enemy push towards Vienna. The 1st Panzergrenadier Regiment group moved back towards Wollersdorf, onto Oberpiesting and then Berndorf and Pottenstein. Constant relentless enemy attacks were endured during this time. These attacks were launched night and day and came from infantry, tanks and the air. Berndorf and Pottenstein came under enemy pressure towards the end of the first week of April 1945. The 1st Panzergrenadier Regiment group held this area against these attacks for six days.

Gerhard Dilling, at that time serving with the 2. *Kompanie*, states that he helped to defend the Pottenstein area against the Russian attacks. He recalled that the 3. *Kompanie* were on the left and the 1. *Kompanie* were on the right. He also recalled that the *LAH* were suffering a lot of losses at this time.

In other areas the Russians completed their capture of Vienna. The American 3rd Army, under Patton, had reached Nuremburg. The possibility of a fight on two fronts was looming for the men of the *LAH*. President Franklin D. Roosevelt died also, and amongst the troops on the ground, there was an expectation that this could alter the American prosecution of the war.

Meanwhile, the Russians were pushing their forces through in many areas. The 1st Panzergrenadier Regiment's positions were treated to a relatively quiet period. The situation was getting critical and to avoid encirclement, the 1st Panzergrenadier Regiment and the rest of the *LAH* were ordered south around the 23rd of April 1945. Gerhard Dilling recalled that they began their withdrawal on the 24th of April. The order to withdraw did not reach all of the men of the 3. *Kompanie*. Some of them were part of a group of around sixty *LAH* men captured. They were last seen being loaded onto an enemy train for movement east, most of them would not survive Russian captivity. The enemy was everywhere and the *LAH* did not have the resources to reverse this situation and help their *Kameraden*. The 3. *Kompanie* had around thirty men who managed to evade capture and together with the remnants of the 1. *Kompanie* they moved westwards.

It was during April that *Untersturmführer* Heinz Scheifes of the 3. *Kompanie* was killed. His replacement was *Untersturmführer* Gerhard Dilling. They moved back through Weissenbach, Hainfeld and onto Furth. By the end of April they were at Kleinzell Fels. These moves continued on from Kleinzell through Reisalpe and onto Lilienfeld, where motorised transport was waiting for them.

Heinz Scheifes: Sixteenth Commander of the 3. *Kompanie*

Date of birth: 05.01.24 *SS number: 476 144*

The only information available on this officer is the fact that he served with the 2nd SS Division *Das Reich* as an *Untersturmführer* during June 1944.

Critical Developments for the *LAH*

The bigger picture was developing fast in the final stages of the Second World War. The Führer of Germany, Adolf Hitler, made his decision to commit suicide in the bunker of the Reichs Chancellery in Berlin. In his Last Will he appointed his successor as Admiral Dönitz. The men at the front heard of this news either by radio or through their commanders. They remained loyal to the orders of the 1st Panzergrenadier Regiment Commander, Max Hansen. They were to protect their present positions and the population against the Russians.

One other major development that directly affected the remaining men of the *LAH*, was the news that the Enns River would form a demarcation line with the Americans. This would provide the focus point for the men in the last few days of the war. Orders were issued that would withdraw the men bit-by-bit in reverse order, meaning that the supply troops would withdraw followed by the infantry and then the armoured troops. During the first week of May 1945 the individual *Kompanie*s and men awaited their turn to withdraw. The Enns River was around 150 miles west of their present positions. The remnants of the *LAH* made their way towards the river, mainly at Altenmarkt. The thought in everyone's mind, what was to come next? Gerhard Dilling states that he commanded the remnants of the 3. *Kompanie* and the 1. *Kompanie* during the last week of the war.

Gerhard Dilling: The Seventeenth Commander of the 3. *Kompanie*

Gerhard Dilling volunteered for the Waffen-SS on the 1st of April 1942, where he took on the role of a radio operator/signaller. As stated previously, he joined the 3. *Kompanie* on the 12th of July 1942. He stayed with them until 1944 and in this time he took part in the battles of Kharkov, Kursk, into Italy and back to Russia in late 1943. He was sent to the *SS-Junkerschule* in Prague from April until December 1944. At the end of March 1945 he re-joined the 1st Panzergrenadier Regiment of the *LAH*, when he served as an *Untersturmführer* and Platoon Leader in the 2. *Kompanie*. He fought alongside the 3. *Kompanie* and the 1. *Kompanie* as the I Battalion retreated back through Hungary and Austria during April 1945. In the first week of May 1945, he took command of the remnants of the 3. *Kompanie*. He stayed with them until they reached the Enns River on the 10th of May 1945. He entered American captivity and stayed there until the end of February 1948. Like many of his *Kameraden*, many of his personal effects were stolen, including photographs of him as an *Untersturmführer*. He was awarded the following medals whilst with the 3. *Kompanie*; Iron Cross First Class, Iron Cross Second Class, Close Combat Clasp, Panzer Assault Badge and the Wound Badge. He was one of only two surviving former 3. *Kompanie* commanders alive at the time of the writing of this book.

The German Surrender and the Final Days of the War

On the 7th of May the general surrender of the German forces was signed at Reims. The *LAH* had to reach the Enns by the 9th of May. It was on the 9th of May that the

Gerhard Dilling photographed in November 1943 as an *SS-Junker*, or Officer Candidate (this had the equivalent rank of *Unterscharführer*). This photograph was taken at a time when Dilling was serving with the 3. Kompanie. Dilling would command the remnants of the 3. Kompanie in the last week of the war, and up until the LAH's surrender. He is seen wearing the Second Class Iron Cross, the Tank Assault Badge and the Hitler Youth Badge. (Gerhard Dilling)

Russians added their signatures to the surrender, thereby bringing the war in Europe to a close. Things were not at an end for the remaining men of the 3. *Kompanie*, nor the rest of the *LAH*.

Crossing the Enns River and Captivity

The men of the 1st SS Panzer Division had difficulty right to the end. All routes west were jammed with civilians and other people trying to escape the clutches of the Russians. The remainder of the I Battalion of the 1st Panzergrenadier Regiment, now under *Sturmbannführer* Wandt, finally crossed the Enns River south of Steyr. They had started off at Weyer and then they moved to Losenstein; they crossed close to Ternberg. The Battalion Commander had ordered that the men go onto captivity with the same high esteem they began with. The men of the I Battalion crossed the river wearing their steel helmets and fully buttoned up collars. They felt proud that they had served the Fatherland well. Gerhard Dilling recalled that the remaining men of the 3. *Kompanie* entered American captivity on the 10th of May 1945.

The men of the 3. *Kompanie* had been in existence for twelve years. Their ranks had seen some remarkable soldiers; Men such as Hinrich Schuldt, Hans-Joachim Schiller, Heinrich Springer and Wilhelm Mohnke. The 3. *Kompanie Kameraden* expected to be treated as honourable soldiers by their victorious western enemies, whom they had fought against on many occasions. They belonged to an elite formation and felt that they had earned the respect of their former enemy. The truth however, was a far cry from this expectation.

Otto Kumm: Last Commander of the *LAH*

Date of birth: 01.10.09 SS Number: 18 727

Otto Kumm was born in Hamburg. He joined the SS on the 1st of June 1934 as part of the *Germania Standarte*. Within three months he was holding the rank of *Untersturmführer* and command of the 2. *Kompanie* within *Germania*, he later moved to the command of the 4. *Kompanie*. In 1936 he was promoted to *Hauptsturmführer* and given command of the 2. *Kompanie* within the *Deutschland Standarte*. Eighteen months later he transferred to the *Der Führer Standarte*. Just prior to the start of the western campaign in 1940 he attended a Battalion Commanders course. He assumed command of the III Battalion of the *Der Führer Standarte* on the 13th of May 1940 and led this Battalion during the subsequent fighting. He received the Second Class Iron Cross on the 30th of May 1940 and the First Class Iron Cross on the 30th of June. He was also promoted to *Sturmbannführer*.

It was during the battles in Russia during 1941 that Otto Kumm would show his abilities. He is credited with helping to forge the excellent reputation that the 2nd SS Panzer Division *Das Reich* gained. He commanded the *Der Führer Standarte* during the opening stages of Barbarossa. He would gain promotion to *Obersturmbannführer*, receive the German Cross in Gold on the 1st of December 1941 and also the Knight's Cross to the Iron Cross on the 16th of February 1942. *Das Reich* was back in Russia and fought alongside the *LAH* at Kharkov. It was for the *Der Führer Standarte*'s actions during this battle that Otto Kumm received the Oakleaves to the Knight's Cross on the 6th of April 1943. He was promoted to *Standartenführer* in the same month.

He was attached to the 7th SS-Gebirgs Division *Prinz Eugen* during mid-1943 and he remained with that Division until the 1st of February 1944. It was on this date that he assumed command of *Prinz Eugen* from Arthur Phleps. He held the rank of *Oberführer* by that stage and he led the Division in the very difficult

The LAH's last commander, Otto Kumm, holding the rank of *Brigadeführer und Generalmajor der Waffen-SS*. He is also seen wearing the Swords and Oakleaves to the Knight's Cross, which he received on the twelfth anniversary of the forming of the LAH, March 17, 1945. (Otto Kumm)

fighting against partisan forces in Yugoslavia. Towards the end of 1944 he was promoted to *Brigadeführer* und *Generalmajor der Waffen-SS*.

His last command was that of the 1st SS Panzer Division *Leibstandarte* Adolf Hitler, which he started on the 15th of February 1945, replacing Wilhelm Mohnke. Just over one month later, he was awarded the Swords and Oakleaves to the Knight's Cross for his leadership of the *Prinz Eugen* Division. The 7th SS-Gebirgs Division had been transformed into a first class formation under his leadership. The *LSSAH* gained a vastly experienced and very capable commander when Otto Kumm took over. He can be regarded as one of the foremost commanders within the ranks of the Waffen-SS, if not the German Army as a whole. The situation in early 1945 was not one that any single commander could have transformed. Otto Kumm led the *LSSAH* in the final bitter fighting in Hungary and Austria up until the surrender in May 1945. He survived the war and was still alive at the time of the writing of this book.

Max Hansen, holding the rank of *Sturmbannführer*. He finished the war with the rank of *Standartenführer* and holder of the Oakleaves to the Knight's Cross. His many other awards can be clearly seen. This much-respected officer commanded the LAH's I Battalion and later the 1st Panzergrenadier Regiment. (Justin Horgan)

Max Hansen: Last Commander of the 1st Panzergrenadier Regiment

Date of birth: 31.07.08 *SS Number: 27 813*

Max Hansen was born in Niebüll, Holstein. He was an early member of the SS and joined the *LAH*'s 1. *Kompanie* in 1933. By 1934 he was holding the rank of *Scharführer*. There is no other information available on his pre-war year activities. He saw his first action with the SS in the campaign in Poland in 1939 where he received the Second Class Iron Cross. This was followed by participation in the fighting in the west during 1940 when he was awarded the First Class Iron Cross. He got command of the 14. *Kompanie* during July 1941, while the Germans were advancing into Russia. His next award was that of the German Cross in Gold on the 29th of December 1942. He was commander of the II Battalion of the 1st Regiment around this time and he was awarded the Knight's Cross to the Iron Cross on the 28th of March 1943. He stayed in command of the II Battalion until July 1944.

He had command of his own *Kampfgruppe* during the Ardennes Offensive in late 1944, which the 3. *Kompanie* were part of. He went on to command the 1st Panzergrenadier Regiment of the *LAH* in late 1945 and led the remnants of that regiment in the final difficult battles until the end of the war. It was during this time that he was awarded the Oakleaves to the Knight's Cross. He was a much-respected officer and was probably one of the *LAH*'s most capable leaders. He endured much in his time with the Waffen-SS. He was wounded no less than twelve times by the time hostilities ended! He was highly decorated also, and besides the awards listed above, he also held the Close Combat Clasp in Gold, the Infantry Assault Badge, the General Assault Badge and the Gold Wound Badge.

CHAPTER TWENTY

SURRENDER AND THE LEGACY OF WORLD WAR II

As mentioned previously, the men of the 3. *Kompanie*, 1st Panzergrenadier Regiment of the *LAH* crossed the Enns River in Austria at Ternberg. They drifted to the west in small groups until they were collected together in camps. They quickly learned the way of the Americans as they had all of their personal possessions taken from them. Everything from medals to watches and photographs were taken. Once in the camps the search began for the suspected war criminals that were wanted by the Allies. High on the American list were men from Peiper's *Kampfgruppe* that had taken part in the Malmedy crossroads incident. This was followed by anyone who had been involved in the concentration camps. Trials and sentencing followed for some of the *LAH*, an occurrence, which repeated itself throughout the late 1940s and 1950s as blame was apportioned for the causes of the conflict.

Victors Justice and the Hungerlagers

As these actions began to take place, the rest of the men of the former 1st SS Panzer Division started their life behind the wire enclosures of the detainment camps. It is known that some of the men from the I Battalion were held in Ebensee, but it is not detailed if any specific 3. *Kompanie* men were held there. This camp and various others such as Altheim and Mauerkirchen quickly became known as Hungerlager, or hunger camps by the men held there. They were fed meagre rations and many of the men, who had survived countless battles against worthy opponents, died from starvation. Around the end of October 1946 many of these camps were closed and the men transferred to camps in Germany. The treatment did not improve however, and the former soldiers of the Waffen-SS were subjected to the indignation of the Allied decision to brand them as war criminals. This removed further rights usually given to prisoners of war and no doubt resulted in further losses to the ranks of the former 1st SS Panzer Division *Leibstandarte Adolf Hitler*.

Civilian Life and Building a Future

Those who did survive the camps, not only in the west, but also in the east, came out of captivity and began to forge a new existence for themselves and their families. Part of the decision to regard them as criminals meant that they were prevented from claiming a pension. Therefore, many of them had to work beyond the normal expected time frame. The younger members were also subjected to this as they passed from youth into old age. Self-help groups were formed and many former *Kameraden* remained in contact. The division of Germany was another legacy of the war as the former Allies descended into a fifty-year 'cold-war'. Once this came to an end, some long lost *Kameraden* came into contact with one another.

At least two former members of the 3. *Kompanie* were discovered after the 'wall' came down in November 1989. These men were probably part of the group of 60 men captured during the retreat in April 1945. At the time of starting this work, there were nearly two dozen former members of the 3. *Kompanie* still alive. Unfortunately, at least two of the people that have made this book possible have died; they were Max Schmidt and Gerhard Franz. It is with the help of some of them that this work has been completed. I will leave it to Günther Junker, the former 3. *Kompanie Kameraden* who fought in the Ardennes Offensive, to have the last word on the 3. *Kompanie* after the war. He stated that there has been one thing that has kept them all together throughout all of their battles, surrender, hunger camps and alienation by their fellow countrymen; that is:

'Loyalty and Honour'.

APPENDICES

Appendix 1
The 3. Kompanie Officer List

Surname, Name	Rank	Rank at date listed
Sator, Emil	*Hauptsturmführer*	August 1933
Mohnke, Wilhelm	*Hauptsturmführer*	October 1933
Polewacz, Harry	*Oberscharführer*	
Stenwedel, Albert	*Scharführer*	
Lindner, Hinrich	*Scharführer*	
Scheide, Rudolf	*Scharführer*	
Schuldt, Hinrich	*Hauptsturmführer*	October 1934
Gross, Martin	*Untersturmführer*	
Streipart, Fritz	*Untersturmführer*	
Wichmann, Kurt	*Hauptsturmführer*	September 1939
Fisher, Franz	*Obersturmführer*	
Janssen, Karl-Wilhlem	*Untersturmführer*	
Schiller, Hans-Joachim	*Hauptsturmführer*	January 1940
Franz, ?	*Untersturmführer*	
von Wallfeldt, ?	*Untersturmführer*	
Witt, Franz	*Untersturmführer*	
Springer, Heinrich	*Obersturmführer*	August 1941
Schiller, Hans-Joachim	*Hauptsturmführer*	Early 1942
Stehr, Eberhard	*Untersturmführer*	
Gessner, Manfred	*Obersturmführer*	July 1942
Flocke, Hans	*Untersturmführer*	
Friese, Hans-Gert	*Untersturmführer*	
Froese, Erwin	*Untersturmführer*	
Hogele, Karl	*Untersturmführer*	
Dahlke, Hermann	*Untersturmführer*	March 1943
Zaag, Günther	*Untersturmführer*	July 1943
Huser, Ferdinand	*Untersturmführer*	October 1943
Kleist, Kurt	*Obersturmführer*	?
Maurer, Paul	*Hauptsturmführer*	April 1944
Harrer, Karl	*Hauptsturmführer*	July 1944
Griese, Wilhelm	*Hauptsturmführer*	December 1944
Reichel, ?	*Oberscharführer*	February 1945
Ertl, Leopold	*Untersturmführer*	March 1945
Scheifes, Heinz	*Untersturmführer*	March 1945
Dilling, Gerhard	*Untersturmführer*	May 1945

Appendix 2
The 3. Kompanie Casualty Lists

Please note that these lists do not cover all of the campaigns that the LAH were involved in and not all of the lists are complete. These lists were provided to the author by Max Schmidt during 2000. The author has also made additions, where the details are available.

Campaign 1: Poland

Name	**Date of Death or Injury**	**Location**
Oberscharführer Rudi Schiller	01.09.39	Nalepa
Rottenführer Werner Mohr	01.09.39	Nalepa
Rottenführer Kurt Schwertfeger	01.09.39	Nalepa
Obersturmführer Franz Fisher	03.09.39	Stolec
Rottenführer Kurt Michaelis	03.09.39	Stolec
SS Mann Kurt Berger	03.09.39	Stolec
SS Mann Willi Lange	03.09.39	Stolec
SS Mann Bruno Schmidt	03.09.39	Stolec
SS Mann Robert Bruning	07.09.39	Pabianice
SS Mann Adolf Thiede	08.09.39	Pabianice
SS Mann Mathias Frick	08.09.39	Pabianice
Sturmmann Hans Ellmerer	09.09.39	Nadarzyn
Sturmmann Werner Schonrock	10.09.39	Oltarzew
SS Mann Walter Boysnen	10.09.39	Oltarzew
Sturmmann Ernst Augustin	12.09.39	Pilaszkow
Sturmmann Ernst Bantow	12.09.39	Pilaszkow
SS Mann Siegfried Dreher	12.09.39	Pilaszkow
SS Mann Hans Nitzsche	12.09.39	Pilaszkow
SS Mann Erich Pfannkuchen	12.09.39	Pilaszkow
Untersturmführer Karl Wilhelm Janssen	14.09.39	Sochaczew
Sturmmann Heinrich Eggers	14.09.39	Sochaczew
SS Mann Harry Nehring	14.09.39	Sochaczew
Unterscharführer Erich Jadecke	14.09.39	Julianopol
Unterscharführer Otto Felleckner	16.09.39	Julianopol
Sturmmann Günther Kube	16.09.39	Julianopol
SS Mann Heinz Pioch	17.09.39	Trojanow
Rottenführer Willi Kutz	18.09.39	Sladow
SS Mann Otto Hohnke	23.09.39	Modlin
Rottenführer Hans Joachim Opelt	24.09.39	Modlin

Campaign 2: The West 1940

Untersturmführer Werner Linde	28.05.40	Wormhoudt
Rottenführer Herbert Sollmann	28.05.40	Wormhoudt
Sturmmann Ernst Lindenberg	28.05.40	Wormhoudt
SS Mann Bernhard Pietsch	28.05.40	Wormhoudt
SS Mann Fritz Frobel	29.05.40	Wormhoudt
SS Mann Theodor Noll	29.05.40	Wormhoudt
Strummann Erich Rokitta	31.05.40	Dunkirk

Rottenführer Gunther Kell	01.06.40	Dunkirk
Rottenführer Henry Peters	12.06.40	Ste. Aulde

Campaign 3: Greece

Untersturmführer Franz Witt	10.04.41	Vevi
Oberscharführer Georg Koch	10.04.41	Vevi
Rottenführer Eugen Brandhoff	10.04.41	Vevi
Scharführer Fritz List	11.04.41	Klidi
Sturmmann Helmut Fiuster	11.04.41	Klidi
Sturmmann Roderich Geserich	11.04.41	Klidi
Unterscharführer Siegfried Richter	12.04.41	Klidi
Rottenführer Johann Huntschel	12.04.41	Klidi
Sturmmann Arthur Lietz	12.04.41	Klidi
Sturmmann Friedrich Schumacher	12.04.41	Klidi
Unterscharführer Johann Ohlrogge	12.04.41	Vevi
SS Mann Karl Heinz Seller	12.04.41	Vevi
Sturmmann Werner Gotz	13.04.41	Klidi

Campaign 4: Russia

Hauptsturmführer Hans Joachim Schiller	31.07.41	Uman
Sturmmann Gehrken	15.10.41	Taganrog
Sturmmann Lippke	15.10.41	Taganrog
Sturmmann Schwillinsky	15.10.41	Taganrog
Sturmmann Steiner	15.10.41	Taganrog
SS Mann Mehnke	15.10.41	Taganrog
SS Mann Plotz	15.10.41	Taganrog
Sturmmann Erich Wildenstein	28.10.41	Rostov
Hauptsturmführer Heinrich Springer	21.11.41	Rostov

Campaign 5: Russia II

Untersturmführer Hans Gert Friese	12.02.43	Kharkov
SS Mann Alois Hausser	12.02.43	Oschgun
Obersturmführer Manfred Gessner	15.02.43	Nowo Bereka
Untersturmführer Hans Flocke	15.02.43	Nowo Bereka
Untersturmführer Erwin Froese	27.02.43	Poreskawaja
Untersturmführer Karl Hogele	27.02.43	Poreskawaja
SS Mann Claus Gronenberg	27.02.43	Poreskawaja
Obergrenadier Walter Ockel	27.02.43	Krasokorsk
Sturmmann Ernst Ruckner	11.03.43	Kharkov
SS Mann Heinrich Kauth	11.03.43	Kharkov
Untersturmführer Hermann Dahlke	05.07.43	Jakowlewo

Campaign 6: Russia III

Scharführer Willy Liebig	18.11.43	Kotscherowo
Unterscharführer Rudi Mahlkuch	29.11.43	Brussiloff
Obersturmführer Kurt Kleist	06.12.43	Shitomir
Sturmmann Waldemar Richert	06.12.43	Shitomir
SS Mann Walter Schuld	06.12.43	Sliptschizy
Oberscharführer Erich Ambrolat	07.12.43	Tortschin
Unterscharführer Hans Pospiech	07.12.43	Tschaikowka

Unterscharführer Helmut Schlog	21.12.43	Baljarka
SS Mann Harald Schminke	21.12.43	Baljarka
Sturmmann Adam Zimmermann	23.12.43	Peremoga
Sturmmann Rolf Franke	24.12.43	Dolgie Polga
Untersturmführer Ferdinand Huser	April 1944	Losaicz
Campaign 7: Normandy		
Hauptsturmführer Paul Maurer	05.07.44	Caen area
SS Mann Gerhard Franz	05.07.44	Caen area
Campaign 8: Ardennes		
Hauptsturmführer Wilhelm Griese	18.12.44	Poteuax
SS Mann Gerhard Franz	23.12.44	Ambleve R.
SS Mann Günther Junker	26.12.44	Vielsalm
Campaign 9: Hungary/Austria		
Oberscharführer Reichel	March 1945	Hungary
Untersturmführer Leopold Ertl	March 1945	Hungary
Untersturmführer Heinz Scheifes	April 1945	Austria

In addition to the above listed casualties, it is known that an *Untersturmführer* Karl Hoffrichter died whilst serving with the 3. Kompanie. Unfortunately, it is known when he died or where.

Appendix 3

Feldpost Number

Each German unit was given a unique field post number. This was used for security purposes amongst other things. The 3. Kompanie's number was 29 707 D. A copy of their field post number stamp is shown below.

Appendix 4
Licence Plates

All vehicles used by the LAH were given an SS licence plate number. In the earlier vehicles these tended to be three or four numerals. As the war progressed and the number of vehicles in use increased, the amount of numerals on the licence plate increased. When checking photos, this is a good indication of when the photo was taken. As an example see the photo on page 38 of the 3. Kompanie in 1940. It is worth remembering however, that you can come across photographs of vehicles with three, four or five digits late in the war. The licence plates would have contained the individual Feldpost Number of the respective Kompanie or in some cases the Division. An example of a typical LAH number plate is shown below. This photograph dates from late 1941. (Hans Vogel)

Appendix 5
Divisional Markings

As detailed during the campaign in the west during 1940, the introduction of unit markings began to make an appearance. The previous photo gives an example of the LAH 'Key-symbol'. This symbol went through a number of changes during the war. Some examples are shown below.

Early LAH Key Symbol (1940)

First variant with shield (1941- 42)

Second variant with shield (1943)

Final variant with the oakleaves added (1944)

Appendix 6
Tactical Markings

One other distinguishing mark that was used on various vehicles was that of the branch of service that the particular unit belonged to. The 3. Kompanie were classed as motorised infantry and as such, their tactical markings would have resembled the illustration below. Again, the photograph on page 38 gives a very good example of the 3. Kompanie's vehicle markings that were used.

Appendix 7
Comparative Ranks

Waffen-SS	British	American
Reichsführer SS	No equivalent	General of the Army
SS Oberstgruppenführer	General	No equivalent
SS Obergruppenführer	Lieutenant General	General
SS Gruppenführer	Major General	Lieutenant General
SS Brigadeführer	Brigadier General	Major General
SS Oberführer	No equivalent	Brigadier General
SS Standartenführer	Colonel	Colonel
SS Obersturmbannführer	Lieutenant Colonel	Lieutenant Colonel
SS Sturmbannführer	Major	Major
SS Hauptsturmführer	Captain	Captain
SS Obersturmführer	Lieutenant	First Lieutenant
SS Untersturmführer	Second Lieutenant	Second Lieutenant
SS Sturmscharführer	Staff Sergeant	Sergeant Major
SS Hauptscharführer	Sergeant Major	Master Sergeant
SS Oberscharführer	Senior Sergeant	Technical Sergeant
SS Scharführer	Sergeant	Staff Sergeant
SS Unterscharführer	Junior Sergeant	Sergeant
SS Rottenführer	Corporal	Corporal
SS Sturmmann	Lance Corporal	Private First Class
SS Obergrenadier	No equivalent	No equivalent
SS Grenadier	Private	Private

Appendix 8
Second War Time Course at Bad Tölz

Bad Tölz Photograph List:

Number 1: *Oberscharführer* Ulrich von Christen. Was killed in action on the 5th of July 1943 as *Hauptsturmführer* and commander of the LAH's 1. Kompanie/1st Panzergrenadier Regiment LAH. Holder of the German Cross in Gold.
Number 2: Unknown.
Number 3: Unknown.
Number 4: Class Leader *Untersturmführer* Rehder (first name unknown).
Number 5: *Oberscharführer* Josef Amberger. Was killed in action on the 21st of August 1944 as *Obersturmführer* and commander of the 8. Kompanie/1st Panzer Regiment LAH. Postumously awarded the Knights Cross on the 31st of October 1944.
Number 6: Unknown.
Number 7: Unknown.

As mentioned in the section relating to Franz Witt, there is a group photograph taken at Bad Tölz during the Second Wartime course. This photograph is reproduced above, with each person numbered to aid identification. It is unfortunately not possible to identify all of the people in this photograph, but the list is the most comprehensive available at the time of going to print.

It is of note that nine of the forty-four people in the photograph would be killed in action during the war. Also, three of the people in this photograph would be awarded the Knight's Cross to the Iron Cross, and four people would be awarded the German Cross in Gold. Overall, 366 people attended the Second Wartime Course at Bad Tölz. Sixty-nine of the attendees would be killed in action, eleven would receive the Knight's Cross and twenty-eight would receive the German Cross in Gold. (Information: Peter Witt)

Number 8: *Oberscharführer* Franz Witt. Killed in action on the 10th of April 1941 as *Untersturmführer* and Platoon Leader within the 3. Kompanie/Infantry Regiment LAH.
Number 9: Unknown.
Number 10: Unknown.
Number 11: *Oberscharführer* Karl-Heinz Ertel. Was awarded the Knights Cross on the 23rd of August 1944 as *Hauptsturmführer* and 1st Ordanance Officer within the III SS General Commando.
Number 12: Unknown.
Number 13: *Scharführer* Hans Jochen Plath. No other information available.
Number 14: *Oberscharführer* Karl Heinz Duhnke. No other information available.
Number 15: *Scharführer* Fritz Scharnath. Killed in action as *Untersturmführer* in the 1. Kompanie/Panzergrenadier Regiment *Germania.*
Number 16: *Oberscharführer* Hans Werner Zech Nenntwig. No other information.
Number 17: *Oberscharführer* Werner Krassowsky. Ended the war as *Hauptsturmführer.*
Number 18: Unknown.
Number 19: *Oberscharführer* Ernst F. Fritscher. Ended the war as *Hauptsturmführer.*
Number 20: Unknown.
Number 21: Unknown.
Number 22: *Oberscharführer* Peter Reese. Killed in action on the 5th of August 1944 as a *Hauptsturmführer* in the 3rd SS Panzer Division *Totenkopf.*
Number 23: *Oberscharführer* Jurgen Hillger. Killed in action as an *Untersturmführer* and Adjutant of Das Reich's Motorcycle Battalion.
Number 24: Unknown.
Number 25: *Oberscharführer* Hans Georg Jessen. Served as a *Hauptsturmführer* in the *Wiking* Division and received the German Cross in Gold on the 15th of December 1943.
Number 26: Unknown.
Number 27: Unknown.
Number 28: Unknown.
Number 29: Unknown.
Number 30: *Oberscharführer* Karl Hecht.
Number 31: *Oberscharführer* Karl von der Recke. Killed in action as *Untersturmführer* in *Das Reich*'s 11. Kompanie.
Number 32: *Oberscharführer* Friedrich Kreigbaum. Killed in action as *Untersturmführer* in the *Totenkopf* Division's 1. Kompanie.
Number 33: Unknown.
Number 34: Unknown.
Number 35: *Oberscharführer* Adolf Braasch. Reached the rank of *Untersturmführer.*
Number 36: Unknown.
Number 37: Unknown.
Number 38: Unknown.
Number 39: *Oberscharführer* Heinrich Oelkers. Reached the rank of *Hauptsturmführer* and held the post of the Ordnance Officer in the XIII SS Army Korps.
Number 40: Unknown.
Number 41: *Oberscharführer* Oskar Pahnke. Served as *Hauptsturmführer* in the 32nd SS Division. Recommended for the Knights Cross right at the end of the war, but never received it.
Number 42: Unknown.
Number 43: Unknown.
Number 44: Unknown.

Amongst the unknowns are the following people:

Hauptscharführer Hans Flugel: Reached the rank of *Hauptsturmführer* and was awarded the German Cross in Gold on the 8th of December 1942. Also awarded the Knights Cross on the 16th of October 1944.
Oberscharführer Heinrich Gunkel: Was awarded the German Cross in Gold on the 2nd of October 1943 whilst serving as an *Obersturmführer* in the *Wiking* Division.
Scharführer Kurt Kiefer: No other information available.
Oberscharführer Fritz Neubert: Reached the rank of *Hauptsturmführer.*
Oberscharführer Hermann Sprecht: Reached the rank of *Hauptsturmführer.*
Bausch: No other information available.
Duppmann: No other information available.

I appreciate that this list is not particularly relevant to the history of the 3. Kompanie, except for the fact that Franz Witt is in the photograph. However, to not list the names of the other known people in this photograph would be to deliberately leave another gap in the history of the Waffen-SS. This list may be of help to other researchers.

BIBLIOGRAPHY

Cross, Robin. *Citadel: The Battle for Kursk.* BCA, 1993.

Lehmann, Rudolf. *Die Leibstandarte I.* J.J.Fedorowicz Publishing Ltd., 1987.

Lehmann, Rudolf. *Die Leibstandarte II.* J.J.Fedorowicz Publishing Ltd., 1988.

Lehmann, Rudolf. *Die Leibstandarte III.* J.J.Fedorowicz Publishing Ltd., 1990.

Lehmann, Rudolf. *Die Leibstandarte IV/1.* J.J.Fedorowicz Publishing Ltd., 1993.

Lehmann, Rudolf. *Die Leibstandarte im Bild V.* Munin Verlag, 1983.

Messenger, Charles. *Hitler's Galdiator: The Life of Sepp Dietrich.* Brassays Defence Publishers,1988.

Meyer, Kurt. *Grenadiers.* J.J.Fedorowicz Publishers Ltd, 2001.

Mollo, Andrew & Page Taylor. Hugh. *Uniforms of the SS: Collected Edition: Volumes 1 to 6.* Windrow & Greene Ltd,1997.

Perrett, Bryon. *Knights of the Black Cross.* Grafton Books, 1986.

Quassowski, Hans & 1. Kompanie Veterans Association. *Twelve Years With Hitler: A History of the 1. Kompanie Leibstandarte SS Adolf Hitler 1933 to 1945.* Shiffer Publishing Ltd, 1999.

Scheider, Jost. W. *Their Honor was Loyalty (2nd Edition).* R. James Bender Publishing, 1993.

Springer, Heinrich. *Stationen eines Lebens in Krieg und Frieden.* Deutsche VerlagsGesellschaft, 1996.

Tiemann, Ralf. *Die Leibstandarte IV/2.* J.J.Fedorowicz Publishing Ltd, 1998.

Whiting, Charles. *Battle of the Bulge: Britains Untold Story.* Suttons Publishing, 1999.

Whiting, Charles. *Westwall: Battle for the Siegfried Line.* Spellmont Publishing, 1999.

Williamson, Gordon. *Knights of the Iron Cross.* Blandford Press, 1987.

Also: Various letters and face to face interviews with surviving Kameraden of the 3. Kompanie and the 1st SS Panzer Division LSSAH from 1998 to 2002.

Also from the Publisher

IN PERFECT FORMATION
SS Ideology and the SS-Junkerschule-Tölz
Jay Hatheway

Includes extensive references to original source material on the underlying SS principles of blood, soil, and struggle as they were formalized in SS ideology. In support of his intricate linkages between ideology and its realized form, Hatheway has obtained over 100 previously unpublished photos of the SS officer training academy Tölz. More than a series of buildings, the structure of the *Junkerschule* was itself a metaphor for the subset of Nazi ideology that was developed by Himmler, Darré and others to create a racially pure vanguard to lead Germany on its path toward Teutonic regeneration.
Size: 6"x9" • over 100 b/w photographs • 192 pp.
ISBN: 0-7643-0753-3 • hard cover • $29.95

HIMMLER'S CAVALRY
The Equestrian SS 1930-1945
Paul J. Wilson

Dressed in black uniforms emblazoned with the SS flash, Heinrich Himmler's horsemen carried the SS banner across the German countryside and to equestrian competitions throughout Germany and Europe. Wilson provides numerous anecdotes, statistics, and capsule biographies of Equestrian SS personnel. This carefully researched study is essential reading for scholars and lay people interested in the history of Nazi Germany, the SS, and the Holocaust.
Size: 6"x9" • 17 b/w photographs • 224 pp.
ISBN: 0-7643-1112-3 • hard cover • $29.95

RIDING EAST
The SS Cavalry Brigade in Poland and Russia 1939-1942
Mark C. Yerger

Riding East details the history of the SS Cavalry Brigade. Heavily documented, the detailed text is supplemented by 109 photographs, previously unpublished. In addition, six maps, six Order of Battle charts, complete officer rosters 1939-142, feldpost numbers, details of primary commanders within the Brigade, as well information on the units and commanders it was subordinated to, complete a comprehensive history of the first combat mounted unit of the SS.
Size: 8 1/2"x11" • b/w photos, documents • 224 pp.
ISBN: 0-7643-0060-1 • hard cover • $59.95

ALLGEMEINE-SS
The Commands, Units and Leaders of the General SS
Mark C. Yerger

The commands, units and leaders of the General SS are finally compiled into a single detailed reference book for both the historian and SS memorabilia collector. The biographical data for individuals alone adds vast detail to this fascinating topic. A detailed index allows referencing of individual commands or personalities.
Size: 8 1/2"x11" • over 120 b/w photographs, maps • 256 pp.
ISBN: 0-7643-0145-4 • hard cover • $49.95